DEER HUNTERS'
ALMANAC

From the publishers of
DEER & DEER HUNTING MAGAZINE

2003
EDITION

Published by

Krause Publications
700 E. State St. • Iola, WI 54990-0001
Telephone: 715/445-2214   fax: 715/445-4087
World Wide Web: www.deeranddeerhunting.com

Please call or write for our free catalog of outdoor publications.
Our toll-free number to place an order or obtain a free catalog is 800-258-0929.

Library of Congress Catalog Number: 92-74255

ISBN: 0-87349-330-3
Printed in the United States of America

W9-AWD-449

CONTENTS

Editor's Note

By Ryan Gilligan

Almanac Helps Fulfill Deer Hunting Goals Great and Small

I suppose I'm an unlikely candidate for writing this column. After all, unlike most of my colleagues, I wasn't born into a deer-hunting family, and as a native of a Minneapolis, Minn., suburb, I spent much of my early childhood far from the deer woods. Who could have predicted that by my late teens, I would spend almost every autumn day deer hunting?

What brought me here? Well, although they aren't deer hunting fanatics, my parents and grandparents deserve most of the credit. Their enthusiasm for fishing, small-game hunting and other outdoors activities fostered a passion in me that eventually expanded to deer and deer hunting.

However, by my early teens, their support and encouragement could only go so far. I was starving for practical information on deer hunting, but they lacked the experience to teach me.

Thankfully, publications like the *Deer Hunters' Almanac* picked up the slack. When I finally grabbed one of those first almanacs from my hometown drug store's shelf, I received more than just awesome photos and entertaining stories about deer hunting — I got the how-to boost I needed to graduate from a mere enthusiast sitting on deer hunting's sidelines to a full-fledged hunter who spent his autumn days perched in tree stands and matching wits with whitetails.

It's been a great experience and I couldn't have done it — at least so quickly — without the help of publications like the *Deer Hunters' Almanac.*

This year's edition should be just as helpful. Whether you're a novice just looking to fill your first tag, or a veteran hoping to fulfill your life-long dream of killing a Boone and Crockett buck, the *2003 Deer Hunters' Almanac* provides information you need to reach your goals.

Do you want to expand your hunting opportunities by starting muzzleloading? Learn how in the easy-to-follow guide beginning on Page 105.

Is hunter density or urban sprawl forcing you to trade your rifle for a slug gun this fall? Turn to Page 93 for Dave Henderson's detailed rundown on today's high-tech slugs. You might discover your slug gun doesn't have to be a handicap.

Have sickening memories of unrecovered arrow-shot bucks left you guessing what to do when a deer steps into range? Check out Daniel E. Schmidt's article on shot placement starting on Page 53.

In addition to these subjects, the following pages will cover topics far too numerous to list here. I hope they help you as much as previous editions have helped me.

Colorado Man Kills His First Whitetail in the Manitoba Woods

When Walter Payne of Woodland Park, Colo., mailed his application for *Deer & Deer Hunting's* 2001 gun-hunting sweepstakes, it never crossed his mind that he might actually win. After all, he rarely hunts and had never killed a whitetail. Despite his expectations, Payne was notified he was the winner in Fall 2001.

WALTER PAYNE and his first whitetail

On Nov. 18, 2001, he boarded a flight to Winnipeg, Manitoba, eagerly anticipating his all-expenses-paid whitetail hunt with Bows 'N Bullets Outfitters.

The next day, after riding horseback to his stand, Payne received his first taste of wilderness whitetail hunting. While watching the spruce and aspen woodlots near his stand, Payne saw several bucks, including a wide-racked 8-pointer that never presented a clear shot. Then, at about 12:30 p.m., a large-bodied 8-pointer walked into a sedge meadow 150 yards from his stand.

Payne settled his scope's crosshairs behind the buck's shoulder and slowly squeezed the trigger. Before the shot's echo had been swallowed by the endless expanse of timber surrounding Payne's stand, his first white-tailed buck had crumpled.

DEER HUNTERS'
ALMANAC

FROM THE PUBLISHERS OF **DEER & DEER HUNTING**

Publisher Hugh McAloon
Associate Publisher and Advertising Manager Brad Rucks

EDITORIAL
Editor in Chief Daniel E. Schmidt
Editor Ryan Gilligan
Associate Editors Joe Shead, Jennifer Pillath
Editorial Intern Leigh Ann Ruddy

ADVERTISING
Sales
Kathy Quinlan • Kyle Franson
Pat Boyle • Karen Glinski
Gary Reichert

Sales Assistant Susie Melum
Sales/Edit Assistant Connie Kostrzewa

CUSTOMER SERVICE
715/445-3775, ext. 257

Published by
Krause Publications Inc.
700 E. State St., Iola, WI 54990-0001
715/445-2214 FAX 715/445-4087
http://www.deeranddeerhunting.com

The first edition of the *Deer Hunters' Almanac* was published in 1992 by Krause Publications. It has been published annually since then.
Address all correspondence to Deer Hunters' Almanac,
700 E. State St., Iola, WI 54990-0001.

Contact Krause Publications about these quality magazines:

Deer & Deer Hunting • Turkey & Turkey Hunting
Trapper & Predator Caller • Wisconsin Outdoor Journal
Bass Pro Shops' Outdoor World

Photo credits: Cover photo by Charles J. Alsheimer.
Big-buck photos in Chapter 2 by text contributors.
Product photos supplied by manufacturers. All other photos, unless otherwise noted, by Ryan Gilligan

Krause Publications
700 E. State St.
Iola, WI 54990-0001

WITH BURGEONING DEER populations prompting wildlife managers to issue bonus antlerless tags, there has never been a better time to donate venison to local food pantries.

1

Vital Concerns For Today's Hunters

Sharing the Bounty

How Hunters Help the Hungry

Some people would label it a "no-brainer." And, I'm sure someone out there has called it a "win-win" situation. But I guess, as cliche as those phrases are, they're accurate.

I'm referring to the hunters-for-the-hungry programs that have popped up across the United States in the past decade. These programs attack two problems: First, our nation is experiencing an increase in white-tailed deer and a decrease in hunter numbers. The effects of this unbalanced equation are thousands of deer/vehicle collisions each year, an increase in urban deer problems, and the threat of Lyme disease and wildlife diseases — to name just a few.

Extra permits have been issued in many states, and season lengths have been modified or adapted to compensate for the deer-herd boom. Kentucky alone hopes to decrease its herd by 10,000 animals this year. Wisconsin, whose hunters set an all-time national record by harvesting more than 625,000 deer in 2000, wants to reduce its herd by hundreds of thousands. Despite 2000's record kill, Wisconsin's deer herd could approach 1.7 million whitetails this autumn. And, all of this must be accomplished when hunter numbers have either remained stagnant or decreased.

How will states encourage hunters to kill more deer than their families can eat?

The second problem is that the United States has — and probably always will have — hungry people who could eat those deer. However, many of them are nonhunters, and that's why hunters-for-the-hungry programs make sense. They allow hunters to kill more deer, which decreases the herd, without worrying about wasting meat.

According to the U.S. Department of Agriculture, 31 million Americans didn't have safe, readily available food in 1999. Of those people, 12 million were children.

This is especially sad, considering children have the greatest need for nutritionally rich foods. Studies indicate that young children who are even mildly malnourished during critical growth periods have poor

TEXT AND PHOTOS BY JENNIFER PILLATH

ALMANAC INSIGHTS

➤ **ALTHOUGH THE NUMBER** of hunters who bought licenses has remained fairly steady since 1998, hunter expenditures have continued to rise, according to the U.S. Fish and Wildlife Service.

More than 15 million hunters bought licenses in 2000, closely mirroring the 1999 statistics of 15.1 million purchasers in 1999. However, expenditures were in excess of $613.9 million for hunting licenses in 2000, up from $580.2 million the year before.

Revenues obtained through license sales support state fish and wildlife agencies, conservation projects and hunting and fishing safety and education programs.

License sales figures are compiled annually by the U.S. Fish and Wildlife Service from information submitted by each state. The figures are part of a formula to determine the amount of funding each state receives through the Federal Aid in Wildlife Restoration and the Federal Aid in Sport Fish Restoration programs, both administered by the Service. Under these programs, hunters and anglers pay an excise tax on hunting and fishing equipment such as firearms, ammunition and tackle. The money is then distributed to the states for fish and wildlife restoration programs.

— *ESPN Outdoors News Service*

➤ **ANTI-HUNTING RESIDENTS** in Beverly Shores, Ind., were unhappy about a 2001 deer hunt that had been approved by the state's Department of Natural Resources and took their frustrations out on the hunt's supporters.

A plan to cull 75 deer in Beverly Shores was approved by the DNR and town-council member John Jannsen. Unfortunately, anti-hunters showed their condemnation by throwing coins at Jannsen's daughter and calling his wife a "deer killer" as she walked the family dog.

— *U.S. Sportsmen's Alliance*

physical and mental development.

The elderly are also greatly affected by food scarcity. In 1999, seniors made up 16.5 percent of all emergency food-pantry clients and 17 percent of all soup-kitchen users. Seniors account for about 18 percent of the population, but by 2030 that figure is expected to nearly double.

Easy as One, Two, Three

Hunters-for-the-hungry programs work on a simple chain system. The programs seek donations from individuals, church groups, corporate entities and other organizations. That money is used to pay state-approved meat processors.

Next in the chain are hunters, who have the easiest role. All they have to do is drop off their deer or venison at a processor.

From there, the meat is processed — usually into hamburger — and given to food pantries and other distribution centers where it, in turn, is handed over to the needy.

Sounds simple, right?

"It's a common-sense approach to what to do with your deer resource," said David Home, founder of Virginia's Hunters for the Hungry.

"The deer herds continue to grow and hunter numbers continue to drop. (Venison) is a product that's not otherwise available," he said.

It's hard to pinpoint where the idea of hunters helping the hungry originated, but nonetheless, it has spread quickly. In 1991, Home, of Big Island, Va., noticed a venison-donation program in Texas. He thought it was feasible, and established a similar concept in Virginia. After two years, the program had grown so quickly that a separate organization was established.

In the first year, 33,000 pounds of venison were donated. In the second year, that increased to 68,000 pounds. In 1999, 182,603 pounds of venison were donated, providing about 700,000 meals. Home figures that Virginia hunters could potentially donate 250,000 pounds per year to the program, providing 1 million meals.

Home's efforts had a domino effect.

In Maryland, Rick Wilson started a similar program in his home county.

"I had no intentions of going beyond that," he said.

By the second year, his program had gone statewide, and in the third year it doubled again.

"I was working on my home phone line at first," Wilson said. "The calls continued. Guys were calling in from their tree stands. One guy called at 2:30 in the morning, wondering where to take his deer."

That hunter had been tracking the deer and wanted to get it to a processor before the meat spoiled.

From those early roots, Wilson's organization has become the umbrella of many state programs. It's now a national program called Farmers and Hunters Feeding the Hungry. Wilson expects it will provide a million meals to the needy per year.

ALMANAC INSIGHTS

➤ **THE AMOUNT OF REVENUE** generated from white-tailed deer license sales varies by state, but it is safe to say that without whitetails, most state agencies would be in trouble. The numbers are staggering. Pennsylvania and Wisconsin take in more than $25 million a year, Michigan and Texas close to $20 million, and Georgia, Minnesota, New York and West Virginia are handed more than $10 million by deer hunters each year. Alabama, Ohio and Virginia get just less than $10 million each year, while Indiana, Kentucky, Louisiana, Missouri and Tennessee receive about $5 million from deer hunting licenses.

➤ **HOW DOES** Quality Deer Management differ from other deer-harvest strategies in its effect on native plant communities? According to a recent study by the University of Wisconsin-Madison, not much.

In the study, graduate student Rebecca Christoffel examined three southern Wisconsin properties that experienced drastically different deer harvests. On one property, hunters were granted access by invitation only and were required to shoot two does before killing a mature buck. The second property was heavily hunted and its harvest composition wasn't regulated. The third property was off-limits to hunting.

Not surprisingly, the unhunted property had a much higher deer density and, therefore, suffered more damage to its native vegetation than the other two areas. Less predictably, however, was that the first two properties, despite their radically different management, experienced equally low pressure on their vegetation.

According to Christoffel, this is because overwinter deer density, not herd composition, is the deciding factor in browse intensity. Therefore, landowners can choose from a variety of management plans without hurting native plant communities.

— *University of Wisconsin-Madison College of Agricultural and Life Sciences*

ALMANAC INSIGHTS

➤ **INDIANA HUNTERS** helped stall a controversial deer birth-control program slated in northern Indiana.

The U.S. Sportsmen's Alliance, Indiana Bowhunters Association and Indiana Deer Hunters filed a legal action challenging the Indiana Department of Natural Resources' granting of the Humane Society of the United States — America's largest animal-rights group — permission to conduct a birth-control program for white-tailed deer.

"It looks to us as if HSUS is not interested in spending the necessary dollars to comply with restrictions to protect both the public and the deer herd," said Rob Sexton, USSA state services director. "Obviously, it was more concerned about the public rela-tions value of this project than the wildlife."

The issue centers on a deer birth-control method involving the adminis-tration of drugs to cause infertility in individual does. This process has failed to work on free-ranging deer popula-tions, and the drug used in this program has not been approved by the Federal Drug Administration.

"These birth-control programs are merely attempts by animal-rights groups to stop hunting," Sexton said. "The risks for someone who eats deer treated with this drug are unknown — this program could prove to be harmful to deer and dangerous to humans."

— *U.S. Sportsmen's Alliance*

➤ **WHITETAILS ARE** "keystone herbivores," that is, they are usually a habitat's primary consumers. As a result, overpopulated whitetails can easily damage plant communities. However, a recent study conducted by ecologists from the University of Wisconsin-Madison suggests exces-sive deer densities might cause mini-mal damage to plant communities in heavily farmed regions. Researchers found that the food available in crop fields buffered native plants.

— *Agricultural and Consumer Press Service*

Lee Dudek, founder of Wisconsin's Hunters for the Hungry, also experienced a growth spurt this past year. His program originated in 1994 when members of his hunting camp in northeastern Wisconsin realized they had more permits than they needed.

"We could only consume so much, and we wanted to put to good use the deer that we harvested," he said.

His program, working in alliance with Paul's Pantry in Green Bay, quickly grew.

In 2000, the Wisconsin Department of Natural Resources had money left over from its crop-damage program to pay for processing. Dudek and Bob Kronstedt of Hunters Against Hunger worked with the state and brought in an increased amount of venison.

"God blessed us with some really substantial growth in 2000," Dudek said.

Dudek's program received 63,000 pounds of meat, of which about 60 percent went to Paul's Pantry.

In Kentucky, the story is some-what different. Twelve years ago, the program started as a regional volunteer effort. Eventually, the Department of Game and Fish joined the mix, funding the program heavily in its first year at the state level.

"Reduction of the herd really depends on filling those extra permits," said Chuck Hartley of Kentucky's Hunters for the Hungry.

This year, the Kentucky organi-zation planned a black-tie fund-

raising event to bring in money for processing. It sold out and drew attention from the governor, national celebrities and several magazines. According to Hartley, the Kentucky program also has the luxury of participation from every major sporting organization in the state.

"We all have our own banquets and we all compete for the sportsmen's money, but we all came together to help with this."

What's So Great About Venison?

Meat is one of the most needed items for food banks because of its expense and short shelf life.

"Food banks really have little meat," Wilson said. "To bring in fresh meat is very inconvenient."

Although nutrients are available from other sources, meat remains the most common source of protein in our diets, also providing a rich source of vitamins and minerals. Protein is essential for its nitrogen and amino acids, which are the build-

THE EXPENSE of obtaining and preserving meat is more than many food pantries can afford. However, donated venison helps fill this vital nutritional niche.

ing blocks for muscles, skin, connective tissues and almost every other body part.

"You have to have meat," said Angie Allard, manager of Paul's Pantry.

In general, Americans tend to overdo it on meat. The Department of Agriculture recommends that we consume two to three servings per day, consisting of about a couple of ounces of meat per serving. On average, Americans eat twice that amount every day.

Put that into perspective. On average, seniors only receive half as much protein as they should. Families that can't afford groceries have an even harder time fitting expensive meat products into the budget.

According to the Department of Agriculture, dairy and meat products remain some of the most

ALMANAC INSIGHTS

➤ **HUNTERS HELPING HUNTERS**, a unique charity organization, was founded to assist hunting families that have experienced a death or serious injury or illness. The organization helps such families pay medical or funeral costs and alleviate financial stress, allowing the family to focus on recovery.

Hunters Helping Hunters began when a group of North American Hunting Club members learned of a fellow hunter whose family was in temporary need because of a loss in the family. The group recognized the need to help such hunters and their loved ones get back on their feet.

Today, the organization has 31 members. To raise funds, Hunters Helping Hunters accepts donations and holds raffles. For example, in 2002, the group raffled a fully guided bear hunt in Maine.

For more information, visit Hunters Helping Hunters' Web site, www.hhh-usa.org.

➤ **THE EARLIEST-KNOWN** art depicting hunting scenes are painted on rocks at Altamira, Spain and Laugerie, France. The paintings are about 20,000 years old.

— Rupert Isaacson, *The Wild Host The History and Meaning of the Hunt*

expensive foods. In June 2000, 1 pound of ground beef cost $1.56. Pork chops were $3.33 per pound, and chicken was $1.07.

Wilson figures that under his program, venison costs 70 cents a pound. Processors work at a discounted rate, charging $35 per deer.

And although a million meals sounds like a lot, it disappears quickly.

"A lot of the meat we receive is close to the (expiration) date or it is hot dogs and sausage," Allard said. "People here really do take (venison). They can use it to make chili or whatever."

Paul's Pantry feeds about 150 families in the Green Bay area daily. It has about 3,500 families registered and provide about 5 million pounds of food per year.

"Venison has been especially well received," said Craig Robbins, director of Paul's Pantry. "People love it."

This sentiment holds true nationwide. Although we hear anti-hunting sentiments from animal-protection organizations like PeTA, most such groups will not speak too loudly against a program that provides meat to those in dire need.

Allard remembers only two complaints in the past six years. Wilson reports similar reactions.

"At the very first feeding program I went to, I thought, 'Oh Lord, what have you done to me,'" Wilson said. "I thought sure that some kid would say, 'Bambi.' I failed to realize what the alternative for these people was."

At Wilson's first event, 150 people attended, and he claims you could hear a pin drop.

"These people came for one purpose," he said. "That's what they were there for."

Home said the public's image of venison was a concern at first, but the worries were short-lived.

"It was certainly a question when we started," he said. "What do you do in urban areas? However, we've had no problem. People are very receptive to venison."

Most organizations also accept packaged meat. In Wisconsin's Hunters for the Hungry program,

20,000 pounds of meat came from hunters who were cleaning out their freezers and realized they couldn't use everything. Of that venison, only about 2 percent had severe freezer burn, making it unusable.

In fact, unless it becomes freezer-burned, pure venison seldom goes bad; it just loses its flavor. Hunters should be careful, however, with ground venison if it has been mixed with pork or beef fat. Pork fat can turn rancid if not used within a few months of being frozen.

Most pantries receive ground meat, so it is a rarity when steaks and other cuts are brought in.

"Check your freezers," said Dudek. "Don't throw anything away."

How You Can Help

Hunters really do have the easiest role in donation programs. Take advantage of any extra permits, and check with your state organization for participating processors. Your state wildlife agency can probably help, or contact someone at Farmers and Hunters for the Hungry. As with any donation, your gift of venison can also be used as a tax deduction.

You can also give financially. Every organization that organizes venison donations is in dire need of funding. FHFH asks for $35 to process one deer. Of course, each organization is thankful for any amount you can give. Also, if you are a member of a sportsmen's club, church youth group, bowling league or anything else, you can donate time or money as a

ALMANAC INSIGHTS

➤ **AS HUNTERS,** we often boast about our financial might. However, animal rights organizations aren't without economic clout. In fact, they have a cumulative budget of almost $400 million.

Not surprisingly, some of the best-funded organizations are the Humane Society of the United States, at more than $37 million, and PeTA, whose budget exceeds $11 million.
— *U.S. Sportsmen's Alliance*

➤ **THE MAGNITUDE** of deer baiting is relatively unknown. In Wisconsin, for example, if you conservatively estimate that 20 percent of the state's gun-hunters (about 138,800 hunters) use bait, and that each of those hunters uses 5 gallons (half the legal limit) of shelled corn per day, that adds up to 694,000 gallons — about 4.58 million pounds — of corn for each day of the state's nine-day season.
— *Mark Toso*

group.

"It's a very benevolent thing ... something that people can feel good about," Hartley said.

"To sit in the woods and know the next deer you harvest is helping the needy is a good feeling," Dudek said. "(This program) has been a real blessing in my life."

Wilson refers to the Bible verse printed on each of his brochures:

"For I was hungry and you gave me something to eat, I was thirsty and you gave me something to drink, I was a stranger and you invited me in."
—*Matthew 25:35.*

Ensure A Successful Hunt

Big Bucks the Benoit Way
*Secrets from America's First Family
of Whitetail Hunting*
by Bryce Towsley

Finally, the long-awaited second book on the tried-and-true hunting strategies of the legendary Benoit family. Although tracking and woodsmanship are emphasized, hunters of all ages, no matter where they hunt, will gain the knowledge needed to bag trophy bucks.

Hardcover • 8-1/2 x 11 • 208 pages
150 b&w photos • 16-page color section
Item# HBB • $24.95

Whitetail
Fundamentals and Fine Points For the Hunter
by George Mattis

Revisit an era of deer hunting when hunters donned wool jackets, congregated in deer camps, and still-hunting was considered a skill. This hardcover reprint is the third Deer & Deer Hunting classic showcasing whitetails and offering valuable insight into the secretive world of white-tailed deer. Learn hunting strategies that were taught decades ago but are still considered essential techniques today, including stalking, using the land's contour to travel, and reading the weather to predict whitetail behavior.

Hardcover • 8-1/4 x 10-7/8 • 240 pages
200 b&w sketches
Item# WHFUN • $34.95

Quality Deer Management
The Basics and Beyond
by Charles J. Alsheimer

Raise quality deer herds with bigger bucks and larger antlers through quality deer management (QDM). Learn how you can participate through land development, proper harvesting, maintaining good doe-to-buck ratios, and establishing nutritious food sources. Contains tips on land management, good forestry practices, controlling antlerless deer herds, and how to sell QDM to neighboring landowners. Even landowners of small plots can participate.

Hardcover • 8-1/4 x 10-7/8 • 208 pages
200+ color photos
Item# QDMGT • $39.95

To order call
800-258-0929
Offer OTB2
M-F 7am - 8pm • Sat 8am - 2pm, CST

Krause Publications
Offer OTB2 • P.O. Box 5009
Iola WI 54945-5009
www.krausebooks.com

Bowhunters' Digest
Advanced Tactics, 5th Edition
edited by Kevin Michalowski

Learn advanced bowhunting tactics from more than twenty top bowhunters including Greg Miller, Bryce Towsley, M.D. Johnson, and Gary Clancy. They'll teach you how to hone your hunting and shooting skills to increase your success. Become familiar with the latest equipment and accessories and find out how to contact archery manufacturers, dealers, and other resources with the state-by-state list.

Softcover • 8-1/2 x 11 • 256 pages
300 b&w photos
Item# BOW5 • $22.95

Legendary Deer Camps
by Robert Wegner

Travel back in time to experience deer camps of famous Americans such as William Faulkner, Aldo Leopold and Oliver Hazard Perry. Rediscover classic hunting traditions such as freedom, solitude, camaraderie, rites of initiation, story-telling and venison cuisine through a series of famous deer camp biographies and rare historical paintings and photographs. This is the second book in the *Deer and Deer Hunting* Classics Series.

Hardcover • 8-1/4 x 10-7/8 • 208 pages
125 b&w photos • 75 color photos
Item# DERCP • $34.95

25 Years of Deer & Deer Hunting
The Original Stump Sitters Magazine
edited by Daniel E. Schmidt

For the first time ever, *Deer & Deer Hunting* magazine opens its vaults and presents a comprehensive look at the articles, photographs, and personalities that built North America's first and favorite white-tailed deer hunting magazine. Heart-warming tributes are given to the magazine's founders, and never-before-published articles provide valuable whitetail insights that cannot be found elsewhere.

Hardcover • 8-1/4 x 10-7/8 • 208 pages
10 b&w photos • 150 color photos
Item# DDH25 • $29.95

Shipping & Handling: $4.00 first book, $2.25 each additional. Non-US addresses $20.95 first book, $5.95 each additional.

Sales Tax: CA, IA, IL, NJ, PA, TN, VA, WI residents please add appropriate sales tax.

How Does Baiting Affect Deer and Deer Hunting?

Loathed by some hunters as lazy and destructive and praised by others as an effective tradition, baiting remains one of deer hunting's most controversial issues. And, with the discovery of illnesses like bovine tuberculosis and chronic wasting disease, baiting disputes will undoubtedly increase.

Deer & Deer Hunting magazine first tackled the subject with Dave Beauchaine's article "Divided We Fall? Baiting Wars Pit Brother Against Brother" in the September 2000 issue. Among other things, the article dealt with baiting's role in disease transmission and hunter conflicts

D&DH revisited the issue in the March 2002 issue with Mark Toso's article, "How Baiting Affects Deer Activity." In the article, Toso cited several studies that indicated daytime deer activity decreases greatly as baiting increases. Interestingly, the studies also showed that nonbaiting hunters were generally as successful as baiters.

After the March 2002 issue hit newsstands, the *D&DH* editorial office was swamped with letters and e-mails from readers on both sides of the baiting controversy.

Here's what some readers said.

➤ After reading Mark Toso's article "How Baiting Affects Deer Activity" in the March 2002 issue, it's obvious the only thing wrong with the article is its title. Toso should have called it "Why I Want Baiting Outlawed in Wisconsin and Michigan."

I have not hunted in Wisconsin, so I can't comment on baiting there. I have, however, hunted in Michigan, and baiting practices there are more extreme than anywhere I've seen.

It is bold and inconsiderate, though, to write an article chastising baiting in general when your main problem and supporting data come from two Northern states.

Many hunters, including myself, have information that makes Toso's data look like a bunch of hooey. For example, I'm the wildlife resource manager for a private wildlife sanctuary in Arkansas, and supplemental feeding there is crucial for the herd's health. I've also encountered baiting and feeding from the dense forests of northern Saskatchewan to the barren South Texas brush country. These areas, among countless others, experience dawn-to-dusk deer activity, including movement by mature bucks. In addition, baiting and feeding in these areas keep herds in excellent health.

Did Toso acquire data from those regions? Has he ever crossed his state line?

If you're bothered by your area's laws, get involved in local politics where you might do some good. Airing your opinions in a nationally distributed article disguised as a biology research project is a futile attempt to change attitudes.

Lance H. Nichols
Des Arc, Ark.

➤ I couldn't agree more with Mark Toso. I've been monitoring baiting and feeding in Michigan and Wisconsin, and I believe the practices will end hunting as we know it.

Through my job as a high school teacher, I interact with young hunters daily. If what I'm hearing from them represents hunting's future, we are doomed.

All of my students hunt over bait. More disturbing is that many of them "hunt" directly over feeders in their yards. Most of them see nothing wrong with this practice.

In his article, Mark Toso cited statistics that showed baiters had equal or lower success rates than nonbaiters. However, my experiences have shown the opposite.

Feeding deer is another major problem. The sheer number of people feeding deer year-round near my northern Wisconsin home is astonishing. Large-scale feeding concentrates deer on private lands, making it almost impossible for deer biologists to successfully manage the herd.

Jay Cornell
Spooner, Wis.

➤ I agree with Mark Toso. Baiting is unhealthy, it increases nocturnal deer activity and it decreases mature buck movement.

However, where I bow-hunt in central Michigan, there are so many bait piles that I see few deer all season. On the other hand, neighboring hunters who use bait see dozens of deer per day.

It is hard to keep children interested in hunting if they don't see deer. When my son starts hunting this fall, how — without baiting — will he compete with the eight nearby bait piles?

Mr. Toso, don't be mad at all baiters. Some of us are just fighting for a deer or two for our children.

Chad Spiekerman
via e-mail

➤ In the late 1980s, my hunting group started baiting deer in national

CHRONIC WASTING DISEASE SPREADING

➤ **ALTHOUGH** it's been diagnosed in Western deer and elk herds for more than 30 years, chronic wasting disease wasn't an immediate concern for Eastern whitetail hunters until February 2002, when three Wisconsin bucks killed during the state's 2001 firearms season tested positive for the fatal brain ailment.

CWD first appeared in captive Colorado deer in 1967, and belongs to the family of diseases known as transmissible spongiform encephalopathies — the same family as "mad cow disease."

Although much remains unknown about the disease and how it spreads, biologists believe it is caused by prions — aberrant proteins — within an affected animal's brain.

The Wisconsin discovery marked the first time CWD had been found in a wild deer herd east of the Mississippi. In fact, the area where the bucks were killed — about 20 miles west of Madison, Wis., — is about 900 miles east of where the disease was thought to be isolated, the confluence of northeastern Colorado, eastern Wyoming, southwestern South Dakota and western Nebraska.

The CWD-infected Wisconsin deer prompted the state to conduct large-scale culling in the area where the bucks were killed to determine the disease's prevalence and control its spread. The discovery also prompted Wisconsin officials to ban baiting and recreational feeding, which concentrate deer and result in nose-to-nose contact between animals.

— RYAN GILLIGAN

forest land east of Eagle River, Wis. At that time, baiting was uncommon, and we had very good results. However, during the last eight years, we've noticed that the deer have become more nocturnal. Plus, baiting is not as effective because of its widespread use.

I believe hunters would kill more deer if baiting were banned, because deer would resume normal feeding

ALMANAC INSIGHTS

➤ **IT'S AMAZING** how time has changed hunting. Just consider this 1948 letter to the editor of *Field &Stream*:

"I've been hearing some rumors about Field & Stream letting ladies take over some of the pages in your magazine. Don't do it! The guy who reads your magazine wants to wear the pants in his family. One thing he wants to remain sole expert and sage on is hunting and fishing. Take that away from him and what has he got left? Nothing. They (women) won't even be able to call him mister anymore. Please don't do it!"

— *Information provided by Tom Conroy, Minnesota Department of Natural Resources*

➤ **DO YOU THINK** animal-rights groups lack the power to disrupt sound wildlife management? If so, think again. In January 2002, animal-rights activists in suburban Princeton Township, N.J., pleaded with a local judge to stop a deer hunt prescribed to reduce crop damage and traffic accidents. Although the hunt was to be conducted at night by White Buffalo Inc., a nonprofit group of deer-control specialists, the activists claimed the plan was dangerous and cruel to animals. The judge believed them.

— *Herm Albright*

➤ **WISCONSIN DEER HUNTERS** were recently asked to rate the factors that most influence their perception of a "quality" hunt. Their answers might surprise you.

According to the survey, 42.6 percent of the hunters said hunts that allow them to spend time with friends and family are the most enjoyable. A slightly smaller percentage, 41.8 percent, said a quality hunt was one that allowed them to merely see deer.

Seeing bucks ranked third, 31.9 percent; while an opportunity to kill a deer ranked a distant fourth with 26.4 percent of the vote. Other factors that made hunts enjoyable to those surveyed included enjoyable weather and the opportunity to spend time alone in the outdoors.

patterns, giving more hunting opportunities during shooting hours. Also, problems like landowner disputes and after-hours shooting would be greatly reduced.

Dennis Scheurer
Seymour, Wis.

➤ I once belonged to a hunting club in Walterboro, S.C., where we were forced to bait because the surrounding clubs were baiting heavily and drawing deer off of our land.

As baiting escalated, deer movement dwindled. The few deer we killed were small and were shot at the fringes of daylight. Larger deer became nocturnal. Our deer harvest fell by almost 40 percent, and I soon quit the club because of the problems baiting caused.

After leaving, I learned baiting had caught the attention of South Carolina biologists who were concerned that the unnatural deer concentrations created by baiting caused inbreeding.

Aside from these concerns, I want my sons to learn about scouting and deer behavior. I've witnessed other children growing up thinking hunting was going to Wal-Mart and buying a bag of corn to pour along an easy access road so they didn't have to exert themselves too much while killing deer.

Roy L. Bibbins
South Carolina

Editor's Note: *If you have questions or comments regarding baiting, e-mail them to Ryan Gilligan at gilliganr@krause.com, or send them via regular mail to 700 E. State St., Iola, WI 54990-0001.*

Do Antlerless Seasons Degrade Buck Hunting?

Exploding whitetail populations have prompted many states' deer managers to issue extra antlerless deer tags and create special antlerless-only seasons. Although they are crucial for controlling deer numbers, these measures have drawn criticism from hunters concerned with maintaining high buck populations, because it's widely assumed that antlerless-only seasons result in disproportionate buck-fawn harvests. However, harvest records show such worries are unfounded.

For example, in Wisconsin's 2000 early "T-Zone" hunt, a four-day antlerless-only firearms season, hunters killed 66,417 deer. Of those, about 53 percent were adult does, 24 percent were doe fawns and 23 percent were buck fawns. In other words, early-season hunters killed about 15,275 buck fawns.

Although that might seem high, keep in mind that those kills were spread throughout the more than 16.25 million acres of deer habitat enrolled in T-Zone that year. Therefore, on average, only one buck fawn died per 1,064 acres of deer range.

That figure was no fluke. In fact, in the almost 40 years the Wisconsin Department of Natural Resources has been aging and sexing antlerless deer kills, the buck-fawn kill percentage has averaged only 21.6 percent, and it has never reached 30 percent.

Even if the buck-fawn harvest during the 2000 early T-Zone hunt had reached 30 percent, that would still equate to just one buck fawn

ALTHOUGH specialized antlerless seasons are often blamed for killing large numbers of buck fawns, harvest statistics prove otherwise.

kill per 816 acres of deer range.

These "losses" are a small price to pay considering the population control antlerless seasons afford wildlife managers. For example, in the 2000 early T-Zone, hunters killed about 51,141 does and doe fawns, which would have produced about .85 fawns apiece the following spring (based on a statewide average of female productivity).

Therefore, Wisconsin's 2000 early T-Zone not only directly removed 66,417 deer from the state's population, it prevented the birth of more than 43,470 deer the following spring, for a net population reduction of about 109,887 deer.

— RYAN GILLIGAN

ALMANAC INSIGHTS

➤ **PROFESSIONAL WILDLIFE** managers and biologists continue to tout the fact that despite decades of research and testing, non-lethal methods of controlling deer are not as effective as hunting.

At a meeting in Howard County, Maryland, research scientists, biologists and wildlife managers made it clear that hunting is the most effective way to control deer populations.

"Even if non-lethal techniques were perfected, they would never replace hunting deer," said Paul Peditto, game project manager for the Maryland Department of Natural Resources. Hunting remains "the most cost-effective way of doing business."

Officials realize there is no trouble-free replacement for bullets or arrows. Robert J. Warren, a wildlife biologist with the University of Georgia, commented about fertility research.

"We do not have any methods that can be used routinely," he said. "We are reducing fertility, but most studies have not yet shown a reduction in deer herds themselves."

Speakers also cited field tests in Maryland and New York, using various methods to prevent deer from conceiving, that all had drawbacks. Dr. Allen Rutberg with the Humane Society of the United States even said that inoculating deer the first time "is often not hard to do, but it gets harder and harder" as the deer grow more wary.

— *U.S. Sportsmen's Alliance*

➤ **"I'M TIRED OF THE** elaborate apologies that we hunters feel obliged to make for our sport. I'm ashamed when some brilliant sportsman finds it necessary to preface his exciting stories with lengthy excuses. I'm sick of letting thin-blooded, tongue-clicking do-gooders make us feel guilty every time we pick up a rifle."

— *Kristin Sergel*

Do You Know Who Hunting's Enemies Are?

Most hunters are well aware of the stance of anti-hunting groups like PeTA and The Fund for Animals, but did you know one of hunting's greatest opponents probably has an office in your hometown or county?

Although we often gloss over its image with thoughts of "rescued" stray cats and dogs, the Humane Society of the United States is hardly benign. For proof, look no further than its official stance on hunting.

"The Humane Society of the United States is strongly opposed to the hunting of any animal for fun, trophy or for sport, because of the trauma, suffering and death to the animals which results. The HSUS also opposes such killing because of the negative effect upon the young who may learn to accept and live with needless suffering and killing."

However, unlike more-radical groups, the HSUS claims to recognize that needs for human subsistence might require killing wildlife.

Groups like Friends of Animals, Inc., have more alarming stances.

"Hunting is cruel. It is deceitful. It is socially unjustifiable. It is ecologically disruptive. Friends of Animals oppose hunting in all its forms."

The group is also frighteningly removed from reality, saying, "The cruelty of hunting involves the gratuitous pain caused wild animals. True, wild predators also hunt, but their killing is not gratuitous. Only humans kill for pleasure."

— THE NATIONAL SHOOTING SPORTS FOUNDATION

Washington Residents Approve of Hunting

With most Americans living in urban areas, it's not surprising that polls and referendums regarding hunting, fishing and trapping often reveal public disapproval for these activities. However, a recent telephone survey by the Washington Department of Fish and Wildlife bucked this trend, indicating widespread public support for hunting.

More than 90 percent of survey respondents — who were hunters and nonhunters — approved of hunting for meat, and many others endorsed hunting for wildlife damage control.

Conversely, few respondents approved of trophy hunting.

These results are surprising considering Washington residents passed a ballot initiative banning foothold and Conibear traps in November 2000. The ban wasn't limited to recreational fur trappers, either. The initiative prohibited animal damage control workers and state wildlife managers from using such traps.

Animal-Rightist Compares Sept. 11 to Poultry-Farming Activities

Ever wonder how bizarre animal-rights activists think? If not, consider the off-the-wall comments Karen Davis, president of United Poultry Concerns, wrote in a letter to the *Vegan Voice*.

"I think it is speciesist to think that the Sept. 11 (terrorist) attack was a greater tragedy than what millions of chickens endured that day and what they endure every day because they cannot defend themselves against the concerted human appetites arrayed against them."

— U.S. SPORTSMEN'S ALLIANCE

ALMANAC INSIGHTS

➤ **WHEN DEER NUMBERS** exceed the land's carrying capacity, heavy browsing destroys the habitat. The physical condition of the deer degenerates and results in lower reproductive rates and survival. Ultimately, growth rates and deer numbers stabilize at some lower density. Unfortunately, when deer numbers exceed the land's carrying capacity, the habitat destruction affects other species, and habitat recovery is slow.

There are many examples of deer populations in various parts of the United States that have grown out of control when hunting was curtailed. Such cases are rare in Missouri, but have occurred in localized situations. Knob Noster State Park in west-central Missouri provides an example of what can happen when a deer population is not managed.

Deer disappeared from the area around Knob Noster in the early 1900s. Between 1945 and 1947, the Missouri Department of Conservation reintroduced about 50 deer into Knob Noster State Park. The population grew rapidly, and by 1953, most plants showed signs of heavy browsing. A severe winter in 1959-60 caused the only documented case of winter starvation of Missouri deer. Seventeen deer were found dead or starving in Knob Noster, and it is likely there were more. If the habitat had not been browsed severely by too many deer, the deer probably would have survived.

➤ **WHITETAILS ARE** important to Missouri hunters. More Missourians hunt deer than any other game animal. The state has more than 530,000 deer hunters, and the annual harvest typically exceeds 225,000 deer. Revenue from deer hunting permits alone exceeds $6.6 million annually. Estimates of total dollars spent by deer hunters in Missouri exceeds $110 million annually, with an additional $220 million in business activity.

DAVID GLITHERO killed this enormous buck on opening day of Ontario's archery season. If accepted, the 197⅜-inch buck will become Ontario's new record nontypical bow-kill.

2

The Big Bucks of North America

Canadian Bow-Hunters Kill Record-Class Nontypicals

When David Glithero and his wife, Rachelle, walked to their tree stands on opening morning of Ontario's 2000 archery season, they had no idea they were beginning a two-year quest for a record-class whitetail.

That morning, Rachelle, who had only been bow-hunting two years, encountered a huge nontypical buck. However, the deer approached her stand head-on, never presenting a shot.

Less than two weeks later, David got his chance. Unfortunately, as the bruiser passed his stand, David misjudged the distance and missed the buck.

The rest of the season passed without either hunter getting another opportunity at the big buck. However, they continued their pursuit through the post-season by searching for the buck's sheds, Their hopes that the buck had survived hunting season were confirmed on Dec. 23, 2000, when David found one side of the buck's distinctive rack.

On Oct. 16, 2001, opening day of the following bow season, David and Rachelle headed back to the Lanark County woodlot where they had been scouting the big nontypical, hoping to cross the big buck's path again.

They didn't have to wait long. At 7:15 a.m., David spotted a big 8-pointer walking toward his stand, but the buck veered out of range. Dejected, David settled back in his stand, doubting he'd encounter more action.

However, seconds after the 8-pointer left, David saw movement in the opposite direction. As he pivoted for a better view, he saw a massive rack moving toward his stand. It was the buck he had missed the previous year!

The buck soon stopped in a shooting lane, and Glithero made a perfect shot. The buck high-kicked its hind legs, and then barreled into the brush.

Minutes later, Glithero descended from his stand and found the buck laying dead 70 yards away.

A year of patience and hard work had paid off. Glithero had killed the buck of a lifetime. Not only that, the buck's preliminary score of 197³/₈ inches surpasses Ontario's standing nontypical bow-kill record, a 168⁶/₈-inch buck killed by Steve Marcinkiewicz in 1995. If accepted, Glithero's buck will become Ontario's record nontypical in the Pope and Young record book.

RYAN GILLIGAN

Alberta Monster Might Rewrite the Books

SERGE PAQUET killed this nontypical while bow-hunting Nov. 24, 2000, in Alberta. At 241³/₈ inches, it is poised to become Canada's largest nontypical bow-kill.

To most bow-hunters, any deer is a trophy — especially when it's your first bow-kill. However, the buck I was fortunate enough to kill in 2000, would be a trophy in anyone's book.

My son, Mark, and I took a day off to go hunting in Strathcona County, Alberta, on Nov. 24, 2000.

I had passed up five bucks earlier in the season, despite never killing a buck with my bow.

We arrived early, but by 10 a.m., I had not seen a deer, and to make matters worse, I had a splitting headache.

I returned to my truck for lunch and had considered ending my hunt for the day, but decided not to because Mark had taken a day off work to hunt with me. After a nap, Mark and I returned to our morning stands.

At 3 p.m., I heard a buck walking in the snow. As the buck appeared and walked into range, I decided to shoot, but had difficulty drawing as I'd undergone elbow surgery a month before. I had to stand to draw, but the buck was already within 20 yards.

Luckily I was able to stand and draw my bow without spooking the deer. At the shot, the buck took off. At first I thought I had missed, but I saw the deer fall before it reached the field edge.

With a preliminary score of 241³/₈, the 31-point nontypical is poised to surpass the previous Canadian record buck by ¹/₈ point!

— Serge Paquet

Iowa Hunter Scores on Public-Land Bruiser

These days, hunters are practically bombarded with stories about the big whitetails that roam Iowa's farm county. Iowa hunts are featured on high-profile hunting videos, touted in magazine articles and sold at top-dollar through guides and outfitters. And although such publicity captures the interest of almost any hunter who sees it, it sometimes also gives the impression Iowa hunts are beyond the means of the average deer hunter.

But believe it or not, with a map, a firm handshake and a little research, many hunters kill big Iowa bucks on do-it-yourself hunts. Don Reese, of Solon, Iowa, is living proof.

Fall 2000 marked Reese's first Iowa bow-season. He didn't have access to much private land, so Reese contacted the Iowa Department of Natural Resources for information on public hunting areas.

Armed with the information he received from the DNR, Reese set his sights on the Sugar Bottom area near the Coralville Reservoir in North Liberty, Iowa. The terrain and habitat seemed to guarantee Reese an encounter with a big buck. However, his perceptions changed drastically when he saw the parcel firsthand. Although the land itself was everything the maps and information he received indicated, he was discouraged by the presence of well-worn bike and walking trails. People had obviously been using the area frequently and Reese wondered how that had affected deer activity.

Although he was disappointed by the area's level of human activity,

A LITTLE HOMEWORK paid off big when Don Reese killed this 133⅜-inch buck on public land in Iowa

Reese still held hopes for the area and hung a stand near some fresh buck sign.

On Nov. 12, 2000, Reese's homework and perseverance were rewarded. At 11:45 a.m., a tall-racked 10-pointer stepped into his shooting lane at 18 yards, giving Reese a quartering-away shot. Reese took careful aim and touched the trigger on his release, sending the arrow through the buck's lungs. The 10-point bruiser went only 40 yards before collapsing.

Reese was overwhelmed. Despite the odds, he had killed the buck of a lifetime. The buck weighed 210 pounds field dressed and gross-scored 133⅝ inches.

— RYAN GILLIGAN

11-Year-Old Kills Monstrous First Whitetail

Successful hunting and fishing just seem to come naturally for Chris Bertholomey of Pacific, Mo. At age 11, he has accomplished hunting and fishing milestones some outdoorsmen never achieve, including placing in archery tournaments, catching and releasing a lunker trout, catching an 8½-pound largemouth bass and killing a boss spring gobbler.

Despite his extensive outdoors experience, Betholomey hadn't killed his first whitetail. He hoped that might change when he participated in a Missouri's special youth gun-hunt in Fall 2001. However, by hunt's end, he was still skunked.

Bertholomey and his father faced more frustration during Missouri's November gun season. After three days of unsuccessful hunting at their family farm, Betholomey and his father traveled near their hometown of Pacific, Mo., to hunt a farm they had bow-hunted earlier in the year.

The move was a gamble. After all, the farm held only 13 acres of woods and the landowner had been seeing only a few small bucks. The hunters had bow-hunted the land for the first time that year, and confirmed the landowner's report. However, they hoped the move would pay off.

It did.

At 4:30 p.m. Nov. 12, Bertholomey and his father spotted a doe crossing a nearby field with a buck hot on its trail.

CHRIS BERTHOLOMEY killed his first deer, this 150-class 10-pointer, while hunting with his dad near Pacific, Mo.

Bertholomey was ready to shoot his first deer, and planned on shooting the doe. As he waited for a better shot, he realized just how big the buck was and decided to try for him. When the buck stepped into the open at 85 yards, Bertholomey, lined up the sights on his .30-30 and fired, dropping the buck instantly.

When Bertholomey and his father walked to the buck, they couldn't believe what they saw. The buck had a 21⅞-inch-wide, 10-point rack that later netted 151⅛ inches.

With a first deer like that, Bertholomey has a dealt himself a tough act to follow!

— Ryan Gilligan

Patience Pays for Georgia Rifle-Hunter

Most of my 2000 Georgia gun-deer season had been frustrating to say the least. Although I had done extensive pre-season scouting, planted food plots and hunted prime deer areas, I had not seen a deer in eight consecutive days of hunting. With my patience running thin, I planned to spend Day 9 hunting a spot on my farm I was confident could break my streak. However, my hunting partner, David Swinwood, persuaded me to change my mind.

The day before, I had hung a stand on a well-used oak ridge that overlooked a clear-cut and river bottom. I wanted to wait a few days before hunting the new area, but Swinwood convinced me I had nothing to lose by hunting the new stand.

Reluctantly, I awoke early the next morning and climbed into the unfamiliar stand by 6 a.m. Although it was a beautiful morning, two hours quickly passed without any apparent deer activity. Frustration and outside obligations had almost lured me out of the stand when I heard a twig snap nearby. The past several uneventful days had made me skeptical, but as I turned, I saw a huge buck standing 50 yards away.

With my heart pounding uncontrollably, I watched the buck through my riflescope. It seemed to suspect something was wrong, and looked like it was about to flee. Anxious to shoot before the deer left the area, I carefully placed my cross-hairs on the buck's chest and fired. The big buck bounded away from my stand and ran gingerly into the river bottom.

MEMORIES OF AN unsuccessful season almost kept Lewis Crook in bed for Day 9 of Georgia's gun-deer season. However, his persistence paid off, and he was soon tagging this big 10-pointer.

Because of the buck's labored gait, I was confident I had made a good shot. However, when I returned with friends to track him, we could find no blood or hair along the buck's path.

I was almost convinced I had missed the buck when Swinwood found a puddle of blood in the river bottom. As I hurried to meet Swinwood on the blood trail, I spotted the big 10-pointer laying 40 yards away.

My long, slow days and countless hours on unproductive stands were forgotten as I tagged my first trophy whitetail.

— LEWIS CROOK

Iowa Hunter Overcomes Pneumonia for Big Buck

It was October 1998, and I had only two weeks to hunt a Conservation Reserve Program parcel near my Iowa home before pheasant hunters interrupted deer patterns for the season. Unfortunately, I was stricken with pneumonia.

With time quickly ticking by, and the pheasant opener rapidly approaching, my health slowly improved. Finally, I grew strong enough to pull my bow back — after cranking down the draw weight for the second time that season.

Although I knew I'd be pressing my luck to head to my stand in my weakened state, the bird hunters were about to take over and I had to get out there before they arrived.

HOWARD SCHMITZ'S dedication has yielded tremendous rewards. In 1998, he overcame pneumonia for a chance to kill this 200-class nontypical, above. In 2001, Schmitz ended a two-year quest for "Grandpa Snaggle Rack" a 160-class buck he first encountered in 2000, left.

I became even more determined to hunt when northeastern winds blew in the night before my hunt. The rare wind let me hunt one of my favorite stands. When I awoke the next morning, Nov. 3, 1998, the thermometer read 35 degrees and the wind was blowing from the northeast at 10 to 15 miles per hour.

Sick or not, I had to hunt my favorite stand. For all I knew, it would have been another 30 days before the wind blew from the northeast again.

Shortly after dawn, I spotted a huge buck in the brush about 180 yards away.

I got his attention with a five-second mild rattling sequence. After he stared in my direction for about 10 seconds, I rattled again, this time slightly longer and louder.

The buck turned and walked toward me, closing the distance to just 15 yards! My arrow hit the buck through the lungs and he walked only 30 yards before falling.

What a rush! I wasted no time climbing down and checking out my prize. Unbelievable! Only once had I seen a deer of his size — and that was one year earlier from the same stand. No doubt this was the same animal. At that time, I thought I was an extremely fortunate hunter just to see a deer like that. However, killing the 200-class brute was hard to beat.

Grandpa Snaggle Rack

After shooting that huge buck in 1998, my good luck continued.

In Fall 2000, I often observed an aggressive nontypical buck, accompanied by a younger buck with a similar rack. In my log I called them "Snaggle Rack" and "Grandpa Snaggle Rack" to differentiate the two bucks. The younger one — age $2\frac{1}{2}$ — was very reckless during the rut, and I could have shot him several times. The elder Snaggle — which I then estimated at $3\frac{1}{2}$ years and 145 inches — was also active during the rut. However, he never offered a shot, leaving me looking forward to the 2001 season.

Unfortunately, 2001 would be more challenging than I had imagined. Large bucks were few and far between, perhaps because of unseasonably warm temperatures.

Persistence paid off, however, on stand No. 35. Shortly after sunrise, Nov. 10, 2001, Grandpa Snaggle Rack made his second appearance of the year. It was a tense 15 minutes as I watched him come from over 200 yards away to check out a small patch of canary grass in search of a doe. At 27 yards, a tough season turned sweet!

Grandpa Snaggle Rack dressed out at 210 pounds. His 14-point rack had a 19-inch inside spread and 24-inch main beams. The rack grossed 167⅝ nontypical Boone and Crockett inches and netted 161⁶⁄₈ inches.

— Howard Schmitz

BOB HIATT shot this heavy-beamed whitetail on the second morning of Kansas' 2001 firearms season.

Hunter Outsmarts Telephone-Pole Buck

During pre-season scouting trips, Bob Hiatt, of Paola, Kan., discovered a buck rub on a telephone pole. He had no idea how large the rub's maker was until Day 2 of Kansas' 2001 firearms season.

Hiatt didn't get a shot on opening day of the 2001 gun-season, but the second day would prove a different story.

At 8:10 a.m. that morning, Hiatt was watching does milling around him. When he glanced behind his stand, all he saw were antlers.

Hiatt shouldered his rifle, aimed at the giant buck and shot, dropping it in its tracks.

The buck's antler bases measure 6 inches in diameter. It is the largest buck ever killed on the Linn County property Hiatt hunts and the largest Hiatt has ever shot.

— Matt Hiatt

Indiana Couple Shares Successful Hunt

By late October 2000, my bow season had been a wash. I had hunted every day of Indiana's archery season, and although I had seen a few decent bucks, no big bucks had given me a chance.

I was hoping my luck would change on Oct. 20, 2000. My fiance, Rachael, was coming home from college for her fall break, and she was planning to sit with me while I hunted.

That evening, after reaching my hunting area, Rachael and I gathered our gear and started the short trek into the woodlot. As we reached our stand trees, I spotted two big bucks running ahead of us.

Instinctively, I grabbed my grunt call and made two loud grunts. The larger buck looked toward Rachael and I, paused and then sprinted at us! Rachael hunkered next to her stand tree, while I prepared for a shot.

When the buck stopped in an opening about 10 yards away, I held my sight pin on its vitals and released the arrow. At the shot, the buck spun around and raced out of sight.

After waiting a few minutes and rethinking what had happened, Rachael and I started to look for my arrow. As timed ticked by without us finding the arrow or blood, I began second-guessing my shot. Ten minutes later, I was almost convinced I had missed when I heard Rachael yell "blood!"

We followed the buck's trail several hundred yards, and

DEREK PHILLIPS and his fiance, Rachael, were still en route to their stands when Phillips shot this Pope and Young-class buck.

Rachael's keen eye for finding blood was a tremendous help.

Finally, we spotted what we had been praying for — the buck laying dead just 20 yards ahead of us.

I was ecstatic. I had killed my first buck, and it was a dandy. Best of all, I was able to share the experience with Rachael.

After the shock started to wear off, I hurried to my truck, drove it to the field and with Rachael's help, heaved the huge-bodied buck onto the tailgate. We then drove home to show our parents.

The buck weighed 235 pounds field dressed, and after the 60-day drying period, scored $126^7/_8$ inches, qualifying it for the Pope and Young record book.

Rachael and I have shared many hunts, but none that matched the excitement of that October evening.

— DEREK PHILLIPS

Wisconsin Hunter Bags 'Junkyard Buck'

As I looked at my busy schedule for the Fall of 2001, I doubted I'd get a chance to kill a deer with my bow. Worse, I was attending college two hours from my central Wisconsin home. Little did I know I'd end my season killing the buck of a lifetime.

I began my season hunting in a mature white pine 150 yards from my parents' house. The first afternoon, a 6-pointer came into view. I was so excited my arms shook, and when I shot, I watched my arrow harmlessly penetrate the soft earth below the buck's body.

Although I was crushed, I vowed to not let it happen again, as I practiced shooting my bow almost daily. However, school continued to keep me away from home and hunting.

I finally found a break in my schedule and drove home to hunt. On that late fall morning I'd been sitting in the white pine for about an hour when the whitetail of my dreams appeared.

The buck strode into view without a sound. I started breathing heavily, so I looked away and tried to relax.

The buck stepped into my shooting lane and stopped. I couldn't believe my good fortune! However, as I reached full draw, the buck quartered toward me, preventing me from shooting. As my arm began trembling with fatigue, the buck turned broadside.

As I released, I saw the arrow shoot past the rest in slow motion. Suddenly the deer shattered the tranquility of the woods as it bounded away.

When the commotion stopped, I scrambled out of my stand and raced home to call my dad at work.

It took him about an hour to arrive, and when I told him how big the buck

MARK KITOWSKI killed this 170-class 14-pointer during Wisconsin's 2001 archery season.

was, he thought I was exaggerating.

My dad grabbed his knife and a camera and we walked to where the buck had been standing.

We found a small speck of blood, then the speck turned into a stream. We found the deer dead after it had traveled 80 yards. I had hit him through both lungs.

The 4½-year-old buck weighed 200 pounds field dressed and his neck had a circumference of 36 inches. His 14-point rack has 25-inch-long main beams and rough scored 176⅛ inches.

Even though I'd never seen the buck before, some of the neighbors had. One family nicknamed the buck "Jaws" because the split left main beam looked like a pair of jaws. Another neighbor had seen the buck while shining near the town dump and nicknamed it "The Junkyard Buck."

Whatever its name, it is truly the buck of a lifetime.

— MARK KITOWSKI

Wisconsin Man Tags Big Buck After Slow Season

In November 2001, Steve Sibinski of New Berlin, Wis., learned patience and perseverance can yield huge rewards.

Earlier that fall, he and his friend obtained permission to hunt a 640-acre farm that had never been bow-hunted. The duo scouted the property briefly in late September and hunted a half-day the following weekend, then stayed off the farm through the low-odds days of October.

On Nov. 6, with the rut nearing its peak, Sibinski and his friend headed back to the farm, arriving at their stands at about 1:30 p.m. Although Sibinski hoped his patience and restraint would yield big rewards, by 4 p.m., he hadn't seen anything.

Suddenly, Sibinski spotted a distant buck walking toward his stand. However, as the buck continued to slowly close the distance, it disappeared within a small standing cornfield.

After several uneventful minutes, Sibinski rattled aggressively, mixing in three long grunts and a doe bleat. He had hardly taken the call from his lips when he spotted the buck emerge from the corn at 50 yards, lower its head and begin charging toward the sound.

When the buck passed within 15 yards, stopping to look for the source of the calling. Sibinski drew and released.

Although Sibinski hit the buck, the arrow penetrated farther back than he intended.

Minutes later, Sibinski descended from his stand and

STEVE SIBINSKI killed this impressive Wisconsin buck while bow-hunting in November 2001.

began looking for blood. What he found didn't bode well. He couldn't locate his arrow and found hair and blood-covered corn along the buck's path. The sparse blood trail stretched several hundred yards, and then disappeared. Considering the situation, Sibinski and his partner decided to back off and return the following day.

The next morning, they picked up the buck's trail where they stopped the night before. After an anxious two-and-a-half-hour tracking job, Sibinski and his friend found the dead buck 250 yards from where they had stopped tracking the previous night.

Sibinski's never-give-up attitude had yielded a beautiful buck!

— Ryan Gilligan

Minnesota Buck Makes the Books

When I headed to my southeastern Minnesota hunting property on the afternoon of Oct. 13, 2001, I was only planning to hang a few stands and cut some shooting lanes. After all, the weather was unseasonably warm, and I thought the conditions had shut down buck activity.

When I had finished my tasks, it was 3 p.m. Although it was against my better judgement, I decided to spend the rest of the evening in the last stand I had hung. I had brought my bow, and I thought sitting in the stand would at least let me see if any does were using the area.

However, the evening exceeded all of my expectations when, about an hour before sundown, I spotted a large-bodied deer moving toward me at about 100 yards. As the buck closed the distance, I could see it had an impressive rack.

Moments later, I held my breath as the buck reached a fork in the well-worn trail, just out of range. One path would lead the buck away from my stand, while the other would likely bring it through my shooting lane at less than 10 yards. As my heart pounded with anticipation, the buck paused, and then began walking toward my stand.

I was at full draw when the buck stepped into my shooting lane — which I had cut only a couple of hours earlier — presenting a broadside 7-yard shot.

A split-second later, my arrow zipped through the buck's lungs, sending him bounding down a nearby hill.

Although I thought I had made a good shot, doubt entered my mind

ALEX HAAGENSEN was only planning to hang tree stands and cut shooting lanes when he headed to his hunting area on Oct. 13, 2001. However, the afternoon eventually yielded a shot at this massive 10-pointer.

as rain started falling, threatening to wash away the buck's blood trail.

Balancing my desire to give the buck time to lay down and the need to find the quickly disappearing blood trail, I waited 10 minutes before descending from my stand and tracking the buck.

Despite my fears, I quickly picked up the buck's trail and soon spotted its rack protruding from the creek bed at the bottom of the hill.

Much to my surprise, the buck was much larger than I had though when I shot it, sporting a massive 10-point rack with split brow tines. What a way to conclude a day I hadn't even intended to hunt!

— ALEX HAAGENSEN

Pennsylvania Teenager Kills Monster Buck

Although most bow-hunters dream of killing a Pope and Young buck, few actually do. Of the fortunate hunters who reach this goal, many must wait until late in their hunting careers. Not so for Jameson Grubb of Coatesville, Pa. In Fall 2001, he reached his big-buck dreams at age 16.

It wasn't easy, however. Grubb had been bow-hunting since he was 12, but had never shot a deer. In Fall 2001, Grubb's prospects weren't looking any better than they had in the previous years. As fall eased into late October, Grubb dedicated himself to hunting as often as possible during the upcoming rut.

On Oct. 23, 2001, Grubb had just climbed into his tree stand when something caught his eye. A big 8-point buck was just about to cross the trail he'd followed as he walked to his stand! Within minutes, the buck bedded down among some pines. Grubb saw the deer rub his antlers from his bed. An hour later, the deer rose from its bed, but never came closer than 50 yards from Grubb.

Grubb saw nothing but squirrels on his next two hunts.

On Oct. 27, Grubb's father hunted, too. As he waited in his stand, he videotaped the same 8-pointer Jameson had seen four days earlier. Grubb's father didn't shoot because he thought the buck might eventually walk past his son. Although the buck did, it passed Grubb's stand along a trail the young hunter couldn't see.

After seeing the video, Grubb was even more determined to

JAMESON GRUBB'S first deer was this 160-class 9-pointer. The buck's greatest spread is 29½ inches.

succeed. He returned to his stand later that evening.

Right away, Grubb saw a buck in the distance. The buck was so far away, Grubb considered moving his stand, but decided not to. It was a good decision.

Two hours later, he heard grunting behind him. When he turned around, he saw a doe standing 25 yards away. Suddenly a huge buck stepped from behind a bush and continued grunting for two minutes, scraping and pawing the ground. Grubb's knees grew weak. Just then, something cracked in the distance and the buck wheeled toward the sound, giving Grubb a chance to draw. Grubb shot and the buck dropped in its tracks.

The 9-pointer was even bigger than the 8-pointer Grubb had seen earlier, sporting a 29½-inch inside spread and measuring 160 inches. Most important, Grubb's long deer hunting drought was over.

— JOE SHEAD

Hunter Scores on Georgia 11-pointer

Although he's a young hunter, beginners' luck had nothing to do with Alabama 15-year-old Blake Turner's success during Fall 2001.

Turner had been hunting since he was 13, under the guidance of his uncle Ronnie Childs. Despite his early efforts, he had missed the few small bucks that presented a shot, because of an apparent case of buck fever. However, although he didn't shoot a buck in his first two years of hunting, he had taken three does his first year and was confident he'd learn to keep buck fever in check.

Turner put his buck fever remedy to the test Nov. 3, 2001, while hunting with Childs in southern Georgia. Turner chose to hunt from a tower stand in a rye field between two bottomland areas. Turner knew there were big deer and the area, and wild hogs were also present. Turner had wanting to shoot a hog all season.

After sitting for about a half-hour, Turner heard hogs snorting and fighting behind him. He raised his .30-06 to the window, but when nothing walked into view after five minutes, Turner eased the rifle back to its resting place in the corner.

He had just set the gun down when a deer walked into the rye field. The sun was shining directly on the deer, and at first, Turner didn't know what it was, but when it moved, he immediately observed antlers. Bucks in the area Turner hunts must have at least three points on the main beam to be legal. When Turner scoped the buck and counted four points on

BLAKE TURNER killed this 120-class Georgia buck on Nov. 3, 2001. The impressive 11-pointer was Turner's first buck.

one beam, that was all he needed. He centered the cross-hairs on the buck's shoulder and touched the trigger. The buck dropped.

Turner radioed his uncle, who told him to calm down. Fifteen minutes later, Turner descended from his stand, and with his uncle, traveled the 105 yards to where the buck had stood. Lying there was Turner's first buck — a 120-class 11-pointer. The young hunter had indeed overcome buck fever.

The buck sported a 17½-inch-wide rack and weighed 155 pounds field dressed.

— Joe Shead

Big-City Bucks Fall to Illinois Bow-Hunters

Mike Neri of Crystal Lake, Ill., is no stranger to killing big bucks. However, he differs from most whitetail hunters. Instead of hunting remote northern forests or distant farm country, he targets bucks in the scattered woodlots and small farms of McHenry County, Ill., just outside of Chicago's sprawling suburbs. His success speaks volumes about the bucks that inhabit the lightly hunted land around America's largest cities.

Neri's 2001 archery season is a perfect example.

After spending summer and early fall 2001 monitoring his hunting land, Neri and his friend Ed Allen had located and patterned several Pope and Young-class bucks, including a drop-tined 160-class buck they had photographed on a remote-sensing camera.

Using what they had learned from scouting, Neri and Allen hung several stands around a beanfield being hammered by mature bucks, and then waited anxiously for opening day of Illinois' archery season.

After the season opened, Neri struck paydirt first. A half-hour before sunset on Oct. 7,

USING A remote-sensing camera, Ed Allen, above, and Mike Neri, opposite page, photographed this 160-class buck in Summer 2001. Allen eventually killed the buck with his bow on Nov. 3. However, the buck had broken off the 6-inch drop tine that once grew below its right G-3.

AFTER SPENDING Summer 2001 scouting, creating food plots and glassing soybean fields near his Crystal Lake, Ill., home, Mike Neri killed this 140-class typical during opening week of Illinois' archery season.

Boone & Crockett Bucks Abound in Chicago Suburbs

Illinois is no secret to bow-hunters. However, when most hunters think about deer hunting in the Land of Lincoln, they think of the Golden Triangle — Pike, Adams and Brown counties, along the state's western border. And for good reason. The relatively small area's rich farm country and river bottom hills produced 274 Pope & Young and 42 Boone & Crockett entries between 1991 and 2000.

Despite these impressive statistics, the P&Y and B&C record books reveal a surprising fact: Bow-hunters might be just as likely to kill a record-class buck within a bustling Chicago suburb as they are in the Golden Triangle farmland.

Need proof? For starters, suburban Will, Kane and McHenry counties accounted for more than 229 P&Y entries between 1991 and 2000. Plus, adjacent Lake and Cook counties yielded more than 31 entries each during the same period, despite being Illinois' most densely populated counties.

Although it's hard to fathom that so many large bucks could exist — much less be killed — so close to one of the country's largest cities, the area's mix of small farms, woodlots and housing developments provides bucks everything they need to grow large: food, cover and protection from hunters.

— RYAN GILLIGAN

he heard leaves shuffling behind his stand. Judging from the sound, he knew it was a deer, but thick cover blocked his view until the animal stepped within 10 yards of his stand. Neri quickly realized the deer was one of the bucks he and Allen had seen during summer. When the buck walked in a shooting lane three yards away, Neri released, sending his arrow through the buck's chest. The 140-inch 10-pointer ran only 70 yards before falling.

Allen got his chance several weeks later on Nov. 3, while he and Neri hunted a farm near where Neri had killed his buck. About an hour before sunset, a large buck walked under Allen's stand, and Allen made a perfect shot. The buck ran into the nearby brush and fell.

Much to both hunters' surprise, Allen's buck was the 160-class drop-tined buck they had photographed in velvet with their remote-sensing camera in late Summer 2001.

Neri and Allen's success not only shows the importance of pre-season scouting, it proves not all big bucks prefer backcountry haunts.

— RYAN GILLIGAN

Pennsylvania Bow-Hunter Kills Nontypical Brute

When Dennis Mauer of Hebe, Pa., retuned from work the afternoon of Oct. 26, 2001, he had little faith in his evening hunting prospects. He knew he wouldn't arrive at his tree stand until after 5 p.m., and the weather was cold and extremely windy. However, he mustered enough hope to warrant loading his bow-hunting gear and heading to the woods.

After reaching his stand, Mauer's hopes diminished further. He just *knew* no deer were going to show. Frustrated, he looked at his watch and silently promised he would head home at 5:45 p.m., despite the fact shooting hours didn't expire until almost 7 p.m.

His premonitions were shattered a few minutes later as a twig snapped behind his stand. When Mauer turned to look, he saw the hindquarters of a deer sticking out from behind a tree a few yards from his stand. As he turned toward the deer, he saw a flicker of movement out of the corner of his eye. A huge buck soon stepped into view and walked stiff-legged toward the other deer.

Trying to not spook the deer beneath him, Mauer stood and picked up his bow. The buck paused momentarily in a small oak grove 35 yards away, and Mauer began to draw. However, as he reached full draw, he realized he couldn't feel his kisser button through his heavy facemask. Mauer depended on the button for shooting, so, while still at half-draw, he scraped the mask below his chin. With the buck at 20 yards, Mauer finished drawing, but

DENNIS MAUER braved wind and cold temperatures to kill this 160-class nontypical in late October 2001.

his arrow squeaked loudly across the rest.

The buck froze and scanned the woods for danger, eventually locking onto Mauer. But it was too late. Mauer's sight pin was already fixed behind the buck's shoulder. Mauer squeezed the trigger on his release, launching his arrow into the buck's vitals.

As the arrow hit, the buck wheeled around, bolted past Mauer's tree, and then disappeared in some distant briars.

Later that night, after returning to the property with a few friends, Mauer found the dead buck near where he had last seen it from his tree stand.

Much to Mauer's surprise, the buck sported 14 points and would later score 161⅞. A low-odds, 35-minute hunt had yielded the buck of a lifetime!

— Ryan Gilligan

Saskatchewan Bruiser Weighs 275 Pounds

In Fall 2001, I hunted near Cumberland House, Saskatchewan, during opening week of the 2001 firearms deer season. It had snowed 4 inches the week before the opener, and temperatures had been in the 20s. Unfortunately, when I got there, unseasonable weather also arrived, bringing warm temperatures, with highs around 50 degrees and lows in the 30s. I knew it would be a tough hunt because big bucks don't move as well in warm temperatures.

My fears proved true on the first day of the hunt. Although I sat from dawn to dusk, I saw only five does and one small buck.

The second day started better. Cooler weather during the night brought a hard frost and temperatures around 20 degrees. As I left camp, I opted to switch stands, because the wind had changed. My new stand overlooked an old pasture overgrown with willow saplings. On each end of it was a poplar ridge that created a perfect funnel.

Around 9:30 a.m. I caught movement at the end of the pasture, and I spotted a large-bodied buck sneaking through the willows. I couldn't believe how big the body was at 110 yards. I now believe in the Bergman Rule, which states that the farther you get from the equator, the bigger the animal has to be to survive the harsh winters.

The buck was slowly working his way through the willows, scent-checking the ground as he went. Just as he was about to enter an opening, he crossed the path I had taken to my stand and he jumped

DESPITE UNSEASONABLY warm weather, Tim Andrus killed this heavy-bodied, 140-class buck during his 2001 Saskatchewan gun-hunt.

back like he had hit an electric fence. My boots must have picked up some type of odor on the trek in. This surprised me because I always practice scent control, wearing an activated-charcoal suit and using scent-eliminating spray.

The buck ran into some willows and began to snort and stamp its hoof, looking toward the spot where he had smelled me. After what seemed like an hour, but was probably about two minutes, he began running toward the same opening. When he hit the opening, I bleated with my voice, stopping him long enough to make the shot.

Although the buck initially seemed uninjured, it piled up 100 yards away.

When I approached the buck, I couldn't believe its body size — it actually made its 10-point, 140-class rack look small! The buck field dressed at 275 pounds!

— TIM ANDRUS

Texas 8-Pointer Ends Five-Year Quest

In Fall 2000, after five years of target practice and learning his way around the deer woods, my 12-year-old son, Chris Farris, was eager for his first chance at a mature buck. While visiting the Flat Top Ranch in Walnut Springs, Texas, he finally got his opportunity.

After arriving at the ranch, we unpacked our gear and prepared for the morning hunt.

After a sleepless, anticipation-filled night, Chris and I headed to our stands. We saw several deer that morning, including a mature 8-pointer that proved his age and wisdom by circling the field before leaving the brush to feed, never giving Chris a shot.

After returning to camp for lunch, we decided to spend the afternoon at the same stand, hoping we could outsmart the big 8-pointer. However, as the afternoon progressed, the wind increased, virtually halting deer movement.

Just before dark, we finally saw a few young deer. As we watched them, a flash of motion caught Chris' eye. Although it was far from our stand, Chris determined it was a mature buck and it was headed right toward us.

When the buck finally stepped into range, it turned its head, giving Chris and I our first good look at its rack. It was the big 8-pointer that had eluded us that morning!

Chris gracefully lowered his binoculars and shouldered his rifle as the buck meandered

FIVE YEARS of anticipation, target practice and study of deer behavior paid of for 12-year-old Chris Farris when he killed this 132-inch Texas 8-pointer in Fall 2001.

through the brush.

Then it happened.

Chris developed a severe case of buck fever. "I see him, but I can't stop shaking!" he said.

I told him to aim at a tree trunk away from the deer and take slow, deep breaths until he could hold a steady aim.

About 30 seconds later, Chris had regained control. He moved the cross-hairs back to the buck's chest and fired, killing the deer instantly.

Chris' big 8-pointer was 7½ years old, and sported a 132-inch rack with 12-inch G2s.

— SHAWN FARRIS

Misty Morning Yields Dream Whitetail

WILLIAM PIERCE shot this wide-racked buck in November 2001 while hunting his farm near Unionville, Va.

The morning started thick with fog and cold with misty rain. I wanted to burrow deeper under my covers, but my wife got up to make coffee.

It was Nov. 24, 2001, and I planned to hunt on our farm in Unionville, Va. Rifle season was on, and the oranges, reds and golds of autumn beckoned.

After two hours, the damp cold began to take its toll. Yelping turkeys kept me from sleepy stupor as I heard a rustle in the woods behind me. Instead of a squirrel as expected, I saw a deer about 60 yards away.

I crept into position, watching him emerge from thick trees into a shooting lane. As he entered the lane, I shot.

After running 20 yards, the buck stopped, then collapsed. I remained motionless for a minute, studying him from my stand. As I walked to the buck, I realized the enormity of the fallen creature. This was a deer like I have only seen on television. The buck had a 25-inch spread, 24-inch main beams and 14 scoreable points. He is the deer of a lifetime!

— WILLIAM PIERCE

Wisconsin Hunter Slugs Big 8-pointer

Opening morning of Wisconsin's 2001 gun-deer season found Paul Gordon of Kohler, Wis., sitting in a stand on his grandfather's land. At about 8 a.m., a large buck entered the field and walked toward Gordon. When it stood 20 yards away, Gordon drew a bead on the buck's neck and dropped it with one shot from his shotgun.

Gordon called his dad on a walkie-talkie and said he'd shot a big buck, but he had no idea how big until the two hunters approached the fallen deer. Gordon's dad told him that any time you walk up to a deer and the first thing you see is antlers, you know it's big.

Gordon's buck sported 8 points and had an 18½-inch spread. The buck dressed at 176 pounds.

— JOE SHEAD

PAUL GORDON shot this 8-point buck in November 2001 while hunting on his grandfather's land.

Teen Has a Knack For Killing Big Bucks

On a particularly cold Nov. 5, 2000, I headed to my stand on my family's northern Wisconsin hunting land. Although my feet were numb by first light, I'd soon forget any discomfort.

At about 7 a.m. a 5-pointer chased a hot doe in front of me into the nearby maple slashing. Seconds later, a forkhorn I had seen the previous day trotted by, following their trail. As I waited for something bigger to show, the hot doe came screaming out of the maple slashings and stopped in front of my tree to catch her breath.

For a couple seconds, I could see the two young bucks at the edge of the maples trying to

JESSE SCHEWE experienced a phenomenal 2000 season. On Nov. 5, Schewe killed a mature 8-pointer, above. A few weeks later, during the state's gun season, Schewe scored again, killing a massive 10-pointer, left.

find her. Suddenly, the three deer froze and looked to the left of me, and I heard a distinct long, low grunt, Just then, I saw something out of the corner of my eye that made my heart pump so hard it shook every part of my body.

An 200-pound buck was strutting toward me — legs stiff and hair flared. I could see the 8-pointer had a wide spread and good mass, so I prepared to shoot, letting the buck pass my stand for a quartering-away shot. When he was at about 10 yards, I drew, grunted to make him stop and tried as hard as I could to

look at the vitals instead of the antlers. With everything in place, I released the arrow.

I saw the arrows fletchings zip into the buck's chest and out the other side, and the buck bounded out of sight.

Although I was sure I had hit the buck well, I gave him a few hours to lie down. After the agonizing wait, I eventually found him piled up 100 yards away. I thought my luck couldn't get any better. However, that was until Wisconsin's 2000 firearms season.

On Nov. 18, the first day of

gun season, I awoke to about four inches of fresh snow and still more coming down with the temperature in the mid-20s. The ideal conditions paid off quickly. A half hour after shooting hours began, I could hear something crashing out of the swamp to my left. I saw flashes of brown through the trees 100 yards away. I desperately tried to find the deer in my scope. What I finally saw amazed me — a huge buck with a monstrous rocking chair of a rack.

However, when I brought my cross-hairs to the opening I saw him last, he was gone. I scanned the woods for what seemed like an eternity. Then I saw him poke his head out of the cover he was hiding in and walk into an opening.

The sound of my shot echoed throughout the woods, and I sat down to catch my breath and let out a sigh of relief. I had hit the buck!

I waited 15 minutes and went to where I had last seen him. I soon found hair and a light blood trail. A few steps later, the trail turned into a wide path of sprayed blood. However, I couldn't see the buck. I took a few more steps along the bucks trail and saw a huge mass of antlers piled into a big maple tree.

After I unloaded my gun, I sprinted to the buck and learned he was even bigger than I thought. The 10-pointer had long, thick beams, forked G2s on both sides and almost foot-long tines. What a way to cap off a dream season!

— JESSE SCHEWE

Bow-Hunter Has Banner Season

DAN YENTER killed this 140-class whitetail Nov. 15, 2000, while bow-hunting in central Wisconsin.

The morning of Nov. 15, 2000, started like most mornings that Dan Yenter of Amherst Junction, Wis., went bow-hunting. He awoke at 5 a.m. and was on stand by 6 a.m., but after that, things became better than usual.

After sitting for an hour and a half without seeing a deer, motion caught Yenter's eye. He saw two deer running through a nearby patch of thick cover. Yenter assumed it was a buck chasing a doe. Yenter grunted but the deer kept going.

Twenty minutes later, Yenter saw a buck approaching. It was walking quickly about 30 yards away. Yenter grunted with his mouth and the buck stopped, but it was obstructed by vegetation, preventing Yenter from shooting. The deer looked at Yenter, then took a step backward. That was all Yenter needed. His shot was well-placed, and the deer dropped after running 75 yards.

The buck's rack grossed $140^{4}/_{8}$ inches.

— JOE SHEAD

Lady Hunter Scores Her First Double

Opening day of the 2001 gun-deer season found me sitting in my cozy deer stand. I didn't have to wait long for action. At 7:10 a.m., I heard something running through the leaves and I saw a doe crossing my shooting lane. The doe walked within range of my stand, but brush prevented me from getting a clean shot.

As the doe disappeared from view, seven more mature does crossed the shooting lane. However, unlike the first doe, the group remained near my stand.

"This is an omen," I thought, "I cannot let this go by."

After taking careful aim, I shot the nearest doe, and I was soon tagging my first deer of the 2001 season.

With venison in the freezer, I had the rest of the nine-day season to hunt for a buck.

On the third morning, the weather was still warm — just perfect for a person who freezes after 15 minutes when she sits still.

I stayed outside until 2 p.m., and only went inside long enough to eat a quick lunch. Then I walked to my ground blind. At 4:10 p.m., a buck came out of the woods along a trail I hadn't expected, but I was ready. I shot the buck, and he ran back into the woods.

I soon went to where I had last seen the buck and immediately found a heavy blood trail. I followed the trail, but did not see the deer. Frustrated, I went back to my stand to take my heavy clothes off and got grabbed my trail-marking tape.

Again I followed the blood trail,

FERNANDE KELLER of Sturgeon Bay, Wis., shot this big buck and a mature doe during Wisconsin's 2001 gun-deer season.

tying a piece of colored tape everywhere there was blood. Suddenly, the trail dried up.

I stood on some high ground to scan the area, and there on my left, 15 feet away, was a big heap of a deer, lying on its side.

I had found my buck! Then I realized how big the rack was. The buck sported 11 tines. I had never seen a deer so big!

Getting the buck to the house was a job for Hercules, but I managed to do it. At 5:57 p.m. I dropped the buck in front of the house.

Patience, persistence, perfect weather and good luck made my hunt successful.

— FERNANDE KELLER

Last-Chance Effort Bags New Brunswick Buck

When Tennesseean Mark Mastellone and his friends planned a semi-guided whitetail hunt in the Canadian bush, they hoped their efforts would yield countless encounters with large-racked wilderness bucks. However, when their hunt finally came to fruition during the first week of November 2000, such hopes seemed lost.

Mastellone and his party were hunting timber-company land near Riley Brook, New Brunswick, and unseasonably warm weather had brought deer activity to a standstill. By the last day of the hunt, several of Mastellone's companions hadn't even seen a deer, and those who had weren't able to connect with a big buck.

As darkness fell the final day, Mastellone spotted two does while he still-hunted along a snowmobile trail. However, by the time shooting hours expired, no buck appeared.

Although that afternoon was scheduled as the group's last day to hunt, Mastellone's brother-in-law persuaded their guide to take Mastellone afield for an extra hunt the next morning.

Early the next morning, Mastellone prepared his gear and headed back to where he had seen the does the night before. By the time he reached the spot and got settled, it was 7:45 a.m. Because of his group's travel schedule, he had only one hour to hunt.

The morning was foggy, overcast and, like the previous days, uneventful. At 8:20 a.m., Mastellone was considering packing up and returning to camp when he heard a deer

MARK MASTELLONE and his hunting partners were mere hours from boarding a flight back to Tennessee when this monstrous New Brunswick 8-pointer presented a shot.

snort nearby. After a few anxious moments, Mastellone saw a buck step into the clearing at 120 yards. Mastellone squeezed the trigger, and at the roar of his 7mm rifle, the deer vanished into the fog.

Mastellone's guide and brother-in-law were nearby when he shot, and soon met him at his stand. When the trio walked to where the buck had been standing, their jaws dropped. The buck was a huge-bodied, thick-racked 8-pointer that weighed 230 pounds field dressed.

Mastellone's last-ditch effort paid off!

— Ryan Gilligan

North Carolina Man Ends Two-Year Hunt

Marty Stine of Oxford, N.C., knew a big buck hung out behind the shop where he worked. After all, he'd been hunting the buck for two years. However, he hadn't been able to outsmart the wide-racked whitetail.

Stine's hunt finally ended on the last day of North Carolina's 2001 bow season. Stine was ready for one last chance at the big buck and was in his stand before daylight. A half hour after dawn, the buck approached the scrapes Stine had doctored with doe estrous scent, lip-curling and trying to find the "doe" he smelled. Stine made an accurate shot, and the two-year quest was over. The 130-class 8-pointer dressed at 160 pounds.

— JOE SHEAD

MARTY STINE hunted this 130-class buck for two years before bagging it.

Michigan Hunter Kills Last-Minute Kansas Whitetail

Richard Remmert of St. Clair Shores, Mich., beat the clock during his Kansas muzzleloader hunt on Dec. 6, 2001.

On the last day of the season, Remmert saw a 170-class, 10-pointer about 285 yards away. He and his guide tried to stalk the buck, but couldn't get close enough. After three fruitless stalks, the duo moved on.

After glassing for a while at a new vista, Remmert spotted an impressive set of antlers about 800 yards away. It took about one minute for the buck to turn its head, but after seeing the buck from a different angle, Remmert quickly decided to pursue the deer.

The hunters sneaked to within 70 yards of the bedded buck, belly-crawling over the last rise. While the deer was looking the other direction, Remmert mounted the muzzleloader on his shooting sticks, shouldered the rifle and fired. The buck sprang from its bed and ran directly at the hunters before falling after a 20-yard sprint. Remmert's 8-pointer grossed $162\frac{1}{8}$ inches.

— JOE SHEAD

RICHARD REMMERT killed this huge 8-pointer on the final day of Kansas' 2001 muzzleloader season.

New Bow Leads to Best-of-Show Buck

Chris Newhart faced a tough decision in Summer 2001. He was shooting well with his bow, but was thinking about upgrading to a heavier draw weight and lower let-off because his bow's let-off was above that allowed by the Pope and Young Club.

He finally opted for the new bow, and after Illinois' 2001 archery season, he's thankful he did.

However, Newhart and his brother-in-law T.J. Johnson didn't have an easy start. Although they hunted extensively during the early season, they didn't have much luck, likely because of warm weather. By early November, they were more than ready for the rut.

After hearing reports of rutting activity, the two hunters planned a hunt for the morning of Nov. 6.

Newhart saw a few does and a small buck early in the morning, but most of the morning was uneventful. At 11:30 p.m., Johnson walked to Newhardt's stand, and the hunters took a break to eat lunch. They later decided to hunt a different area in the afternoon.

The hunters were in their new stands by 2 p.m., but they feared it was too warm for much deer activity. Newhart saw a few does, but as darkness approached he was starting to count the day as a bust.

Moments later crunching leaves to Newhart's right caught his attention, but he figured it was a squirrel. When he looked, however, he saw a huge buck walking toward his stand.

CHRIS NEWHART'S 14-pointer took first place in the typical archery and best-of-show categories at the 2002 Illinois Deer and Turkey Classic.

Newhart rose from his seat and clamped his release on the string loop. However, he needed to find a shooting lane, because the deer was shielded by limbs. Matters got worse when the mammoth buck looked at him. Newhart froze. After a few tense moments, the deer flicked its tail and began walking away. As the buck passed Newhardt's last shooting lane, Newhardt grunted with his voice, stopping the buck for an instant. Newhart released his arrow and the buck dashed away, falling within sight.

The silence of the woods was broken by Newhart's triumphant yell, which was echoed by Johnson, who'd watched the whole encounter.

The massive 14-pointer scored 184⅝ typical and won first place in the typical archery category and best of show at the 2002 Illinois Deer and Turkey Classic.

— JOE SHEAD

How to Age a White-tailed Deer

Biologists and deer researchers agree that analysis of tooth replacement and wear — though not perfect — is the most handy and reliable field method for aging whitetails. That's because, regardless of where they live, whitetails lose their baby "milk" teeth and wear out their permanent teeth on a fairly predictable schedule.

At birth, white-tailed fawns have four teeth. Adult deer have 32 teeth — 12 premolars, 12 molars, six incisors and two canines.

Aging analysis often is based on the wear of the molars, which lose about 1 millimeter of height per year. It takes a deer about $10\frac{1}{2}$ years to wear its teeth down to the gum line. Therefore, it's difficult to determine the age of a deer that's older than $10\frac{1}{2}$ years.

Most importantly, the ability to estimate a deer's age based on the wear of its teeth is something most hunters can learn with a little study and practice.

To order a full-color poster of our complete guide to tooth aging, call (888) 457-2873.

Instructions: Cut one side of the deer's jaw all the way to its socket. Prop open the jaws and compare the lower jaw to these photos to estimate the deer's age.

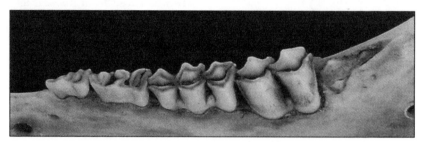

Fawn

Few hunters have difficulty aging a white-tailed fawn, whose short snout and small body are usually obvious when viewed up close. If there is doubt, simply count the teeth in the deer's lower jaw. If the jaw has less than six teeth, the deer is a fawn.

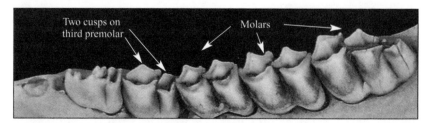

Two cusps on
third premolar

Molars

Yearling: At Least 19 Months

About 1 year, 7 months, most deer have all three permanent premolars. The new teeth are white in contrast to pigmentation on older teeth. They have a smooth, chalk-white appearance and show no wear. The third molar is partially erupted.

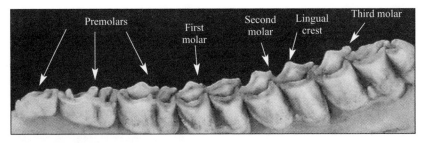

2¹⁄₂ Years

The lingual crests of the first molar are sharp, with the enamel rising well above the narrow dentine (the dark layer below the enamel) of the crest. Crests on the first molar are as sharp as those on the second and third molar. Wear on the posterior cusp of the third molar is slight, and the gum line is often not retracted enough to expose the full height of this cusp.

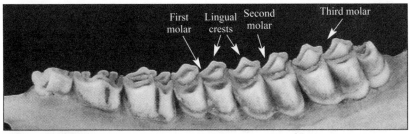

3¹⁄₂ Years

The lingual crests (inside, next to tongue) of the first molar are blunted, and the dentine of the crests on this tooth is as wide or wider than the enamel. Compare it to the second molar. The dentine on the second molar is not wider than the enamel, which means this deer is probably 3¹⁄₂ years old. Also, the posterior cusp of the third molar is flattened by wear, forming a definite concavity on the biting surface of the teeth.

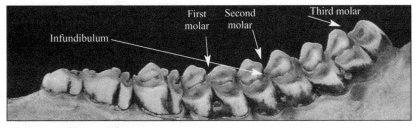

4¹⁄₂ to 5¹⁄₂ Years

At this point, it's often hard to distinguish between the two age classes. The lingual crests of the first molar are almost worn away. The posterior cusp of the third molar is worn at the cusp's edge so the biting surface slopes downward. Wear has spread to the second molar, making the dentine wider than the enamel on first and second molars. By age 5¹⁄₂ wear has usually spread to all six teeth, making the dentine wider than the enamel on all teeth. Because the first molar is the oldest, it wears out first. Also, by 5¹⁄₂, there might be no lingual crests on the first and second molars, although rounded edges might appear like crests. A line drawn from lingual to outside edges of first and second molars generally touches the enamel on both sides of the infundibulum.

Bow-Hunting Receives Boost from Pope and Young Club

The formation of the Pope and Young Club arose from a need to show the world the bow was an effective, viable hunting tool. Most hunters and state game agencies of the 1940s and 1950s believed the bow was little more than a toy, and few recognized it as a hunting weapon.

It was Glenn St. Charles and a group of dedicated bow-hunters who conceived the idea of pulling together all the nationwide bow-hunting successes they could document. Their idea was to bring all of the information together and show it to those who believed bow-hunting was ineffective.

Today, the bow is accepted nationwide.

Although few people in the non-hunting world think of the hunter as a conservationist, the hunter has always been one. Aldo Leopold, the father of the modern conservation ethic, was a bow-hunter and advocate of land stewardship. It was Theodore Roosevelt — an avid hunter — who conceived the idea of the Boone and Crockett Club, of which P&Y is modeled after.

— REPRINTED COURTESY OF THE POPE AND YOUNG CLUB

Will Your Big Buck Make The Books?

The Boone and Crockett scoring system, with few changes, is essentially the same one developed by a committee of Boone and Crockett Club members and staff in 1950. The system was developed in the 1940s with valuable additions by Grancel

Where to Write

For more information on white-tailed deer records, contact:

Boone and Crockett Club
The Old Milwaukee Depot
250 Station Drive
Missoula, MT 59801
Phone: (406) 542-1888

Pope and Young Club
15 E. Second St., Box 548
Chatfield, MN 55923
Phone: (507) 867-4144

Fitz. It was Fitz, who had his own scoring system, that emphasized antler symmetry in the rack's final score.

A B&C score chart for typical-antlered bucks is included on the facing page.

For B&C record-keeping purposes, official scores can be disputed, even years after the original measurement. Repeat measurements are allowed because of the enduring nature of white-tailed deer antlers.

Scoring a rack begins with careful reading of the official score charts reproduced in this book. Be sure to follow the instructions carefully. After taking a rough measurement, the owner must contact a volunteer B&C measurer to get an official measurement for the records program.

An official measurement cannot be made until the rack has dried 60 days after the date of kill. A drying period is necessary to allow for normal shrinkage. The drying period also ensures shrinkage will be relatively the same for all trophies, an impossible condition if "green" scores were allowed.

Boone and Crockett Score Sheet

OFFICIAL SCORING SYSTEM FOR NORTH AMERICAN BIG GAME TROPHIES

Records of North American
Big Game

BOONE AND CROCKETT CLUB®

250 Station Drive
Missoula, MT 59801
(406) 542-1888

Minimum Score:	Awards	All-time
whitetail	160	170
Coues'	100	110

TYPICAL
WHITETAIL AND COUES' DEER

Kind of Deer: _____

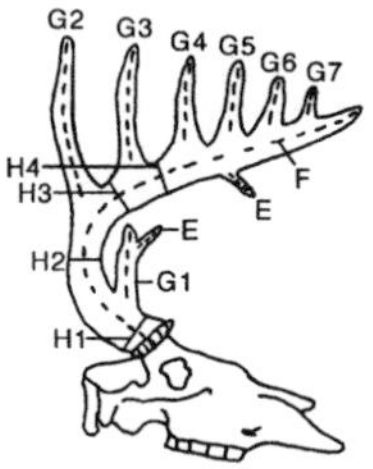

Detail of Point Measurement

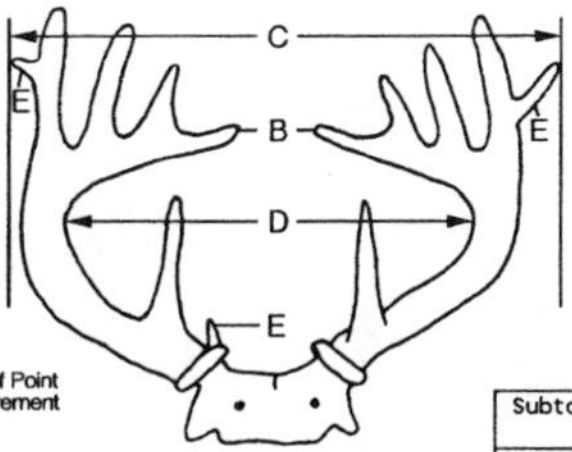

Abnormal Points	
Right Antler	Left Antler
Subtotals	
Total to E	

	Column 1	Column 2	Column 3	Column 4
SEE OTHER SIDE FOR INSTRUCTIONS				
A. No. Points on Right Antler / No. Points on Left Antler	Spread Credit	Right Antler	Left Antler	Difference
B. Tip to Tip Spread / C. Greatest Spread				
D. Inside Spread of Main Beams / (Credit May Equal But Not Exceed Longer Antler)				
E. Total of Lengths of Abnormal Points				
F. Length of Main Beam				
G-1. Length of First Point				
G-2. Length of Second Point				
G-3. Length of Third Point				
G-4. Length of Fourth Point, If Present				
G-5. Length of Fifth Point, If Present				
G-6. Length of Sixth Point, If Present				
G-7. Length of Seventh Point, If Present				
H-1. Circumference at Smallest Place Between Burr and First Point				
H-2. Circumference at Smallest Place Between First and Second Points				
H-3. Circumference at Smallest Place Between Second and Third Points				
H-4. Circumference at Smallest Place Between Third and Fourth Points				
TOTALS				

ADD	Column 1		Exact Locality Where Killed:
	Column 2		Date Killed: Hunter:
	Column 3		Owner: Telephone #:
	Subtotal		Owner's Address:
SUBTRACT Column 4			Guide's Name and Address:
			Remarks: (Mention Any Abnormalities or Unique Qualities)
	FINAL SCORE		

Copyright © 1997 by Boone and Crockett Club®

(Sample — Not for Official Use)

MOST BOW-HUNTERS have been taught to wait for the quartering-away shot. It's the best angle, we're told, for causing massive damage to a whitetail's vitals. Why, then, do many bow-hunters hesitate to take such shots while hunting?

3

Advanced Bow-Hunting Tips & Tactics

What is the Most Lethal Shot for Bow-Hunting?

The scene would have made most bow-hunters ecstatic. With the October sun nearly below the horizon, dozens of whitetails poured out of a distant pine grove and trotted for a lush ryegrass field. Lines of square-nosed does trekked across the field and headed for a secluded corner bordered by white oaks.

"That's your corner," the landowner said while handing me a cup of homemade hot apple cider as we stood on his driveway. "There are so many deer out there because we haven't allowed anyone to hunt this land in years.

"Shoot as many as you want," he continued. "Just make sure you take clean shots. The neighbor to the north won't let you trail deer on his land."

Talk about pressure. I'm confident in my shooting ability, but restrictions like that make me extra cautious.

I returned to the property the next afternoon with a portable tree stand, four doe tags and high hopes. After hanging the stand high in an oak, I pulled up my bow, quiver and backpack, and settled in for what was sure to be an action-packed hunt.

While nocking an arrow, I couldn't help but think about what the landowner said. Looking down at a well-used deer trail, I decided on the spots where deer had to stand before I could think about shooting.

"This arrow doesn't leave my bow-string unless a deer is quartering away," I told myself.

Within 30 minutes, I heard leaves shuffling behind my stand. Leaning into the tree and peering backward, I spied seven deer on the trail. They were beneath my stand in no time. Three of them were mature does.

With acorns falling steadily to the forest floor, the deer weren't going anywhere. I decided to shoot the largest doe when given the right opportunity. That took awhile. Although she was standing broadside only 20 yards away, I wanted to be certain my arrow did maximum damage when it hit her. The doe fed for a couple of minutes before lifting her head and turning toward the field.

Thwack!

My arrow hit the doe about two inches to the left of where I was aiming,

BOW-HUNTING HISTORY

➤ **MODERN BROADHEADS** have a history dating back farther than most hunters realize. The Peck and Snyder Co. introduced the first commercially manufactured broadhead in 1878. The first broadhead advertised appeared in 1923, and was manufactured by California By-Products.

In the 1920s, Wisconsin's Roy Case introduced the Kiska broadhead. In 1930, after acquiring written permission from the Wisconsin Conservation Department, Case killed a spike buck with the Kiska — the first recorded bow-kill during a modern deer season.

In 1934, Wisconsin implemented the first archery-only hunting season in North America. Joining Case in the crusade to create archery-only seasons were such legends as Aldo Leopold, a wildlife professor at the University of Wisconsin; Fred Bear, an archery industry king in progress from Michigan; and Larry Whiffen, a prominent archery promoter and manufacturer from Milwaukee.

Their combined efforts brought about the little 1934 bow-hunt. Only antlered bucks were legal during that hunt, and the license cost $1. Otis Bersing, a deer hunting historian, wrote that 40 archers participated.

In his 1949 book *Fifteen Years of Bow & Arrow Hunting in Wisconsin*, Bersing wrote that the first hunt's "participants were a small group, viewed tolerably, looked upon as queer, and at times ridiculed. They reported a kill of one lone buck."

This group included an eight-man crew led by Leopold. His crew included four family members and some colleagues, and their camp consisted of straw beds inside Leopold's 10-by-12-foot Army tent. The men didn't bring home a deer, but they got five shots, two taken by Leopold himself.

After Case killed his buck in 1934, conservation wardens inspected his broadhead and set its ⅞-inch cutting width as the minimum size for a hunting broadhead. That standard is still in place in many areas today.

but I wasn't worried. Considering the doe's angle at the moment I shot, I knew she wasn't going far. The doe ran just 45 yards before collapsing.

Although I knew the broadside shot would likely have been just as deadly, I was glad I waited for the angling-away shot. The entrance wound was a little far back, but the broadhead sliced the liver, parts of both lungs and the heart.

A Broken Record?

It seems bow-hunters have been taught since birth to wait for the quartering-away shot. It's the best angle, we're told, for causing massive damage to a whitetail's vitals.

Hunter education instructors preach the shot's benefits by showing deer anatomy overlays on overhead projectors. The National Bowhunting Education Foundation has even produced a shot-placement video that emphasizes, among other things, the lethality of angling-away shots.

Why, then, do some hunters refuse to acknowledge the angling-away shot as the best shot for bow-hunting?

The answer is rooted in the results of several major bow-hunting surveys. One was conducted by this magazine in 1997 when it asked its readers about their bow-hunting habits.

More than 2,000 hunters responded, providing an error rate of just 3 percent. According to the survey, the average *D&DH* reader would feel comfortable taking a 31-yard shot at a 14-point buck standing broadside. The same hunters said they would only feel comfortable taking a 21-yard shot at a 14-point buck if it was angling away.

Here's the amazing part: None of the hunters said they would pass on the 31-yard broadside shot, yet 6.2 percent said they wouldn't shoot if the buck was angling away at 21 yards.

What's even more interesting about the *D&DH* survey is it involved some highly experienced bow-hunters. Those responding had an average of 12.7 years of bow-hunting experience. In addition, 49 percent had killed a deer while bow-hunting the previous year.

These statistics weren't an aberration. The *D&DH* survey was modeled after a study conducted by the Minnesota Department of Natural Resources, which revealed similar tendencies.

D&DH Contributing Editor Jay McAninch is president of the Archery Manufacturers and Merchants Organization. McAninch was a wildlife research biologist for the Minnesota DNR in the early 1990s when he supervised a study that asked similar questions. The study was conducted by Michael Osterberg, who presented the findings in his thesis at West Virginia University.

In the study, Minnesota bow-hunters were asked to pretend they were in a tree stand and saw a 14-point buck approaching. They were then asked whether they would shoot if the buck was standing at various angles and distances.

More than 98 percent of the hunters said they would shoot if the buck was standing broadside at 15 yards. Only 79 percent said they would shoot if the buck was angling away.

EQUIPMENT INSIGHTS

➤ **HIGH-SPEED** compound bows are prone to noise because they're built to transfer enormous amounts of energy. A lot of things can cause bows to be noisy when shot, including cams, risers and limb pockets. Shock and vibration from the shot typically transfers into the bow's exterior parts, making for a less-than-pleasurable shooting experience. In fact, excess vibration can cause avid shooters to develop tendinitis.

Besides robbing a bow of peak performance, shock and vibration cause premature wear to accessories. Many add-on products, such as stabilizers and "cat whiskers" help quiet bows, but those products do not cure inherent flaws. Fortunately, today's bow companies have addressed the problem head-on, and are working on more efficient designs.

Remember, high-speed bows cannot be completely tamed of noise and vibration. Despite technology, a bow is a primitive device that transfers energy from two bow limbs to an arrow shaft. Therefore, it's inevitable that some energy will be transferred to the bow as the arrow leaves the string.

➤ **THOUSANDS** of bow-hunters care little about flinging arrows at sound-barrier speeds. If you're in that group — and you just want a bow that's accurate and easy to tune — consider the advice from Golden Eagle Archery pro-staff member Bob Foulkrod.

Foulkrod says the ideal hunting bow for experienced finger and release shooters is one that has a brace height of about 7 inches — the distance from the back of the riser to the bow-string. Longer brace heights allow for a more stable-shooting bow that "forgives" imperfect shooting form. Bows with longer brace heights don't shoot as fast as those with short brace heights, but the improved accuracy is worth the trade-off.

Beginning bow-hunters should consider bows with brace heights in the 9-inch range.

With the buck standing 40 yards away, 58 percent said they would attempt a broadside shot. Only 22 percent said they would shoot if the buck was angling away at 40 yards.

The Age Factor

According to the Osterberg study, a hunter's age can dictate what types of shot angles he prefers. Unfortunately, the study revealed that adults were often more willing to take poor-percentage shots.

Of the hunters who said they would attempt a low-percentage shot at a buck standing 15 yards away, 49 percent were age 28 to 42; 30 percent were age 12 to 27; and 21 percent were older than 43.

Of the hunters who said they would take a conservative shot — broadside or angling away — at the same distance, 53 percent were age 28 to 42; 30 percent were older than 43; and 17 percent were age 12 to 27.

These statistics indicate bow-hunters exhibit more confidence with their shooting abilities as they approach middle age, then revert to conservatism as they mature.

The Real World

Data from an in-depth bow-hunting study at Minnesota's Camp Ripley indicate that hunters are even more reluctant to wait for angling-away shots during actual hunting situations.

In her thesis, *Aspects of Wounding of White-tailed Deer by Bow-Hunters,* for West Virginia University, Wendy Krueger found that less than one-third of the successful Camp Ripley bow-hunters killed their deer with angling-away shots. According to the 1992-93 study, more than 66 percent of successful hunters waited for broadside shooting opportunities before releasing their arrows. Only 28 percent of successful hunters waited for angling-away shots. The study consisted of four two-day hunts – two in 1992 and two in 1993. In the four hunts, 7,293 hunters killed 693 deer. McAninch supervised the study.

"In approaching this question, we found a bit of discrepant feelings among bow-hunters in which shot they thought was better if they were forced to choose," he said. "Clearly, they said they thought the broadside shot presented a bigger target than the quartering shot. In some ways, I agree. If you place a circle around the vitals, the broadside shot presents a bigger target. That seems to shrink when the deer is angling away."

Although the broadside shot might appear to present a larger target, it really doesn't. In fact, many hunters argue that the quartering-away shot actually offers a bigger target because a deer's vital area isn't flat like a paper plate.

For example, an arrow that enters the paunch and angles forward might miss the near lung, but it will invariably hit the liver and opposite lung as it passes through. Therefore, the quartering-away shot allows for a greater margin of error. Conversely, if a shooter botches a broadside shot and shoots right or left, the arrow will miss the vitals altogether.

Tim Poole, executive director of the NBEF, agrees that the angling-away shot presents the best shot opportunity.

"In a way, it's parallel to the issue

NONLETHAL HITS are less likely on quartering-away shots, because the angle allows you to drive an arrow through a deer's intestines and still hit the liver, a lung and possibly the heart.

of not shooting does," Poole said. "In some hunters' minds, the taking of does doesn't make sense. It's not in their scheme of how to manage wildlife. I see the lack of willingness to take the quartering-away shot in a similar fashion.

"They might rationalize it as less effective. To them, the broadside shot appears to be a better shot. What I don't think they realize is that with the quartering-away shot, they will also shoot the arrow through the diaphragm, liver, and possibly a kidney. These are all vital organs, and destroying them results in a clean and quick harvest."

Poole was quick to add that although angling-away shots are best for whitetails, they should not be used on bigger animals like elk and moose.

IF POSSIBLE, wait for a quartering-away shot — even if it means passing up broadside shots. Why? This Illinois doe, for example, appeared to be broadside, but was actually quartering slightly toward the hunter. Although the arrow sliced the lungs, it angled through the paunch, resulting in a hard-to-follow blood trail.

More Mess?

With angling-away shots clearly the better choice, why don't more hunters wait for them? One reason might be because some bow-hunters aren't keen on driving an arrow through any part of a deer's paunch because of the mess it might make. Let's hope that's not a wide-held excuse. If it is, bow-hunters would admit to passing on a more effective killing shot in favor of trying to save some field-dressing time.

"The whole notion of puncturing the rumen is way overdone," McAninch said. "It's the same thing with the scent glands in (a buck's) legs. People treat them as if they're poison or something.

"The truth is, even if you slit the rumen, there's almost no way you can ruin the meat. You might lose a backstrap near the abdominal cavity if it gets tainted with stomach contents, but even then you can save almost all of the meat if you just take the time to clean it out.

"The angling-away shot is so deadly that you shouldn't have to think twice about it."

Improving Your Odds

Granted, an arrow must go well awry, but a hunter can make a mistake on a broadside shot. If the arrow sails eight or nine inches right or left, it will hit the abdomen or front shoulder. Even those types of shots can kill deer, but they increase the chances of losing a deer.

That possibility is more remote on the angling-away shot, because as the angle becomes more pronounced, a hunter can drive an arrow through a deer's intestines and still hit the liver, a lung and possibly the heart. In short, the angling-away shot invariably kills the animal quickly.

Furthermore, the 45-degree angle makes for a much easier passage and entry to the kill zone. Besides hitting a lung, the arrow might also nick the liver, making for an even more lethal hit.

"When you take a quartering-away shot, for all practical purposes, you have just improved your chances of killing the deer," McAninch said.

That's not to say McAninch believes hunters should hold out for quartering-away shots at all costs. "In some regards, the quartering-away shot is somewhat tougher to make. This has more to do with experience. The first time you do something – even if it's taking a high-percentage shot — it takes some getting used to."

McAninch saw this type of behav-

The Angling-Away Shot: No Need For Do-Overs?

On a sweltering August afternoon, two buddies grab their bows and head for a 3-D range. They're both excellent shooters, and they soon get caught up in a friendly competition as to who will finish with the most kill-zone shots.

Halfway through the course, they come upon a broadside target that's 40 yards away.

"No problem," says the first shooter as he draws his bow and steadies his aim.

Without warning, a mosquito lands on his forehead and proceeds to do what mosquitoes do best.

"Ouch!" he says while releasing the shot. The arrow smacks the target solidly in the rumen area – just inches from the vital ring. "No fair," he says. "That has to be a 'do-over.'"

Unfortunately, there is no such thing as a "do-over" in the deer woods. You make the shot, or you don't, and that's often the difference between a short blood trail and one that requires you stay up all night.

The angling-away shot is the closest thing a bow-hunter can get to a sure thing. While the perfectly executed angling-away shot will take out the lungs and heart of a white-tailed deer, even a poorly placed shot invariably causes massive destruction to the thoracic cavity and leads to a quick kill.

Over the past six years, I have killed 15 deer with angling-away shots. I'm not proud to admit this, but some shots were not perfect. The angle of the shots, however, allowed my arrows to penetrate the vital areas on each deer, killing them quickly and efficiently.

For example, I recently shot a doe while bow-hunting from a tree stand 15 feet above the ground. The arrow hit several inches high and to the right of where I was aiming. Although the broadhead punctured the intestines, it still passed through the deer and destroyed the right lung. That deer ran just 65 yards before collapsing.

I saw another example of the quartering-away shot's effectiveness when I shot a mature Texas doe. I had watched the deer for several minutes as it milled around the oak tree I was hunting from. Although I had several opportunities for a broadside shot, I waited until the doe angled sharply away before releasing my arrow. The arrow struck the doe squarely in the stomach — five or six inches off target. However, thanks to the angle, the arrow passed through the liver and opposite lung before shattering the deer's left shoulder bone. The doe died after running about 75 yards.

The most extreme example I've experienced involved a Wisconsin buck. When I released the shot, the bow-string caught my jacket sleeve, and the arrow hit the buck just in front of the right flank — missing its mark by at least 10 inches. Still, it drove through the rumen, sliced the liver and destroyed the opposite lung. I saw the buck collapse after it ran about 80 yards into a clear-cut.

If any of those deer had been standing broadside when I missed my mark, I would have probably been trailing purely gut-shot deer.

And I would have also been wishing for three "do-overs."

– Daniel E. Schmidt

ior firsthand when he supervised a deer-removal project in a Minnesota suburb. To control a sprawling herd, the community hired FBI-trained sharpshooters. The shooters were instructed to only take head and neck shots at deer as they approached bait stations. Some of the shooters were also hunters, and they struggled with the concept of not aiming for the chest.

"These guys could put a bullet on a dime at 500 yards, yet they were apprehensive," McAninch said. "It was a classic case of dealing with the unfamiliar. We all don't like to do things we're unfamiliar with."

McAninch said this phenomenon carries over into the bow-hunting debate on shot placement.

"I don't know this for a fact, but I think hunters shy away from the angling-away shot because it appears to narrow the shooting window, and

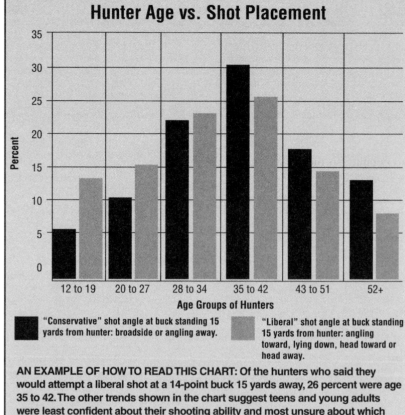

Hunter Age vs. Shot Placement

Age Groups of Hunters

Percent

"Conservative" shot angle at buck standing 15 yards from hunter: broadside or angling away.

"Liberal" shot angle at buck standing 15 yards from hunter: angling toward, lying down, head toward or head away.

AN EXAMPLE OF HOW TO READ THIS CHART: Of the hunters who said they would attempt a liberal shot at a 14-point buck 15 yards away, 26 percent were age 35 to 42. The other trends shown in the chart suggest teens and young adults were least confident about their shooting ability and most unsure about which shot angles are best.

Source: Impacts of Bowhunter Attributes on Hunting Behavior and Outcomes in Minnesota, Michael S. Osterberg, West Virginia University.

the average hunter fights the problem of having a lot of confidence in his shooting ability," he said. "Perhaps they're showing a little bit of conservatism."

Mind Over Matter

McAninch's insights into the behavior of trained sharpshooters probably explain why most hunters feel more comfortable taking broadside shots over angling-away shots at whitetails.

In the surveys, most shooters

began hunting at younger ages and typically learned how to hunt from their parents. Because most of today's middle-aged deer hunters are first-generation bow-hunters, perhaps their inclination for not waiting for angling-away shots was passed down to their children in subtle ways. For example, most archers are guilty of placing their 3-D deer targets in permanent broadside positions. This isn't bad, but it doesn't train shooters to wait and then execute the most devastating shot: the angling-away shot.

"You just don't see people practicing angling-away shots," McAninch said. "It's mind-set and habituation. That doesn't mean they don't want to take it. They aren't taking it because they don't think about it. And that goes for guys who know the quartering-away angle is a higher-percentage shot. They've been conditioned to believe the broadside shot is acceptable, so they take it when it comes along."

Conclusion

Shooting schools, hunter education programs and backyard practice sessions have taught us the broadside shot is acceptable for bow-hunting. However, this conditioning has perhaps caused many hunters to form a mind block that the broadside shot is the most lethal.

It's not. The angling-away shot presents more room for error, and it allows hunters to inflict more damage to a whitetail's vitals, thus increasing the chance for a quicker kill.

True, many hunters will argue that "dead is dead," and that they've killed piles of deer quickly and humanely with broadside shots. That's admirable, but it misses the point, which is this:

If you have an opportunity to increase your bow-hunting success, you should learn more about it.

The angling-away shot offers that opportunity.

Editor's Note: To better understand how shot angles affect blood trails, recovery times and the distance deer travel after being shot, use the Blood Trailing Log, found on pages 193-196.

SHOT-SELECTION FACTS

➤ **SOME HUNTERS** believe the compound bow has caused bow-hunters to take longer shots than they would if they were shooting a recurve or longbow. Is this assumption accurate?

According to *Deer & Deer Hunting* surveys, most bow-hunters who use compounds still prefer their shots be 20 yards or less, and the average distance of a killing shot from a compound bow is 17 yards. In a study at Wisconsin's Fort McCoy, the average killing shot with a compound was 19 yards.

Believe it or not, those shooting distances are shorter than the average bow-shots taken by Wisconsin archers from the late 1930s through mid-1950s — 20 years before the first compound bows hit the market!

From 1939 to 1954, Wisconsin archers took 2,864 shots at whitetails, and the average shooting distance at deer was 27.3 yards. In addition, nearly 38 percent of shots were taken at running deer. Obviously, today's bow-hunters — 93 percent of whom use compounds — are more conservative in their shot selection.

➤ **CAN HABITAT** and cover affect the shooting distances of today's bow-hunters, especially between compound shooters and traditional shooters? Some hunters assume Western bow-hunters in more open habitat are more likely to take longer shots than Eastern bow-hunters in dense woodlots.

According to *Deer & Deer Hunting*, the shooting distances in these regions aren't as different as you might think. For example, according to a study of South Dakota bow-hunters, compound shooters felt most comfortable with shots less than 40 yards, and traditional archers felt most comfortable with shots less than 30 yards. However, at ranges farther than 50 yards, 20 percent of compound shooters and 15 percent of traditional shooters still shoot.

While there is a difference in shooting decisions between 30 and 40 yards, those distinctions blur at short and long distances.

Mossy Oak Camouflage

HIGH-SPEED COMPOUND BOWS are prone to noise because they're built to transfer enormous amounts of energy. However, many bow companies have developed more efficient designs.

Taking the Buzz Out of High-Performance Bows

Technology isn't always a good thing because it sometimes brings trade-offs. Take the compound bow, for example. Many of us grew up shooting compounds that used wheels, not cams. And, although those bows weren't lightning fast, they were relatively quiet.

Things changed in a hurry when manufacturers added two cams — and eventually just one cam — to their new bows. Arrow speeds increased dramatically, and let-off percentages skyrocketed.

All was good. Well, sort of.

The new designs allowed average archers to shoot greater distances with improved accuracy because the new bows launched arrows at unheard of speeds. Most of those bows, however, were anything but quiet.

What are bow companies doing to tame shock, recoil and vibration?

A lot.

What Causes Noise?

High-speed compound bows are prone to noise because they're built to transfer enormous amounts of energy. A lot of things can cause bows to be noisy when shot, including cams, risers and limb pockets. Shock and vibration from the shot typically transfers into the bow's exterior parts, making for a less-than-pleasurable shooting experience. In fact, excess vibration can cause avid shooters to develop tendinitis.

Besides robbing a bow of peak performance, shock and vibration cause premature wear to accessories. Many add-on products, such as "cat whiskers," stabilizers and Sims Limb Savers, help quiet bows and help them perform better, but those products do not cure inherent flaws. Fortunately, today's bow companies have addressed the problem head-on, and are now working on more efficient designs.

It's important to note that high-speed bows cannot be completely tamed of noise and vibration. Despite technology, a bow is a primitive device that transfers energy from two bow limbs to an arrow shaft. Therefore, it's inevitable that some energy will be wasted and transferred to the bow as the arrow leaves the string. With that in mind, let's take a look at the companies that are working overtime to make the best-performing bows for deer hunters.

Leading Off

Mathews Archery has been a leader in bow design and archery innovation. Mathews not only invented single-cam technology, it took the concept one step further

DANIEL E. SCHMIDT

ARCHERY NEWS

➤ **FOR THE FIFTH CONSECUTIVE** year, traditional bow-hunters raised thousands of dollars to defend archery and bow-hunting through their participation in the McMahon Eagle Eye contest.

The McMahon Eagle Eye contest was held across the United States this past year, with the proceeds benefiting the Wildlife Legislative Fund of America. The WLFA and its Bowhunter Defense Coalition have been at the forefront in the fight to protect bow-hunting.

Funds raised from this program have been used to defend bow-hunting in areas such as Little Rock, Ark., Waterville, Maine and Akron, Ohio. They have also been used to help protect bow-hunting on the 93 million-acre National Wildlife Refuge System.

Recently these funds have been used to combat a birth-control program for deer in northern Indiana. These birth-control programs, which have proven unsuccessful in controlling free-ranging deer populations but are politically attractive to some elected officials, would seriously threaten bow-hunting in many urban areas nationwide.

The contest involved several qualifying events, which were usually held in conjunction with an archery or other sporting event. All proceeds were donated to WLFA.

During the event's five-year run, the program raised $30,000.

➤ **HOW DO GUN-HUNTERS** view bow-hunters? According to a 1999 survey funded by the Archery Manufacturers and Merchants Organization, 72 percent of gun-hunters view bow-hunting favorably. Only 3 percent viewed bow-hunting unfavorably.

by unveiling perimeter-weighted cams.

A perimeter-weighted single cam features a coin-sized disc that's placed within the upper end of the cam. When the bow is fired, the weight catapults in the opposite direction of the limbs, counteracting limb momentum. The result is dramatically decreased recoil and noise.

Although single-cam technology greatly improved bow performance, Mathews further reduced bow vibration and noise through parallel limb design and Harmonic Damping. Older two-cam bows were generally noisy because variations in the limbs often meant the two limbs were fighting each other during the shot. In the case of the new Mathews bows, limbs are almost parallel and the upper and lower ends of the riser feature built-in dampers. The dampers, which are made of rubber and feature center-floating brass or aluminum weights, act as bushings that absorb vibration.

High Country Archery addresses vibration and noise problems by incorporating carbon technology into risers, limbs and limb pockets. High Country bows feature a limb-mounted system that equalizes the timing and limb-tip load while absorbing vibration. Inside the limb pockets are specially designed pads that absorb up to 80 percent of the shot vibration. The company uses carbon risers that reduce noise and overall weight while increasing arrow speed. Carbon acts as a natural damper to shock, noise and vibration.

Browning takes noise taming to another level with its Sorbothane vibration system. Sorbothane is a visco-elastic composite material that absorbs shock and vibration. What's more, it retains its dampening properties over a broad temperature and frequency range.

Browning engineers learned that bows are quieter when material is layered between a bow's riser and limbs. This prevents the bow from transferring noise and shock through the limb pocket to the riser.

When it comes to limb pockets, Alpine Archery is considered by many as a trendsetter. Alpine bows feature individually machined-aluminum limb pockets that fit precisely in machined limb tracks. This precise fit allows the bow to fit together seamlessly and, as a result, provides quiet and smooth operation.

Quiet Technology

Although most archery companies are focusing on limbs and limb pockets to quiet their high-performance bows, others are adding technology.

The North American Archery Group — makers of Golden Eagle, Jennings and Fred Bear bows — made a splash this year when unveiling ZenCam technology. Golden Eagle offers this futuristic cam on the Z-Fire bow. The ZenCam is mounted on the riser, while two concentric wheels occupy the limb tips. The result is a smooth-drawing bow that produces little, if any, hand shock. The cam, which eliminates the need for a cable guard, is designed so it can't go out of time.

Bows are also quieter if they feature machined-aluminum limb pockets. In years past, companies built bows with metal limb pockets, and the metal-on-limb contact made for noisy-shooting bows. Today's Fred Bear bows feature

DESPITE IMPROVING technology, today's high-speed bows still produce excess noise and vibration. That's where stabilizers and limb-silencers can make a big difference in shooting performance.

machined-aluminum pockets and friction-killing composite components that soften vibration. Jennings bows also use this concept. For example, the Jennings T-Master Extreme features machined-aluminum limb cups that fit precisely on the riser. The placement of these cups near the limb pockets helps reduce noise and vibration.

The "third wheel" Force-Multiplier concept was unveiled last year by BowTech to increase speed. BowTech's Generation 3 features a riser-mounted second cam that, in addition to shooting arrows at 330 feet per second

ARCHERY INSIGHTS

➤ **WHEN BOW-HUNTERS** encounter the whitetail in early fall, they are trying to kill an animal whose bloodstream resembles a "working hospital." At this time of the year, the total protein in a deer's bloodstream peaks and the arterial system probably contains high levels of vitamin K1 and K2. Discovered in 1934 by a Danish scientist, vitamin K, well-known as the antihemorrhagic vitamin, greatly assists the whitetail in speeding up the blood-clotting process.

The clotting process begins when a broadhead hits an artery but doesn't completely severe it. Platelets adhere to collagen fibers in the connective tissue and release a substance that makes platelets sticky. The platelets then clump together to form a plug that provides emergency protection against blood loss.

➤ **THE INCREASED** effectiveness and selectivity by bow-hunters has led to increased antagonism with some gun-hunters, even though 85 percent of bow-hunters also gun-hunt. While jealousies have likely always existed between the groups, the increased emphasis on buck-hunting has often deepened such feelings.

But harvest data suggest bow-hunting has not greatly reduced gun-hunting opportunities. Even in intensively bow-hunted Wisconsin, gun-hunters have accounted for 79 percent of the state's total buck kill the past five years. During that time, the state has experienced three of its all-time high gun-buck harvests: 171,891 in 1995, 159,256 in '99 and 151,575 in '98. Those three years also produced the state's all-time high buck bow-kills: 45,492 in 1999, 42,010 in '98 and 39,379 in '95.

➤ **ACCORDING TO** a 1999 bow-hunting survey funded by the Archery Manufacturers and Merchants Organization, 57 percent of bow-hunters hunt mostly on private land, 22 percent hunt primarily on public land. About 21 percent hunt public and private land equally.

(IBO), helps substantially reduce hand shock.

Parker Bows licensed the technology and introduced its Force-Multiplier bow this year.

Hoyt USA also builds vibration-taming features into its bows. For example, the Hoyt VorTec features moderate reflex riser geometry. This design allows for a stiff, lightweight riser that calms recoil without passing vibration to the shooter.

The Sand Trap

BowTech's bows are as high-tech as they come, but for all the innovative engineering in this company's bows, a common substance — sand — is used to all but eliminate shot sound and vibration.

BowTech's engineers experimented with many products to quiet limb pockets, and they concluded that lightly packed sand absorbed the most energy. As a result, the company designed encased limb pockets filled with sand. It's hard to argue with the result. I test-shot the company's latest bows at this year's Archery Manufacturers and Merchants Organization trade show, and found them as quiet as new bows from bigger companies.

Exterior Solutions

For 2001, PSE joined Sims Vibration Laboratory to create the bow-mounted No Vibration system. The system features machined aluminum donuts that house rubber-like material. The donuts are mounted to the upper and lower limb bolts, and they act as shock and vibration absorbers.

The NV system is sold separately and can be used on most modern compounds and recurves.

Leven Industries, inventor of the famous Doinker stabilizers, introduces the Doinker Doe-Nut. Similar to the PSE device, the Doe-Nut features three interchangeable weight-control rings. The Doe-Nut can be slid forward or backward on a stabilizer rod to absorb 20 percent to 30 percent of shot vibration.

Quiet Bows

Thousands of bow-hunters care little about flinging arrows at sound-barrier speeds. In fact, many prefer the quiet characteristics of recurves and longbows.

If you're in that group, check out the new traditional bows from the Fred Bear Bowhunting Equipment Co. The Fred Bear Montana longbow, for example, features a 64-inch reflex-deflex design that reduces hand shock and improves arrow flight. Also consider the Bear Kodiak Mag, which features beefy, black fiberglass laid over select hardwood laminates.

Conclusion

The days of noisy, hard-to-control compound bows are passing us by. If increased arrow speed and smooth shooting are your goals, visit your pro shop and shoot a few of today's new bow designs. Regardless of which bow you buy, you can be assured a pleasurable test ride.

HUNTING THE RUT

➤ **ALTHOUGH THE GENERAL** timing of the whitetail's breeding season is set by changing photoperiod, many factors can interact to determine when, or if, a doe breeds.

Why does the rut appear frenzied one year and almost nonexistent the next? According to *Deer & Deer Hunting* Research Editor John Ozoga, the answer is partially linked to a herd's access to nutrition. Poorly nourished adult does achieve sexual maturity later than normal, and sometimes don't breed at all. By comparison, well-fed yearlings — and even 7-month-old fawns — can breed successfully.

Given these facts, hunters should learn to expect the unexpected when hunting the rut.

➤ **ABOUT THE LAST** weekend in October, Northern hunters should switch from pre-rut to rut-hunting strategies. The food sources that were excellent during the pre-rut will still offer opportunities, but the hunter who begins incorporating calling, rattling, decoying and scrape- and rub-line tactics will have the upper hand when the rut unfolds.

The key to understanding the whitetail rut is realizing it's not one frenzied period. It's made up of three phases consisting of seeking, chasing and breeding. Each phase is distinctly different and often requires different strategies for success.

For detailed predictions on the best times to hunt the rut in your region, check out the articles by Charles J. Alsheimer in the October and November issues of *Deer & Deer Hunting.* Alsheimer's predictions are also included in the annual *Whitetail Calendar*, available from Krause Publications, (800) 258-0929.

➤ **RECENT RESEARCH** and *D&DH's* 2000 scrape survey show there are no hard and fast rules when it comes to scrapes or scrape-hunting. Whether you hunt where scraping behavior is intense, or where it is a low-odds affair, here's how to use recent findings to your advantage.

Tree-Stand Safety Begins at Your Archery Shop: Informed Hunters Look for the TMA Label

Grab a pencil, and take this quick quiz:

1. Are your tree stands TMA-approved?

2. Do you shop for stands with the TMA label?

3. Do you know what the TMA is?

If you answered "no" or "don't know" to any of these questions, you need to do some homework. And you might want to re-evaluate your tree stand selections. Why? Your life could depend on it.

The Treestand Manufacturers Association, just 6 years old, is dedicated to making hunting from high places as safe as possible. Unfortunately, few hunters know the TMA exists. In its 1999 survey on tree-stand safety, *Deer & Deer Hunting* discovered 71.1 percent of hunters weren't aware of the TMA and its goals.

"These things come in baby steps," said Jeff DeRegnaucourt, a commercial insurance agent who is the TMA's communications coordinator. "We're winning the battle, but we haven't won the war."

The History of the TMA

The TMA formed in 1995. A similar effort to develop manufacturers' standards in the late 1980s failed when industry leaders struggled to define common goals. In late 1995, DeRegnaucourt and Norb Mullaney, consulting engineer for the Archery Merchants and Manufacturers Organization, drafted the TMA's first testing standards.

The TMA is simply a testing organization. Standards do not dictate a

TO EARN the Treestand Manufacturers Association stamp of approval, a fixed-position tree stand must meet standards for load, stability and adherence to trees.

stand's design or what type of material is used. To receive the TMA stamp of approval, a fixed-position tree stand must meet standards for load, stability and adherence to trees. Climbing stands are tested for load, stability, repetitive loading and adherence to trees. All manufacturers are allowed to join TMA and have their stands tested to see if they meet the standards.

Stands that measure up can carry a "TMA Certified" sticker, which is sold to manufacturers by the TMA. The manufacturer is also allowed to use the TMA logo on the stand's packaging.

The TMA board of directors includes co-chairmen Ray McIntyre of Warren & Sweat and Ron Woller of

Summit Specialties. John Louk of Ol'Man Treestands is secretary/treasurer, and Brent Hunt of Trophy Whitetail Products is a board member. The TMA is looking to fill one more board seat.

Safety Standards

The TMA tree-stand testing process is thorough and unbiased. Stands are tested by Law Engineering, a Jacksonville, Fla., company with no other ties to the hunting industry. The company requires all applicants to provide proof they have written quality-assurance plans. From there, a manufacturer can submit a tree stand for testing. If the stand meets the safety requirements, Law Engineering purchases the same model of stand from a retail outlet and tests it. This step ensures the manufacturer is adhering to its quality-control plan.

"These are good tests," DeRegnaucourt said. "They're not unduly harsh, and they're not designed to eliminate competition. They make sure consumers can identify tree stands with structural integrity, and they answer the consumer's most important question: 'Will this thing hold me?' "

TMA is working on standards for ladder stands, climbing sticks, tripods and fall-restraint systems. DeRegnaucourt said one manufacturer, Fall Woods, makers of the Seat-O-The-Pants full-body harness, has already agreed to be tested.

John Woller, president of Summit Specialties, said most manufacturers view the TMA stamp as the final check for what they already know: Their stands are safe. However, he said it's crucial that consumers look for the TMA sticker on stands because

MOSSY OAK BLIND-HUNTING TIPS:
NATURAL CAMOUFLAGE

Technological advancements have made life much easier for hunters, and ground-blind hunters haven't been left out of the mix. Today's commercially made blinds are light, durable, portable and effective. However, a little extra effort can make these blinds even better.

After setting up your portable blind, prune some nearby limbs and use them to further conceal your position. Then, drag brush against the blind's base to add that final touch of natural camouflage.

Whether you hunt with a commercially manufactured blind or build your own, it's vital that the blind hides your outline and blends into its surroundings. Although today's portable blinds are effective on their own, putting in the extra effort can yield tremendous rewards.

that's the only proof a stand meets the requirements.

"Yes, it's expensive to have stands tested," he said. "But it's worth it."

Educating Consumers

Besides making quality tree stands, TMA members are also devoted to educating consumers on tree-stand safety. The most important part of that message is to use fall-restraint equipment while hunting from tree stands.

"It absolutely boggles my mind that a guy can spend $200 on a tree stand, $1,000 on a rifle and up to $700 on a

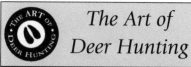

The Art of Deer Hunting

BY TOM CARPENTER

Mastering the Art

Like much of our world, deer hunting has gone high-tech, offering today's hunter pungent scents, powerful rifles, countless gadgets, climbing tree stands, space-age clothing, lightning-quick bows, deer calls for every occasion and a detailed understanding of deer behavior.

However, there's much more to deer hunting than cold, calculating science and technology. It is also an art — a careful blend of knowledge, understanding, patience and aggressiveness. It's knowing what to do, and when.

Equipment and data can't teach these ideas. They are *The Art of Deer Hunting*, and you'll find pieces of this lore sprinkled throughout the following pages.

bow, but he's too damn cheap to spend $70 on a fall-restraint system that ensures he comes back home safe and sound," DeRegnaucourt said.

Unfortunately, even the most expensive safety equipment doesn't help much if a hunter doesn't wear it from the time he leaves the ground to climb to his stand until the time he climbs down. According to the *D&DH* survey, 88.2 percent of hunters who fell from tree stands were not using a safety belt or harness when they fell.

"That bothers me," DeRegnaucourt said. "We have to work with states to educate kids and adults on the impor-

tance of always wearing fall-restraint devices from the time they go up (a tree) until the time they come down. "If people just did that, we would save at least 10 lives a year."

A Slow Train

Despite the TMA's myriad benefits, many manufacturers are slow to embrace it. As of September 1999, the TMA had 23 members, despite the fact the United States has more than 50 tree-stand manufacturers. DeRegnaucourt said he wonders why more companies aren't in the TMA. The TMA is an open organization and manufacturers can join at any time. Annual dues are $250, and manufacturers are charged $1,600 for tests.

DeRegnaucourt said some smaller manufacturers hesitate at a stipulation that requires them to carry liability insurance, which can cost up to $25,000 a year. To that, DeRegnaucourt says, "If a manufacturer can't afford it (insurance), he can't afford to be in this business. This is serious business."

McIntyre, who has owned and operated Warren & Sweat the past 17 years, concedes testing isn't cheap. He said his company manufactures more than 50 types of tree stands, and he has spent nearly $100,000 on TMA testing. McIntyre said tests ensure consumers receive safe products.

"Tree-stand companies are major players in this (hunting) industry," McIntyre said. "The TMA has caused even the major companies to be more aware and careful about the products going out. The end product going to consumers is a lot safer and stronger than ever before."

McIntyre said consumers, for their own safety, should demand sport shops, retail outlets and mail-order

Mossy Oak Camouflage

catalogs carry only TMA-tested products. Unfortunately, those demands sometimes fall on deaf ears. Several companies import tree stands made in China and Mexico and sell them at rock-bottom prices.

"Do those stands pass TMA tests?" McIntyre asked. "I don't know. Have they even been tested? I don't know that, either."

A Self-Regulating System?

The formation of TMA has brought some changes, including lower insurance premiums for manufacturers. How? The legal system now has standards and precedents to draw on during litigation, DeRegnaucourt said.

A 1997 lawsuit in South Carolina supports this point. According to DeRegnaucourt, a man sued a major tree-stand company after he reportedly fell 30 feet from a climbing tree stand he had placed on a power pole. The man claimed the stand slid all the way down the pole without digging into the wood. DeRegnaucourt said Law Engineering representatives, citing information from TMA tests of

THE TMA TREE-STAND testing process is thorough and unbiased. Stands are tested by Law Engineering, a Jacksonville, Fla., company with no other ties to the hunting industry.

the stand, testified the man's claims were false, and that the stand could not fall without engaging at some point. The defendant's lawyers also argued that TMA standards showed the tree-stand company exceeded all safety standards and that the man's injuries were caused by his failure to use the stand properly.

The jury deliberated 30 seconds before siding with the tree-stand company.

DeRegnaucourt added that TMA standards not only ensure consumers they're buying safe products, but they help safeguard manufacturers from frivolous lawsuits.

Woller agreed. He predicts the TMA will soon be embraced by all serious tree-stand manufacturers. "We want this to be an association for all tree-stand manufacturers," he said.

— Daniel E. Schmidt

How to Select Fletchings for Your Hunting Arrows

For hunting arrows tipped with broadheads, three 5-inch feathers or four 4-inch feathers work best. Individual differences in equipment and shooting style sometimes require the use of larger feathers. It is also possible that good flight can be achieved with smaller feathers. Test shooting is the best way to decide which setup is right for you.

It's important to remember that broadheads need more guidance than field points. Without proper guidance, a broadhead will cause the arrow to yawn or fishtail during flight. Yawning arrows cause inconsistent flight patterns, and lose velocity and penetration.

Use the following question-and-answer segment to determine which setups are right for your arrows:

➤ **Should I use right- or left-wing feathers?**

You can shoot either wing successfully. An arrow does not rotate noticeably until it is well clear of the bow. Left-wing feathers should be used to rotate the arrow counter-clockwise, while right-wing feathers rotate the arrow clockwise.

➤ **How can I determine the alignment of the feather on my arrows?**

Two methods can be used to determine right- or left-wing alignment. First, look at the nock end of the arrow (aligned as though the arrow is ready to be shot), and rotate it so one fletching is on top of the shaft.

FEATHER SPLICING

Cut quill only here ⟶

Cut quill only here ⟶

Butt quills together in clamp and fletch

(Smooth webs together after glue has set and the clamp has been removed.)

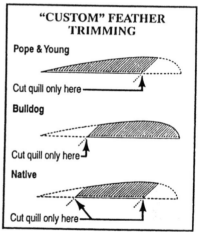

"CUSTOM" FEATHER TRIMMING

Pope & Young

Cut quill only here ⟶

Bulldog

Cut quill only here ⟶

Native

Cut quill only here ⟶

If the "catch lip" is to the left of the web, it is a right-wing feather. If the "catch lip" is to the right of the web, it is a left-wing feather. (See diagram.)

The second method involves holding the forward end of the die-cut (pointed end) or full-length feather (larger end) toward yourself. Look down from the top, and rotate the feather so its web is horizontal and its natural curve droops the end pointed away from you downward ("shedding rain" as opposed to "catching rain"). If the web is to the right of the quill base, it is a right-wing feather. If the web is to the left of the quill base, it is a left-wing feather.

➤ Should I use straight, offset or helical fletchings?

For compound bows, it is recommended that shooters use offset or helical fletchings on all arrows. Offset and helical fletchings cause arrows to rotate in flight just like the rifling in a gun barrel causes a bullet to rotate. This is important for arrows because the rotation acts like a gyroscope to stabilize the arrow during flight.

Helical fletchings offer more stability than a simple offset, and therefore should be the first choice for all broadhead-tipped arrows.

➤ How much fletching offset should I use?

If the forward end of a 5-inch feather is offset $\frac{1}{16}$-inch from its rear, this equals about three-quarters of one degree. This works well for most offset or helical-fletched arrows.

➤ How should I prepare my arrow shafts for the fletching process?

Begin by wiping the fletching area of the arrows with alcohol, then lightly scuffing the area with 600-grit sandpaper or fine steel wool. It's wise to perform a final alcohol wipe before starting the fletching process.

— FOR MORE INFORMATION ON FLETCH-INGS, CONTACT TRUEFLIGHT MFG., BOX 1000, MANITOWISH WATERS, WI 54545

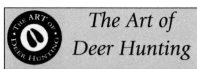

The Art of Deer Hunting

BY TOM CARPENTER

Shot Placement Part 1:
Bow-Hunters

Don't lose sleep over arrow speeds and broadhead grains. Instead, concentrate on sending your arrow through a deer's vitals.

Broadside:
Aim halfway up the body, behind the shoulder, avoiding the shoulder blade. This shot destroys the lungs. Hitting slightly low, high or back will still be lethal.

Quartering-Toward:
Wait for a better angle. Bones and muscles shield the deer's vitals, presenting a small target. Plus, the deer is more likely to see you draw.

Quartering-Away:
Aim between the rear ribs, toward the opposite shoulder. The broadhead angles through the entire chest cavity.

Facing Toward or Away:
Wait for a better angle. If a better shot doesn't present itself, let the deer walk.

BOW-HUNTING TIPS

➤ **WHEN HUNTING** whitetails in suburban areas, wait until the wind and weather are perfect for your stand, thus reducing your impact on the area by eliminating low-odds hunts. Also restrict your hunting to afternoons, because bucks typically feed in agricultural fields in the pre-dawn darkness. Therefore, walking to your stand in the morning might alert them to your presence.

➤ **BROADHEADS SHOULD** be checked for flight after shafts have been paper tuned. It's not uncommon for the impact point of a broadhead to be different than a field point.

Set up a broadhead target 20 to 30 yards away. Using the same arrow (with field point) that you used for paper tuning, shoot at the target. This will give you a reference point. If the shot is off, make the necessary adjustments to your sights.

Remove the field point and install a broadhead onto the shaft. Use the same aiming point, and shoot again. If the broadhead hits close to where the field point did, shoot the same arrow several times to be sure you are within a respectable group size.

The shot group is the key. If you are shooting good groups but the impact is off from your aiming point, simply make sight adjustments.

➤ **A BROADHEAD'S LETHALITY** hinges on its degree of sharpness. Just because a broadhead is new doesn't mean it's as sharp as it can be. Sharp blades are more likely to slice a whitetail's arteries and veins on contact, while less-than-scalpel-sharp blades can push past arteries without cutting them. Invest in a broadhead sharpener and touch up each blade of each broadhead in your quiver before every hunt. You owe it to your quarry to ensure quick, clean kills.

For mechanical broadheads, deploy the blades and sharpen them individually. Replace rubber "O" rings that show signs of wear.

Selecting Accurate, Hard-Hitting Broadheads

Quality broadheads aren't cheap, and it's easy to spend a lot of money trying to determine which ones are right for you. With that in mind, follow this simple, four-step game plan to reduce your costs and select the perfect broadhead for your setup:

1. Conduct your own field test.

Most broadheads are sold in three- and four-packs, so get two or three of your hunting partners to split the cost of several packs of broadheads.

2. Research what types of broadheads are out there. You will want to try mechanicals and fixed-position heads, so do some homework and select three or four different brands of each category that you want to try.

Don't let cost scare you from trying what you want. For example, if three shooters spend $40 apiece on a field test, they could shoot at least six brands of broadheads. Furthermore, they will know exactly what heads they want to shoot, rather than spending $40 on two packs of one brand that "looks good."

3. Set up a test course. Present huge soft targets — foam blocks work best — and start by shooting the broadheads from short distances (10 to 15 yards).

First, however, organize the shoot. Give each shooter one broadhead from each pack. Shoot one arrow at a time, plot its performance on a sheet of paper, and retrieve the arrow before shooting again. You can ruin a lot of arrows, and perhaps a few broadheads, if

Jim Schlender

TO FIND THE BEST broadhead, pool your money with bow-hunting friends and buy several brands and styles. Doing so allows you to test-shoot various models at minimal expense.

the impact point of a broadhead to be different than a field point.

1. Set up a broadhead target 20 to 30 yards away. Using the same arrow (with field point) that you used for paper tuning, shoot at the target. This will give you a reference point. If the shot is off, make the necessary adjustments to your sights.

2. Remove the field point and install a broadhead onto the shaft. Use the same aiming point, and shoot again. If the broadhead hits close to where the field point did, shoot the same arrow several times to be sure you are within a respectable group size.

3. The shot group is the key. If you are shooting good groups but the impact is off from your aiming point, simply make sight adjustments.

— NEW ARCHERY PRODUCTS

you allow shooters to shoot several broadheads at the same 6-inch circle on the target.

4. Select the broadhead that shoots best for you, and purchase six or more that will be used strictly for hunting. Also, purchase replacement blades for heads you use. You will save a lot of money.

Finally, use the original field-test broadheads as your practice heads. And, unless your broadheads fly exactly like your field points, always practice with your broadheads.

— DANIEL E. SCHMIDT

Proper Tuning For Today's Broadheads

Broadheads should be checked for flight after shafts have been paper tuned. It's not uncommon for

BOW-HUNTING TIPS

➤ **RESEARCH BY ARROW** manufacturers shows that 400 grains is the magic weight for a carbon, graphite or composite hunting arrow for it to produce deep penetration and excellent flight characteristics. However, it's wise to remember that because graphite shafts are about four times stronger than aluminum, very small changes in diameter change the stiffness of the arrow.

➤ **ANY WELL-PLACED** broadhead will quickly and efficiently kill a deer. However, not all broadheads are created equal. Your job in finding the best head for your setup involves finding a broadhead that offers outstanding penetration, unmatched cutting ability, indestructible construction and incredible flight characteristics. That might sound like a tall order to fill, but it isn't. In fact, the selection process can be entertaining and educational.

The Perfect Stand: 10 Tips for Tree-Stand Hunting

The tree stand has unarguably changed the face of deer hunting. From the early days of hand-sawn boards and nails pounded in trees to today's lightweight ladder, fixed-position and climbing stands, tree stands have earned a place among the most effective ways to bow-hunt whitetails.

However, with a little extra effort and caution, you can ensure that your tree-stand hunts are fun, safe and successful. Consider these 10 tips when setting up your next stand site.

Tip No. 1:
Never Use Homemade Stands

If you've been deer hunting long, you've probably built your own wooden treestands. And, whether your stands were elaborate ladders or planks wedged in forked limbs, you have probably hunted in a less-than-safe perch.

Today, hunting from homemade stands is ridiculous. Weather, animals, poor materials and faulty construction make any homemade stand — even a seemingly safe one — a tragedy waiting to happen. Considering that, you should always use a Treestand Manufacturers Association-approved tree stand made with steel or aircraft-grade aluminum.

Although wooden box-blinds stilted on treated lumber are sometimes considered safe, you should never trust your life to them.

ALTHOUGH TODAY'S tree stands are much safer than the homemade stands many hunters once used, you should always wear a quality safety harness while tree-stand hunting

Tip No. 2:
Follow Manufacturer Directions

Even while using one of today's modern tree stands, hunting from high places is a relatively dangerous proposition. Therefore, it's vital to read the directions supplied with your tree stand and follow them to the letter. Learn how to operate your stand — especially the included safety harness — long before opening morning.

This is especially important with climbing tree stands. Regardless of your stand's design, familiarize yourself with all of the stand's functions at ground level. Test your ability to use the stand before you leave the ground.

Tip No. 3: Slow Down

Hurrying is always a bad idea, but haste while using tree stands can be deadly. Take your time ascending and descending from trees. If you're late getting into position for a hunt, so what? No hunt is worth your life.

Rushing into position probably causes more tree-stand injuries than anything else. Always use a rope to pull up your bow or gun, and make sure your gun is unloaded and your arrows are enclosed in a quality quiver.

Tip No. 4:
Use a Safety Harness

Always use a safety harness — even while climbing. However, don't let a safety harness lull you into a false sense of security. Use the same caution you always would.

It's also a good idea to carry a sharp knife in an easy-to-reach pocket. If you lose your footing and end up hanging by your safety strap, you'll be able to cut yourself free.

In addition, never stay in a tree stand if you're extremely tired. If you feel fatigued, descend from your stand and take a nap.

Finally, always tell someone where you are hunting and leave a map to your stand.

Tip No. 5: Use a Flashlight

While moving to and from your stand during low light, always use a flashlight. This will decrease

ARCHERY INSIGHTS

➤ **IN SOME PARTS** of the United States, particularly the Northeast, almost entire states have a suburban feel because of dense human populations. As a result, bow-hunting has a more obvious impact on statewide harvests. In New Jersey, for example, archers in 1994 bagged 37 percent of the statewide antlerless harvest and 41.5 percent of the buck harvest.

➤ **WISCONSIN HAS** at least five deer management units in suburban areas where bow-hunting has made an impact on overall deer harvest. This is most obvious when comparing "metro" harvests to statewide averages. From 1995-99, bow-hunting in metro units accounted for 37 percent of the combined gun/bow harvest, including 44 percent of the buck kill and 32 percent of the antlerless kill. During that same time statewide, archers accounted for 17 percent of the combined gun/bow harvest, including 21 percent of the buck kill.

Other Wisconsin data also suggest metro archers are more willing to help reduce herds. From 1995-99, 51 percent of 7,799 deer registered by metro archers were antlerless. Meanwhile, 48 percent of 376,563 deer registered by archers statewide were antlerless.

the odds that another hunter will mistake you for a deer.

To help find your way to and from your stand, mark a trail using reflective thumbtacks. The tacks are inconspicuous during daylight, but glow brightly when struck by a flashlight beam after dark.

Tip No. 6: Choose a Healthy Tree

Tree-stand safety begins with choosing the right tree. Proper stand trees are alive, healthy and meet your stand's circumference requirements.

Mossy Oak Camouflage

IT'S ALMOST IMPOSSIBLE to get within range of hard-hunted whitetails if you're skylined. Therefore, choose stand trees with the most background cover. If your stand tree lacks suitable cover, attach leafy limbs to the trunk around your stand.

Never climb into a dead tree or one with too many bends or twists in the trunk. Avoid old, slick-barked trees and trees with crumbling bark. In addition, closely inspect your tree for insect damage that might weaken the tree.

Tip No. 7:
Pruning Saws Are Invaluable

A folding limb saw is an indispensable tool for tree-stand placement. Such saws let you prune your way into almost any tree and create shooting lanes in the brush around your stand. You can also use a limb saw to clear a trail to you stand, ensuring you'll reach your stand quietly, without depositing scent on limbs and brush.

If you hunt public land, check state and federal regulations to make sure cutting limbs, using tree stands and installing screw-in steps is legal where you hunt.

Tip No. 8: Pack Light

Reduce the amount of stuff you take into the tree, such as books, cameras and food. Too much gear can be a distraction. Take only vital equipment. Climbing into a tree stand while towing up a daypack or overstuffed fanny pack can be dangerous. Besides, items like books are distracting and might prevent you from seeing the buck of a lifetime.

Tip No. 9: Watch Your Back

Most bow-hunters learn the importance of background cover early in their hunting careers. After all, it's almost impossible to get within bow range of a nervous whitetail if you're skylined.

Considering this, the next time you find a prime stand site, select the tree that offers the most concealment. To help do this, look up at the surrounding trees like an approaching deer. Set up in the tree with the most limbs, leaves and other cover to keep you from being silhouetted.

If no trees offer background cover, but the spot is too promising to pass up, make your own cover by cutting smaller limbs and brush and tying them around your stand.

Hang your stand and cut shooting lanes as far in advance of your hunt as possible, especially if you're bow-hunting. This lets your scent dissipate.

Tip No. 10: Play the Wind

When you find a good stand site, consider your area's most common wind direction. Hang your stand so your scent blows away from where you anticipate deer will approach. Do not hunt a stand if the wind is wrong.

— MOSSY OAK CAMOUFLAGE

BOW-HUNTING: SUBURBIA'S SAVIOR?

➤ **BOW-HUNTING IS** proving effective, or at least a major contributor, in controlling deer herds in urban, suburban and smaller "site-specific" areas such as parks, refuges and arboretums. This is not a modern phenomenon, but it has evolved in recent years. In the 1950s through the early 1980s, agencies often used high concentrations of bow-hunters to control "confined" deer herds. For example, bow-hunter densities ranged from 125 to 200 per square mile to control deer on Howland Island, N.Y., from 1952 to 1957. And at Blackbeard Island, Ga., bow-hunter densities averaged 118 per square mile during herd-control hunts between 1972 and 1982.

Recent confined bow-hunts have taken a lower-profile approach. Even though these early management bow-hunts were safe and addressed firearms-discharge laws, most wildlife managers decided the "beat-the-bushes" approach to deer control wasn't the best way to operate in relatively quiet parks, refuges and suburban neighborhoods.

➤ **HOWARD J. KILPATRICK**, a wildlife biologist with the Connecticut Wildlife Division, administers an urban deer-control bow-hunt in Groton Long Point. He estimates this hunt, which uses experienced bow-hunters who must pass a shooting test, has reduced the herd by up to 52 percent. However, he notes that such hunts can't be effective if hunter access is restricted in good deer habitat.

➤ **WHEN PLANNING FOOD PLOTS** near fingers of woods, keep prevailing winds in mind. Food plots provide deer with added nutrition, but they can be tough places to hunt if proposed stand sites are upwind of the plots. Also, be aware that fallow fields often need to be worked extensively before being planted. Consult a farm cooperative or agricultural agent to determine soil pH. Generally speaking, soil pH must be at least 6.0 to grow lush fields of clover and rye grass.

Can't Bring Bucks Into Bow Range? Try Soft Calls

Despite all that I had ever believed about deer calling — which I had mostly gleaned from overly dramatic hunting video footage — I refrained from blasting the young 8-pointer with loud, aggressive grunting and rattling. Instead, following advice I'd received earlier that afternoon from Woods Wise Calls' Jerry Peterson, I made two barely audible doe bleats.

Even as I called, I thought, "This is ridiculous. It's the peak of the rut. How are a few wimpy bleats I can hardly hear going to get that deer's attention, much less pull him across this cornfield?"

However, I became a believer when the young buck instantly swiveled its ears toward the sound and marched my way. Seconds later, the buck was nibbling browse mere feet from my stand tree.

According to Peterson, the buck's response made sense. After all, I was "speaking" to him in a gentle, nonthreatening way that simply said "come to me."

Loud, aggressive calling, which gets most attention in videos and magazine articles, sends a much different message. Peterson said using such calls is like approaching a small child and yelling for him to come to you. The child will probably stay put or run the other way.

On the other hand, if you ask the child the same question in a soft, soothing voice, he'll probably cooperate. The same is true for deer.

When grunting — whether hunting the pre-rut, rut or post-rut —

ALTHOUGH loud, aggressive grunting and rattling get the fame, soft contact grunts and bleats attract deer more consistently.

short, soft grunts typically attract bucks and does of all ages more consistently than bold, rut-style calls.

Subtle bleats also work well. And, during the rut, these calls serve double duty, because their low-key sounds comfort and attract does, fawns and immature bucks, while convincing dominant bucks that a doe is nearby.

When rattling, try to imitate playful sparring, and reserve fight-to-the-death imitations for the peak of the pre-rut, when bucks are desperate to establish a hierarchy.

Loud grunting and rattling are sometimes great for attracting bucks. However, they're effective for only a short time each year. On the other hand, subtle calls work well throughout the season.

— Ryan Gilligan

Today's Hot New Bows

■ **Mathews'** Legacy takes vibration dampening to a higher level. Along with parallel limbs, perimeter weighting and Mathews' Harmonic Damping System, the Legacy's string suppressors reduce noise and vibration. The innovative features are attached to the limb tips where their rubber-like tips push against the string upon release. The bow also features Mathews' Roller Guard cable system, which reduces cable wear.

■ Measuring 35¼ inches axle to axle and weighing 4 pounds, 1 ounce, the **Jennings** TrophyMaster provides high performance in a small package. The bow features Jennings' Carbon Twill limbs, a SwingArm cable guard, an adjustable damping system, perimeter-weighted one-cam design and reverse-balanced TechTwist string. The TrophyMaster produces arrow speeds of up to 308 feet per second (IBO) and comes in Realtree Hardwoods camouflage.

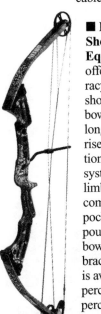

■ **Precision Shooting Equipment's** Nitro offers speed, accuracy and smooth shooting. The bow features a long reflex riser, the NV vibration-reduction system and short limbs mounted in compact, pivoting pockets. The 3-pound, 10-ounce bow has a 6-inch brace height and is available with 65 percent and 85 percent let-off.

■ **Browning** releases the Eclipse SLX bow. The Eclipse features locking limb bolts, Contour XP limbs, Cyber-Cam SX cam, machined aluminum reflex riser, Radial-Lok pivoting limb pockets and ImpacStop vibration-dampening inserts. The bow measures 36 inches from axle to axle and produces arrow speeds of up to 310 feet per second (IBO). Browning offers the Eclipse SLX in 65 percent or 75 percent let-off.

THANKS TO CONSTANTLY improving lens coatings and construction methods, today's riflescopes are better than ever, providing unsurpassed clarity, durability and low-light performance.

4

Expert Insights for Rifle & Shotgun Hunters

Seeing the Light of Day With Today's Riflescopes

I was doing my best to ignore the swarm of mosquitoes buzzing around my head when I noticed movement at the edge of a nearby soybean field. It was early September, and I was taking part in a crop-damage hunt on a friend's farm. However, the 80-degree heat was more conducive to bass fishing than deer hunting.

As I peered through the thick, soupy haze that hung over the field and scanned the still-green woods, I made out the outline of a mature doe, all but concealed by thick grapevines at the field's edge. As the sun began to dip below the horizon, the doe cautiously stuck her head out of the leaves and took a calculated step into the field.

With sweat flowing down my temples and soaking the collar of my light coverall, I slowly shouldered the borrowed rifle and tried to find the doe in the less-than-quality scope. Between the hazy air and fading evening light, I might as well have been looking through a glass of chocolate milk. As I strained to look through the scope, the wind shifted toward the doe. Suddenly alert, she lifted her head, stamped a hoof and ambled back into the grapevines. The only blood shed that hot evening was taken out of me by mosquitoes.

Making Improvements

Of course, riflescopes have spelled doom for countless whitetails. Scopes magnify and clarify distant game, and help hunters hit targets more consistently at long ranges. Whether they're low-magnification, fixed-power scopes or high-magnification, large-objective variable models, most scopes can drastically improve accuracy. However, as I learned during that hunt, low light and foul weather can render a tack-driving scope-and-rifle combination useless.

Hunting conditions are rarely like those on the range. It's always cold, hot or wet, and deer are most active during early morning or evening. Although fortunate hunters squeeze the trigger and watch whitetails crumple in their

TEXT AND PHOTOS BY RYAN GILLIGAN

ALTHOUGH THEY CREATE a larger exit pupil, large-objective riflescopes aren't necessarily the best choice for hunters because they must be mounted unusually high to allow for bell clearance. Instead, hunters are better served to invest in a smaller-objective scope with quality glass and lens coatings. Such scopes often transmit as much or more light than large objective models.

scopes' field of view, untold others before them looked through their scope at the moment of truth to find fogged lenses or an image so dark they couldn't see their target, much less shoot it. Fortunately, today's scope manufacturers are constantly developing technologies that optimize performance in various hunting conditions.

By surveying today's array of high-quality scopes, and sorting through the hype and technical buzz words, you can find a scope that fits your hunting needs.

The Better to See You With

Scopes rely on light. Light increases contrast and clarity, refracts to magnify the image and enhances detail at longer distances. Therefore, scopes that let in the most light and use it most efficiently usually perform best, especially at dawn and dusk, when deer are most active.

A scope's ability to use light is the product of several factors, including lens size, glass quality and anti-reflective coatings. These elements and their relation to each other make the difference between a scope that provides clear, bright images at long distances all day, and a scope that limits your hunting to periods of good light.

Objective Lens Size

A scope's front objective lens affects performance by dictating the size of the scope's exit pupil, which is the shaft of light that passes through the ocular lens to the shooter's eye. Exit-pupil size is calculated by dividing the size of the objective by the scope's magnification. For example, a variable scope set at 3X with a 40 mm objective lens has a 13.3 mm exit pupil, while at 9X, the same scope has a 4.4 mm exit pupil. This figure is important because of how it relates to the dimensions of the human eye.

"The human pupil dilates from 2 mm in brightness, to 7 mm in darkness. In low-light hunting, most hunters need a 5 mm exit pupil," said Jon LaCorte product marketing manager for Nikon.

Therefore, scopes with higher magnifications and smaller exit pupils often produce dim images because they fill less of the shooter's eye. Many manufacturers offer scopes with objectives as large as 50 mm in diameter. However, the trend might be based more on fickle tastes and catchy terms like "light gathering" than actual improvements in performance.

"The term 'light gathering' is a misnomer. It has no meaning in the technical sense," said Ken Woytek plant manager for Millet Industries. "Brightness and resolution are what people look for in adverse conditions. That's what people are thinking of when they say 'light gathering.'

"The big motivation for hunters to go to a big objective came out of Europe, where hunting is done at long ranges in extreme low-light conditions. That caused a big stampede to big objective lenses here."

MOSSY OAK BLIND-HUNTING TIPS:
PLAYING IT SAFE

If you're planning to rattle or grunt from a ground blind, make safety a priority when selecting a location.

Sitting on the ground while making sounds that resemble bucks fighting is an excellent way to increase your chances of seeing big deer, but you must make sure other hunters won't mistake your movement as a target.

Choose a calling location with a solid cut bank, large tree or other impenetrable obstacle behind you.

Also, be on the lookout for other hunters moving toward you. If you see another hunter approaching, don't shout or wave. Address them in a calm voice and let them know what and where you are.

A little defensive thinking goes a long way toward preventing accidents.

Large objective lenses increase the size of the light shaft hitting the shooter's eye. However, for most magnifications, a large-objective scope provides a larger exit pupil than the human eye can use. For example, in a 3X scope with a 40 mm objective, the 13.3 mm exit pupil created is far larger than the 5 mm pupil of the shooter. This is useful in snap-shooting situations, because it lets a hunter see the target quickly and shoot.

However, that advantage is often overridden by problems with shooting such scopes. The larger the objective lens, the higher the scope must be mounted to allow for bell clearance. As a result, a hunter with a large-objective scope must raise his head higher to see through the scope, causing less comfortable, less accurate shooting.

Lens Coatings

Considering the limitations of objective lens size, most hunters are best served by a scope that features well-coated lenses, rather than one with an exaggerated objective. In fact, a scope with a small, well-coated lens will likely outperform better than one with a large, poorly coated objective, especially in low light. That's because all glass surfaces reflect light. With scopes, reflection means increased glare, stray light within the scope tube, and decreased light transmission — all of which hinder scope performance.

"Any air-to-glass surface gives up up to 4 percent of incoming light to reflection," Woytek said.

According to Woytek, a typical scope lens, depending on its power, has an index of refraction — a relative measurement of reflection ability — of 1.6. In comparison, plate glass has a index of refraction of about 1.3. The higher the density of a piece of glass, the greater its ability to reflect. Therefore, high-magnification scopes can reflect more light. That's where lens coatings earn their keep.

By coating lenses with salts such as magnesium fluoride, most manufacturers reduce light reflection to a fraction of a percent per lens surface. By doing so, more light is allowed

Leupold Offers the VX-II

Leupold's VX-II riflescope is modeled after Leupold's Vari-X II. The scope features Multicoat 4 lens coatings and ¼ minute audible and tactile click adjustments. Leupold offers the VX-II in 1-4x20 mm, 2-7x33 mm, 3-9x40 mm and 3-9x50 mm fixed-objective models, and in 4-12x40 mm and 6-18x40 mm adjustable-objective models. The VX-II is available in several finishes and seven reticles.

through the scope and to the shooter's eye, increasing brightness, clarity and contrast.

Lens-Coating Advancements

High-tech lens coatings pick up where lens size leaves off in producing clear, bright images. However, coatings and how they are applied vary between manufacturers.

Although many manufacturers fully coat all glass surfaces on interior and exterior lenses, some do not. Before buying a scope, make sure all air-to-glass surfaces of each lens are coated. If only a select few lenses are coated, the result is reflected light within the scope tube.

"We do a special multicoating so instead of spraying or dipping, we put lenses in a vacuum with four crucibles," said Chuck Miller of Millet Industries. "We super-heat the crucibles, vaporizing the coating material. When the material settles, it coats the lenses evenly — right out to the edge of all the lenses, without any pooling."

The Art of Deer Hunting

BY TOM CARPENTER

Shot Placement Part 1: Gun-Hunters

You can sweat over ballistics tables and bullet styles, but putting your projectile in the right place is the real key to effective shooting.

Broadside:

Aim halfway up the body, behind the shoulder. This shot penetrates the lungs.

You may also aim high on the shoulder. If executed properly, this shot causes nerve damage, breaks bone and destroys the lungs.

Quartering-Toward:

Aim for the near shoulder. This will break the shoulder and angle the bullet through the chest.

Quartering Away:

Angle the shot from the back of the body cavity toward the opposite shoulder. The shot will destroy most vital organs and might break the shoulder.

Facing Toward or Away:

The angle presents a small vital area. Wait for a better shot.

And, although the process increases expense, applying multiple coats of anti-reflective coatings significantly improves performance. Although even one anti-reflective coating helps reduce reflection, the more coats the better. Some manufacturers offer scopes with 30 layers of coatings. However, such performance comes with a price tag. Hunters are best served in price and performance by a scope with lenses that have at least a few coatings.

Reticle Type

Choosing a scope with an appropriate reticle is also important. During midday, fine reticles work well because they provide the greatest precision. However, when shooting at dawn or dusk against a dark background, thicker reticles make aiming faster and easier.

Recently developed illuminated reticles go a step further. By contrasting sharply with the target and standing out in low-light conditions, electronically illuminated reticles help hunters acquire their target quickly and take advantage of light.

However, not all illuminated reticles function the same way. For example, Kahles manufactures scopes that feature etched glass illuminated reticles, rather than more common flash-dot reticles. Flash-dot reticles work by projecting a beam of light to the scope's internal aiming point. Because of this artificial light projection, the amount of stray light inside the scope tube increases, hindering light transmission.

"Flash-dot systems reduce light transmission by up to 10 percent," said Greg Jones, product manager for Kahles.

In etched-glass reticles, the cross-hairs are etched into a plate of glass separate from the scope lenses. The artificial light powering the reticle comes in from the edges of the glass. Because etched glass reticles don't project light through the scope tube, there is no stray light to interfere with light transmission.

Construction Advancements

Although lenses and optical components get much attention, improvements in scope materials and manufacturing techniques have a profound effect on quality. For example, new lightweight, strong materials such as titanium have contributed greatly to scope durability and performance afield.

The increasing influence of computer design has also played a role in improving scope performance.

"I think computer-aided design and manufacturing processes have really improved scope performance," said Pat Mundy, public relations representative for Nikon. "Twenty years ago, if you changed the power on a variable scope, you had a point-of-impact shift. Now you don't, thanks to better design and manufacturing tolerances.

"Tolerances are extremely tight, and lenses can be spaced more precisely. Nowadays, you're getting first-rate quality with every scope because the tolerances are so tight – within ten-thousandths of an inch."

Today's scope manufacturing techniques also help hunters contend with wet, cold conditions. No matter how much light a scope gathers or how clear its view, it won't do you any good if it's fogged up. To combat this, most manufacturers purge their

GUN-HUNTING INSIGHTS

➤ **THE *STANDARD CATALOG* of *Firearms, 11th Edition,*** is a comprehensive reference guide. The book features information on more than 12,000 firearms.

Rifles and shotguns are listed with a detailed grading system to help readers determine retail prices. The book also examines gun-collecting issues, firearms legislation, and provides a manufacturer index .

For more information, contact Krause Publications, Book Department PR01, Box 5009, Iola, WI 54945-5009, or visit the Web site: www.krausebooks.com.

scopes of oxygen and fill them with nitrogen. This keeps the inside of the scope dry, preventing moisture from accumulating on lenses in changing temperatures, which prevents fogging.

Conclusion

Thanks to high-tech lens coatings, innovative reticles and construction advancements, today's scopes serve hunters better than ever. Modern riflescopes provide unsurpassed clarity, accuracy, durability and low-light performance.

Remember, no single factor makes or breaks the way a scope works. Instead, realize that a scope's reticle, construction, lens size and anti-reflective coatings play important roles in how the package will function when the moment of truth arrives.

By taking advantage of these advancements in scope technology and selecting a scope that fits your hunting style, you'll be well prepared this fall.

How to Mount a Riflescope

A state-of-the-art scope is useless if it is mounted incorrectly. Although your local gun shop should be up to the task, doing the work yourself can save money and add another rewarding dimension to your hunts.

Follow these steps to meld your rifle and scope into a tack-driving combination.

Tools required
✓ Hex wrench set (English)
✓ Gunsmith screwdrivers
✓ Scope-mounting adhesive
✓ Gun oil
✓ Long cotton swabs
✓ Soft cotton cloth
✓ Acetone, ether or other cleaning/degreasing agent
✓ Riflescope bore-sighting device and arbors
✓ Scope alignment rods
✓ Shims
✓ Rubber hammer
✓ Rifle vise
✓ Short steel ruler
✓ Lapping kit
✓ Reticle leveler

Instructions
1. Place the gun's safety in the "on" position. Unload firearm and remove bolt, cylinder, clip, etc. Make sure the chamber is empty.

2. Remove old bases or rings. If the gun is new, you might have to remove the factory screws from the receiver. These screws protect the scope's mounting holes until needed.

3. Degrease the base screws and the receiver's mounting holes.

4. Temporarily install the bases. Shimming might be required under part of the base if the top of the receiver is not parallel to the axis of

WHEN THE SCOPE is mounted on the gun, make sure there is at least ⅛ inch of clearance between the bell of the scope and the gun.

the bore. Mismatches might require a different set of bases.

5. Install the scope alignment rods into the rings and place them on the firearm. If there is a misalignment, some shimming might be required. Very small adjustments can be made later by tapping the base with a rubber hammer.

6. Remove the rings when the rods indicate the system is aligned. Apply a light coating of gun oil to the underside of the base and the top of the receiver.

Also install the base and screws, using adhesive. Be sure the adhesive does not drip into the action. Use cotton swabs to clean spillage.

7. Re-install the rings with the alignment rods. Again, if there is a small alignment problem, tapping with the rubber hammer might correct it. If there's gross misalignment, shimming might be required.

8. Once you are satisfied the rings and the base are aligned, install the riflescope in the rings. Degrease the inner surface of the rings and the area of contact on the scope.

Inspect the fit of the rings to the

riflescope. Some inexpensive rings are not perfectly round, making for a poor fit between the ring and the scope's body tube.

If you're using Weaver-style rings, install them loosely, then attach them to the base. For Redfield-style rings, attach the twist-lock front ring by using a 1-inch metal or wooden dowel.

When the scope is mounted, ensure there is at least $\frac{1}{8}$ inch of clearance between the bell of the scope and the gun. Also, make sure the action isn't touching the scope during cycling.

9. Set up the bore-sighting system on the firearm. Adjust the ring screws so the scope can rotate, but not wobble. Adjust the distance the scope is from the eye to prevent injury during recoil — about 3 inches.

10. Turn the scope to high power and adjust the windage and elevation controls so the image of the bore-sighting grid and the scope reticle doesn't move with each other as the scope is rotated.

11. Gently rotate the scope in the rings so the horizontal portion of the reticle is level when the gun is held in the shooting position. To aid this adjustment, use a bubble level or reticle leveler. Next, tighten all rings and base screws. Use adhesive on the screws, and let set overnight.

12. Adjust the windage and elevation controls to place the center of the reticle on the center of the bore-sighting grid. Shimming might be required to bring it in alignment with the bore. If so, consider using a system with windage control.

13. With everything secure, the riflescope is now ready for the range. The shooter should pick a common distance — 25, 50 or 100 yards — and adjust accordingly. Remember, ammu-

Use a Partner to Sight-In Your Rifle with Two Shots

The best way to sight in your deer rifle is to shoot from a bench and steady rest at a paper target 50 to 100 yards away.

If your scope is equipped with an adjustable objective, be sure it is adjusted to the range at which you are sighting.

The traditional method of sighting a rifle from a solid rest is to aim at the bull's-eye and carefully fire one or more shots. Note the vertical and horizontal distances between the resulting bullet holes and the desired point of impact. Adjust the scope the required number of clicks to move from the initial point of impact to the desired point of impact. Fire additional shots and make adjustments as required to achieve the desired result.

The "two-shot" sighting method is much easier, but it requires another person's help.

With the rifle on sandbags, take careful aim at the bull's-eye and fire one shot. Arrange the rifle back on the bags and aim at the bull's-eye again. Without moving the rifle, have a friend adjust the scope reticle while you watch through the scope. Direct the person to move the reticle until it's centered on the first bullet hole. Now the rifle should shoot where the scope is looking.

Fire a second shot to confirm the rifle is sighted. You might need to perform some fine tuning, but this method is quick, easy and accurate.

— For more information, contact Pentax, 35 Inverness Drive E., Englewood, CO 80112.

nition, outside temperature, temperature of the barrel and cleanliness of the barrel all affect a gun's accuracy.

14. Make sure the scope's rings and bases are tight.

— FOR MORE INFORMATION ON SCOPE MOUNTING, CONTACT BUSHNELL SPORT OPTICS, 9200 CODY ST., DEPT. DDH, SHAWNEE MISSION, KS 66214.

EARLY "PUMPKIN BALL" SLUGS are no match for today's high-tech sabots. Modern slugs not only produce energies and velocities similar to some centerfire rifle rounds, they offer amazing long-range accuracy.

Today's Slugs Push the Performance Envelope

"The buck on the left is 191 yards away," said outfitter-guide Scott Denny, as he peered through a laser range-finder at a group of bedded pronghorns on the high plains of east-central Wyoming. "We can get closer if we stay behind this little ridge to the right."

"No. I'll try it from here," said Steve Meyer, readying his gun on a bipod for the shot. "How fast do you think that wind is?"

"I dunno. Ten mph, maybe a little more," said Denny, switching from range-finder to binoculars.

Meyer carefully lined up the cross-hairs, shifted them for windage, and slowly exhaled while pressing the trigger.

"Boom!"

At the report, the antelope rose and were soon running full speed, intent on getting somewhere else quickly.

All but one. The targeted buck never got out of its bed, and was lying in a twisted pile with one leg in the air.

It was a nice shot. For a shotgun.

Meyer was shooting a 12-gauge Browning A-Bolt with a Winchester Partition Gold slug. With a muzzle velocity of more than 1,800 feet per second, more than 1½ tons of energy at the muzzle, a lead-core projectile, and partitioned copper jacket, it's only technically a shotgun slug.

Sighted dead-on at 150 yards, the slug offered a point-blank range (plus or minus 3 inches elevation, assuring no need of holdover) at 178 yards. Meyer, who was part of the slug's design team at Winchester-Olin, allowed two inches of holdover at 191 yards and six inches of wind drift.

"Shotguns?" had been Denny's surprised reaction when Meyer uncased his A-Bolt and I pulled out my Tar-Hunt RSG-12 custom-bolt gun. However, he was converted after watching us shoot rifle-like 100-yard groups from a makeshift bench.

Denny was also at my shoulder the first day of the hunt, when my 117-yard offhand shot killed a buck out of a milling herd.

"I'm impressed," Denny said. "I wasn't so sure at first, but after seeing those things in action, I figure that's all you need anywhere they're legal."

The Slobberknocker

Clint Amiotte, ranch hand for the Triple U in Fort Pierre, S.D., was also skeptical a few days later when we showed up with shotguns to kill a bison.

Although bison aren't particularly wary, they're extremely tough. A typical 6½-year-old bull weighs

BY DAVE HENDERSON

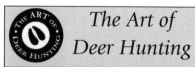

The Art of Deer Hunting

BY TOM CARPENTER

Stay Just a Little Bit Longer

Many gun-hunters leave the woods an hour or two after sunup, thinking, "The best hour of the day is gone, I'll try again later." However, this is usually a mistake. After all, there is an art to deciding when to leave your stand.

When you're considering leaving your stand, chant to yourself, "Stay just a little longer." Even if it's a little cold or you haven't seen a thing, wait it out just a little longer, and then wait a little longer again. And again. Convince yourself that deer are trying to get back to where you are waiting. Tell yourself this, and outwait everyone else.

I learned the effectiveness of this simple technique a few years ago, when a big buck was frequenting my hunting area. Soon after arriving at my stand, I noticed at least six hunters within sight across the surrounding fields. Although the morning was uneventful, I remained in my stand. Shortly after the last of the other hunters had left, I shot a large buck.

Staying just a little longer had paid off.

between 1,800 and 1,900 pounds, and has a heavily furred neck and shoulders and large, dense bones. Amiotte wasn't sure a shotgun slug could effectively work its way through the heavy fur, let alone the muscle and bone.

Eric Fischer, a fellow Table Mountain hunter who traveled with us to the Triple U, borrowed my Tar-Hunt and killed the first bull with a well-placed shot to the neck.

"Whoa," yelled Amiotte, who had seen hundreds of buffalo shot on the ranch, but none with a shotgun. "That shotgun slug is a real slobber-knocker, ain't it?"

Well, that's one word for it.

How do antelope and bison relate to deer? If a shotgun can take down an antelope at nearly 200 yards and drop a bison in its tracks, imagine what it can do on whitetails.

Exciting New Loads

The Partition Gold is part of a vanguard of impressive new loads that have been pushing the envelope in slug performance. These loads have been described as "rifle fodder disguised as shotgun slugs." Despite its flashy ballistics and design, the Winchester load isn't the fastest or hardest-hitting slug on the market.

Hornady's 12-gauge H2K Heavy Mag is the fastest slug ever made, approaching 2,000 fps at the muzzle, and Lightfield's 3-inch Commander throws a $1\frac{1}{16}$-ounce slug fast enough — 1,800 fps — to produce nearly 3,300 foot-pounds of energy at the muzzle and 1,550 foot-pounds at 100 yards.

Not wanting to be left out of the velocity blitz, Federal Cartridge loaded its Premium Barnes EXpander to achieve a muzzle velocity of 1,900 fps through a 30-inch test barrel at the company's development facility in Anoka, Minn. Hunters can expect about 1,830 fps in a 24-inch barrel and 1,800 fps in a 22-incher.

Federal simply loads its ¾-ounce

20-gauge Barnes EXpander in a 2¾-inch 12-gauge hull with the appropriate powder load to boost the velocity.

As if that isn't enough, Brenneke USA plans to produce a unique 1-ounce, 1,690 fps sliding-copper jacket slug with a soft aluminum nose. The introduction was announced at the 2000 Shooting, Hunting and Outdoor Trade Show, but production was postponed to allow German designers to develop a softer nose.

"Brenneke has always built slugs for penetration rather than expansion," said Brenneke USA President Tom Turpin. "But you just can't sell a slug in the United States unless it expands. We softened the nose for marketing sake, but it's still a penetration slug."

The idea of producing alloy instead of lead projectiles started in 1993 with the Remington Copper Solid, which was milled out of solid copper bar stock rather than swedged or cast from molten lead like previous slugs. The slug turned out to be much too hard for most applications, but other designers fell in line with the slug's bullet-like construction after it became clear the concept hadn't alarmed hunting law-enforcement agencies.

Too Far?

"We're seeing a whole new concept in slug design," said a veteran industry observer who works for a major slug manufacturer. "It's a bold move when you consider just why we shoot slugs in the first place."

The insider recently offered his

Brenneke Introduces Innovative Sabot

Brenneke's SuperSabot offers deer hunters another effective option for obtaining maximum accuracy and downrange power from today's slug guns. The slug features a 490-grain, .63-inch-diameter wadcutter projectile that provides 58 percent more frontal area than conventional 50-caliber sabots. This increased area lets the SuperSabot transfer more energy on impact.

Brenneke offers the SuperSabot in 2¾- and 3-inch 12-gauge models, which produce 1,526 fps muzzle velocities and 2½-inch groups at 100 yards.

blunt opinions on slug designs, on the condition of anonymity.

"Obviously, some municipalities make us shoot slugs because slugs don't have the long-range potential of rifle cartridges," he said. "Frankly, it's dangerous from our standpoint. We are now making slugs that we always knew we could make but never did because we were afraid of the repercussions. We're pushing the envelope, and you've got to wonder how far we'll be allowed to take this before somebody puts up a stop sign."

These high-velocity, exotic 2000 design innovations came on the heels of Federal's 1997 loading of the 12-gauge Barnes EXpander and

TODAY'S SLUGS offer shotgun performance once reserved for rifle rounds. Dan Schmidt used Winchester's Partition Gold slug to kill this Wisconsin whitetail at 167 yards.

the 1998 redesign of the Remington Copper Solid. Both were readily expandable copper bullets loaded in shotgun sabots. They were powered at a manageable 1,450 fps, which was the norm for sabots since the early 1990s.

These projectiles were rear-weighted — a departure from previous slugs, which, except for the original Copper Solid, had been constructed nose-heavy for stability. A bullet is stabilized more by rotation and airflow over the surface — particularly how the air flows over the base of the projectile.

Ballistics

The Winchester Partition Gold sabot features a Nosler-style partition .50-caliber, 385-grain bullet manufactured at the Winchester-Olin plant under the Combined Technologies agreement with Nosler. Its ballistic coefficient is .220 compared to .101 for Winchester's hourglass-shaped Hi-Impact sabot.

By comparison, conventional Foster slugs have a ballistic coefficient of about .060.

The high-velocity Federal Barnes EXpander, essentially a solid copper 325-grain bullet with a ballistic coefficient hovering around .200, should yield about 2,500 foot-pounds of muzzle energy in a normal barrel, retaining more than 1,500 foot-pounds at 100 yards and nearly 1,400 foot-pounds at 125 yards.

Hornady loads a 300-grain XTP Mag bullet with a ballistic coefficient of .200. This load achieves more than 2,000 fps in a 30-inch test barrel, which translates to 1,930 fps in a 24-inch slug barrel or about 1,900 in a 22-inch version — figures I confirmed through extensive testing with an Oehler 35P chronometer.

Lightfield's Commander is a different design than its popular 2¾-inch Hybred, which features a soft, .67-caliber, 1¼-ounce pure lead nose with an attached plastic wad. The Hybred's lead is so soft it oozes and has difficulty shedding sabot halves if pushed past 1,500 fps.

To build a faster slug, Lightfield engineers designed a Delrin sleeve that stays with the slug until impact rather than falling off like sabot halves. The Commander's slug is a different shape and weighs an eighth-ounce less than the Hybred, but travels 370 fps faster. Lightfield will introduce a 3½-inch version this fall.

I hunted Alabama's White Oak Plantation with the new 3-inch Commander in January 2001, and killed two does. I recovered a perfectly upset version of the Commander, with its sleeve and wad still intact from a doe I killed with a 110-yard quartering-away shot.

What does the increased velocity of the new slugs mean in terms of trajectory? Well, the rule of thumb for a 100-yard zero with past sabot loads was to center them at least 2½ inches high at 50 yards. According to my experience and calculations, the new Winchester, Federal, Hornady and Lightfield Commander loads need only be ¾ to 1 inch high at 50 yards to zero at 100 yards. In fact, Meyer and I printed them 2 inches high at 50 yards for a 150-yard zero.

These shotgun slugs rival the performance of a .45-70 centerfire rifle. The improved ballistic coeffi-

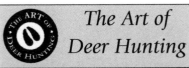

The Art of Deer Hunting

BY TOM CARPENTER

Vested Interest

Gear weighs a deer hunter down. After all, how can anyone comfortably carry calls, cameras, raingear, ammunition, extra clothes and binoculars, not to mention basic necessities such as food and water?

Fanny packs usually aren't big enough, and their weight pulls your pants down like overstuffed pockets do. Backpacks are difficult to shoot with, and they encourage you to over-pack.

One of the best solutions to the gear dilemma is to wear a blaze orange vest like those worn by small-game or bird hunters. These vests have shell loops for slugs. If you're a rifle-hunter, stitch these loops in half to hold rifle cartridges. Such vests also have ample pockets for must-have gear and a big, roomy game bag for food, water and peeled-off clothes.

By wearing a game vest, you get all of your bulky gear out of your pants pockets, while avoiding unwieldy fanny packs or backpacks.

It's just a littler piece of the deer hunting art that works wonders for mobile hunters.

cients, 400- to 500-fps increases over standard sabot loads, and the bullets' expansion and penetration characteristics simply flatten deer. The new slugs boast previously unheard of muzzle energies of around 3,300 foot-pounds and retain 2,000 foot-pounds of energy at 125

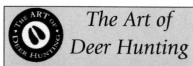

The Art of Deer Hunting

BY TOM CARPENTER

Deer Driving Part 1:
Handling 'Squirts'

Gone are the days when several hunters could line up along a woodlot, walk through and send deer filing out the other side to be shot by standers. Most self-respecting whitetails don't do that anymore — at least where I hunt — probably because the deer that did have been removed from the gene pool.

To outsmart today's savvy whitetails with deer drives, start by thinking of drivers as pushers, because they probably won't force deer to go where they don't want to. Instead, pressured deer will probably run parallel to drivers or circle behind them, "squirting" out in unlikely places.

Anticipating where deer will squirt and positioning posters to intercept them is an art. The hardest part is convincing yourself or a hunting companion that the best posting spot is far from the pushers' path. However, these unorthodox methods sometimes pay off. In fact, because of modern whitetails' tendency to squirt, I often don't place standers in traditional hotspots.

yards — 600 foot-pounds more than expanding copper slugs. What's more, these slugs still have 1,500 foot-pounds available at 200 yards.

Matching Gun to Slug

Winchester and Hornady had difficulty designing the new high-velocity loads because the increased pressure made it difficult to cleanly separate the sabot from the slug when it left the muzzle. Both companies have conquered the problem by stiffening the sabots, but the fast stuff still isn't for every shooter.

"Some say the fast slugs need a faster twist rate, but I think interior barrel diameter is more of a factor," said Randy Fritz, owner of Tar-Hunt Custom Guns and research and development coordinator for Lightfield. "I think you're going to find that most guns made in the last three years will shoot them fine, but anything made before that might or might not handle them well.

"That's because in 1997, the Shooting Arms and Ammunition Manufacturers Institute created a standard bore size for 12-gauge rifled barrels — minimum .719, plus .003 — and the newer guns will have standardized barrels, whereas earlier guns might be virtually any size."

Conclusion

Slug performance has taken giant strides, and hunters are reaping the benefits. Today's slugs achieve rifle-like performance, and manufacturers continue to make improvements. However, considering why we shoot slugs in the first place, slug technology might be nearing its limit.

New Slug Offers Superior Performance

Winchester Ammunition took slug shooting to a new level when it introduced the Winchester Supreme Partition Gold slug in 2000. Never before had a sabot shot so accurately and provided so much knockdown power for long-range shots at whitetails.

AS ITS NAME SUGGESTS, Winchester's Platinum Tip slug features a 400-grain platinum-tipped bullet housed in a reverse-tapered jacket. The design ensures total weight retention and rapid expansion on impact. The load also produces 2,567 foot pounds of energy at the muzzle.

Well, Winchester one-upped itself in 2002 when it unveiled the Platinum Tip sabot. The load's 400-grain platinum tip bullet features Winchester's patented reverse-taper jacket and notching technology, a design that offers superior expansion and weight retention on impact. The 12-gauge slug produces muzzle velocities of 1,700 feet per second with 2,567 foot-pounds of energy.

The Platinum Tip is 15 grains heavier than the Partition Gold, it is only 150 fps slower.

I field-tested the new slug while attending the 2002 Shooting, Hunting and Outdoor Trade Show in 2002, and was impressed with the load's performance. When shot into gelatin blocks wrapped with whitetail hides, the Platinum Tip exhibited impressive expansion and penetration. The penetration tests showed the slugs provide greater wound channels, while the mushrooming characteristics are more impressive than those produced by the Partition Gold.

The Platinum Tip slug also showed to be a consistent performer when shot out of less-than-ideal slug guns.

— DANIEL E. SCHMIDT

Ballistics for the Winchester Platinum Tip Slug

Velocity in Feet Per Second

Muzzle	50 Yards	100 Yards	125 Yards
1,700	1,565	1,428	1,365

Trajectory Heigh in Inches

25 Yards	50 Yards	100 Yards	125 Yards
.6	1.3	0	-2.2

Energy in Foot Pounds

Muzzle	50 Yards	100 Yards	125 Yards
2,567	2,176	1,810	1,654

The Dos and Don'ts of Proper Gun Cleaning

Most hunters appreciate the importance of proper gun cleaning. However, even the most experienced hunters sometimes make gun-cleaning mistakes that reduce their firearm's accuracy, performance and lifespan. Here are a few pointers for keeping your favorite deer gun in its prime.

➤ **Always clean from the breech to the muzzle.**

When you fire a gun, powder residue and dirt foul the barrel, but stay out of the receiver. By running a brush or patch from the muzzle, you push dirt and residue into the chamber. This frequently causes problems with lever-action and autoloading rifles and shotguns.

➤ **Center the rod in the firearm's barrel while cleaning, and do not let it rub against the bore.**

A firearm's bore is a record of the gun's cleaning history. When a cleaning rod rubs a firearm's bore, it creates marks and scratches, hampering accuracy.

➤ **Always use a clean patch.**

Reusing cleaning patches is like cleaning a floor with a dirty mop. During normal use, abrasive dirt collects in rifle and shotgun barrels. By reusing patches, you redeposit dirt and push it into the gun's chamber and neck. The next round you fire through the gun picks up this dirt as it leaves the chamber, thus eroding the throat.

➤ **Never run a brush down the barrel first.**

A brush picks up dirt, moisture and powder residue and redeposits it in the receiver and chamber. Also, never dip a brush in solvent, as this enhances this effect.

➤ **Use only a few drops of solvent or lubricant.**

Although many people think the more solvent the better, this damages

CLEAN YOUR FIREARM thoroughly after each hunt. Doing so will ensure optimum performance and extend the weapon's lifespan.

firearms. Use only as much solvent as the patch can absorb. If you use too much, the solvent or oil will drip into the trigger mechanism, causing a gummy trigger, or into the stock, destroying the wood.

➤ **Put the patch on the cleaning rod correctly to ensure it fits within the barrel as tightly as possible.**

Doing this lets the patch mold itself to the bore and scrub deep within the rifling.

➤ **Run successive patches down the barrel until they come out clean.**

After doing this, cleaning is finished. If you plan to store the gun for an extended period, run a loose, oiled patch down the barrel and let the oil stay in the bore.

➤ **If you plan to shoot the gun immediately after cleaning, run a dry, tight-fitting patch down the bore.**

This removes any excess oil or solvent, eliminating the need for a fouling shot.

— *Otis Technology, Inc.*

Revive a 'Shot-Out' Rifle

Neglected gun barrels can frequently be brought back to life with a special cleaning procedure called "deep cleaning." This procedure can return a "shot-out" rifle to a tack-driving deer gun.

If you have a rifle that isn't shooting consistently and is extremely difficult to clean, this might be worth trying.

✓ With the gun in a cradle or vise, install a bore guide. Attach a jag to a cleaning rod. Place a patch on the jag and saturate it with solvent. Push the patch slowly through the bore.

✓ Put a clean patch on the jag. Using your fingers, work bore compound into the patch until it's saturated. Be sure to use a bore compound that won't harm the barrel.

✓ Run the saturated patch into the bore. Mentally divide the barrel into four equal lengths. Using short strokes, work the rod into each area, using at least 10 strokes in each area. As the patch becomes looser, replace it with another one saturated with bore compound. Continue scrubbing until the patch moves through the bore with uniform smoothness.

✓ Remove bore compound residue from the barrel with patches moistened with carbon solvent. Run patches through the bore until no residue remains. Clean the compound from your cleaning rod, jag and bore guide.

✓ Resume standard cleaning.

— *Ian McMurchy*

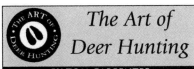

The Art of Deer Hunting

BY TOM CARPENTER

The Simplest Stand

I learned one of deer hunting's oldest tricks on my first hunt, and it is still my most foolproof way to make a good, quiet stand while hunting on the ground.

Clear away all leaves and debris around the base of the tree or other cover you are using to break up your outline. However, go beyond just a foot-shuffle area — clear a little path around the entire tree. This takes only about one minute, and the sounds you'll make won't be especially alarming to nearby deer. A deer might approach from any direction, and you might need to move to shoot.

It sounds elementary, and it is. But many of us, especially gun-hunters, hunt from the ground. If you conceal your silhouette and don't crunch leaves as you fidget, shift your weight or take aim, you'll have better odds of eating venison this winter.

How to Check Smokeless Powder for Deterioration

Although smokeless powders basically don't deteriorate when stored properly, safe practices require a recognition of the signs of deterioration and its possible effects.

Powder deterioration can be checked by opening the cap on the container and smelling the contents. Deteriorating powder has an irritating acidic odor. Don't confuse this with common solvent odors such as alcohol, ether and acetone.

Make sure powder is not exposed to extreme heat, because this causes deterioration. Such exposure produces an acidity that accelerates further reaction and has been known to cause spontaneous combustion. Never salvage powder from old cartridges, and do not attempt to blend salvaged powder with new powder. Don't accumulate old powder stocks.

The best way to dispose of deteriorated smokeless powder is to burn it out in the open at an isolated location in small, shallow piles not more than 1 inch deep. The quantity burned in any one pile should never exceed 1 pound. Use an ignition train of slow-burning combustible material so the person can retreat to a safe distance before powder is ignited.

For a free copy of the *2001 Basic Reloaders Manual*, write Hodgdon Powder Co., Box 2932, Dept. DDH, Shawnee Mission, KS 66201, or call (913) 362-9455.

Average Centerfire Rifle Cartridge Ballistics

Cartridge	Weight	Velocity in feet per second			Energy in foot pounds			Trajectory in inches			Box Price
		Muzzle	100 yds	200 yds	Muzzle	100 yds	200 yds	100 yds	200 yds	300 yds	
.270 Win.	130 gr.	3,060	2,776	2,510	2,702	2,225	1,818	+2.5	+1.4	-5.3	$17
.270 Win.	150 gr.	2,850	2,585	2,336	2,705	2,226	1,817	+2.5	+1.2	-6.5	$17
.30-06 Spfd.	150 gr.	2,910	2,617	2,342	2,820	2,281	1,827	+2.5	+0.8	-7.2	$17
.30-06 Spfd.	180 gr.	2,700	2,469	2,250	2,913	2,436	2,023	-2.5	0.0	-9.3	$17
.300 Win/Mag	150 gr.	3,290	2,951	2,636	3,605	2,900	2,314	+2.5	+1.9	-3.8	$22
.300 Win/Mag	180 gr.	2,960	2,745	2,540	3,501	3,011	2,578	+2.5	+1.2	-5.5	$22
.300 Wby/Mag	150 gr.	3,600	3,307	3,033	4,316	3,642	3,064	+2.5	+3.2	0.0	$32
.300 Wby/Mag	180 gr.	3,330	3,110	2,910	4,430	3,875	3,375	+1.0	0.0	-5.2	$32

Source: *2001 Gun Digest*, Krause Publications

Find Gun-Hunting Gear on the Web

Looking for more information on gun-hunting equipment? Check out these Web sites:

Ammunition
Federal:
www.federalcartridge.com

Hornady:
www.hornady.com

Remington:
www.remington.com

Winchester:
www.winchester.com

Riflescopes
Bushnell Sport Optics:
www.bushnell.com

Leupold:
www.leupold.com

Nikon:
www.nikonusa.com

Simmons:
www.blount.com

Swarovski/Kahles:
www.swarovskioptik.com

Firearms
Browning:
www.browning.com

Ithaca:
www.ithacagun.com

Marlin:
www.marlinfirearms.com

O.F. Mossberg & Son:
www.mossberg.com

Remington:
www.remington.com

Savage Arms:
www.savagearms.com

Sturm, Ruger & Co.:
www.ruger-firearms.com

Tar-Hunt Slug Guns:
www.tar-hunt.com

Thompson/Center Arms:
www.tcarms.com

Weatherby:
www.weatherby.com

U.S. Repeating Arms:
www.winchester-guns.com

Cleaning Products
Birchwood Casey:
www.birchwoodcasey.com

Hoppe's:
www.hoppes.com

Outers:
www.outers-guncare.com

Safes and Gun Locks
Americase:
www.americase.com

Heritage Safe:
www.heritagesafecompany.com

Winchester Safes:
www.fireking.com

Reloading Equipment
Corbin:
www.corbins.com

Hornady:
www.hornady.com

Lee Precision:
www.leeprecision.com

Lyman:
www.lymanproducts.com

Mayville:
www.mayvl.com

MTM Case-Guard:
www.mtmcase-guard.com

Stony Point Products:
www.stonypoint.com

Hearing Protection
Walker's Game Ear:
www.walkersgameear.com

Publications
Krause Publications:
www.krause.com

Today's Hot New Deer Rifles

■ **Remington** introduces short-action .300 and 7mm Model Seven Magnums. Combining bullet velocities and energies similar to long-action calibers with the easy-to-handle Model Seven design, Remington's short-action Model Seven Magnums are excellent for whitetail hunting. Remington offers the rifle with a laminated stock and blued barrel, a synthetic stock and stainless steel barrel and in the rugged Alaskan Wilderness model.

■ **U.S. Repeating Arms** adds .270 and 7mm models to the Winchester Short Magnum rifle line. WSM rifles offer power, accuracy and performance with a shorter action than conventional rifles. The Winchester WSM rifle features a three-round magazine, 24-inch weight-contoured barrel and classic short, control-round-feed action. Winchester offers the .270 and 7mm in Classic stainless, laminated and featherweight models.

■ **Weatherby's** Mark V Super Big GameMaster provides varmit-rifle accuracy in a deer-hunting package. The rifle weighs 5³/₄ pounds and sports a 24-inch Krieger Criterion hand-lapped barrel. The Mark V SuperBig Game Master's barrel flutes are heat dissipating with an 11-degree parabolic target crown.

■ **Tikka** presents the Hunter Stainless Synthetic. Tikka's Whitetail Hunter Stainless Synthetic rifle is built to withstand brutal field conditions. The rifle's action and barrel are made of high-grade stainless steel and its composite fiberglass stock is reinforced with polypropylene for increased durability. Tikka offers the Whitetail Hunter Stainless Synthetic in several popular whitetail calibers, including 7 mm Rem. Mag., .270 Win. and .30-06.

ALTHOUGH SIDE-HAMMER muzzleloaders still see action, in-line muzzleloaders dominate modern blackpowder hunting. The change has increased hunting opportunities and helped deer biologists manage booming herds.

Facts for Modern Muzzleloading

By the 1870s, muzzleloading firearms were all but obsolete. The military firearm advancements of the Civil War had paved the way for brass cartridge technology, and shooters were quick to purchase the new weapons. Although muzzleloaders remained in circulation for years after the large-scale introduction and use of brass cartridges and breech-loading firearms, the age of the frontstuffer was over, and most hunters never looked back — at least, until about 20 years ago.

Starting with a few hard-core traditionalists, flintlocks and percussion-cap rifles once again saw action in the deer woods. And, although the influx of muzzleloading hunters was initially a trickle, it became a torrent after the establishment of specialized muzzleloading seasons and equipment improvements, such as in-line Pyrodex Pellets, sabot bullets and in-line ignitions.

Today, it's difficult to turn on a Sunday morning hunting show without seeing a muzzleloader hunt, and it's even harder to wander a sporting goods store without being bombarded with specialized muzzleloading guns and accessories.

Although this might seem like a bunch of hype to hunters for whom muzzleloaders have always been merely props in period movies, the muzzleloading boom is more than justified. After all, muzzleloaders provide hunters an added challenge and another chance to hunt whitetails each season. What's more, muzzleloaders give wildlife managers another tool for controlling expanding deer herds.

However, despite muzzleloading's recent advancements, hunting with a frontstuffer remains daunting for hunters who have known only modern centerfires. Everything from loading to shooting to cleaning requires extra care, and the equipment is vastly different than what most hunters are familiar with.

If you're thinking about taking a muzzleloader afield for the first time this fall, or if you're an experienced muzzleloader who wants to brush up on the latest equipment and techniques, the following pages are for you. They feature great information on muzzleloading loads, projectiles and today's most innovative rifles. In addition, they provide valuable how-to information on gun cleaning, sighting methods and long-range shooting. Plus, you'll find a comprehensive list of contact information on today's leading muzzleloading equipment manufacturers.

Sighting-In Your Muzzleloading Rifle

1. Be sure your muzzleloader has good iron sights, or, if it's topped with a scope, be sure the mounts are secure. A shooter cannot properly sight-in a rifle with lousy open or peep sights, or a scope that's going to wiggle out of place.

2. Make sure the firearm is sound. Tighten all screws, including the sight screws.

3. Be sure of your load. Inaccurate loads will not print consistently. All things must be equal — especially the charge — to ensure tight shot groups.

4. Use a benchrest, and use it right. Make sure that both the forend of the rifle and the toe of the stock are well padded and secure on the benchtop. A rifle should be set up so that it all but aims itself when properly resting on the benchtop. The shooter should be comfortable with both feet flat on the ground and spread apart a bit for stability. If recoil is a problem, the left hand for a right-handed shooter can be used to grip the forestock. If recoil is not a problem, it's best to rest the left hand flat on the bench. The right hand should control the aim and the trigger.

5. Use a target you can see — one with a well-defined aiming point.

6. Start by just getting a shot on paper. Do not frustrate yourself with 100-yard shots. Save those for later. Start by dialing the gun in at 10 to 15 yards. Adjust sights to hit dead center at close range, then move out to 100 yards.

7. Know your trajectory before shooting. There's no point in sighting-in a big-game rifle with its top load at only 50 yards. Skilled shooters should be able to sight-in a round ball at 75 to 100 yards. Therefore, top loads should increase your range to 150, 175 and, in some cases, 200 yards.

— *The Complete Blackpowder Handbook,* Krause Publications

Muzzleloader Projectiles

Round Balls

The Round Ball

The earliest and most traditional projectile; an all-lead sphere. Used with a lubed patch; either pre-cut or trimmed during loading (with a patch knife). A .50-caliber round ball weighs approximately 175 grains. Using 100 grains of FFG Black Powder, muzzle velocity is about 2,000 feet per second. At 100 yards, terminal energy will be only half of what a conical delivers.

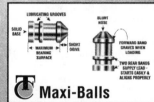

Maxi-Balls

Lead Conicals

An all-lead, conical-shaped projectile, with grooves to hold a lubricant. Although weights might vary, the most popular weight used (.50 cal.) for deer is approximately 350 grains. Using 100 grains of FFG black powder, muzzle velocity is about 1,400 fps. At 100 yards, terminal energy will be about twice that of a round ball.

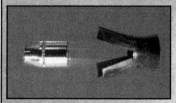

Mag Express Sabots

Sabots

A jacketed bullet (usually .44 or .45 cal.) housed in a plastic or polymer sleeve. The weight of a .50-caliber bullet is usually between 240 and 250 grains. Using 100 grains of FFG black powder, muzzle velocity is approximately 1,600 fps. At 100 yards, terminal downrange energy is between 1,100 and 1,250 ft lbs; on par with a 350-grain all-lead conical. At longer ranges, 150 yards or greater, down-range energy starts to surpass that of a conical because of the higher retained velocity.

Muzzleloading Supplies

Barnes Bullets
Box 215
318 S. 860 E., Dept. DDH
American Fork, UT 84003

Connecticut Valley Arms
Box 7225, Dept. DDH
Norcross, GA 30091

Goex Black Powder
Belin Plant, Dept. DDH
1002 Springbrook Ave.
Moosic, PA 18507

Gonic Arms Inc.
134 Flagg Road, Dept. DDH
Gonic, NH 03839

Hodgdon Powder Co.
6231 Robinson, Dept. DDH
Shawnee Mission, KS 66202

Hornady
Box 1848, Dept. DDH
Grand Island, NE 68802

Knight Rifles
234 Airport Road, Dept. DDH
Centerville, IA 52544

Markesbery Muzzle Loaders Inc.
7785 Foundation Drive, Suite 6
Florence, KY 41042

Muzzleloading Technologies
25 E. Hwy. 40, Suite 330-12
Roosevelt, UT 84066

Prairie River Arms
1220 N. 6th St., Dept. DDH
Princeton, IL 61356

Remington Arms Co. Inc.
870 Remington Drive, Dept. DDH
Madison, NC 27025-0700

Thompson/Center Arms
Box 5002, Farmington Road
Rochester, NH 03867

Traditions
1375 Boston Post Road, Dept. DDH
Old Saybrook, CT 06475-0776

White Shooting Systems
25 E. Hwy. 40 (330-12), Dept. DDH
Roosevelt, UT 84066

Testing Pyrodex Pellets

While examining Pyrodex Pellets, one word comes to mind: consistency. Each pellet weighs about 37 grains and consists of 50 grains of powder.

A random sample of five Pyrodex Pellets weighed 36.8, 36.7, 36.7, 36.9 and 36.9 grains, with an average of 36.8 grains. The same test performed on five two-pellet sets yielded 73.2, 73.6, 73.4, 73.8 and 73.3 grains, for an average of 73.46 grains.

That's close enough to 71.5 grains weight, considering muzzleloader propellant efficiency, or lack thereof, to call it a 100-volume charge. And this size charge with proper bullets is considered a whitetail load for most muzzleloaders, while some frontloaders are allowed even more powder.

Weighing five three-pellet sets, these figures were produced: 110.2, 110.0, 110.6, 110.8 and 110.6 grains, averaging 110.44. That's about 140 grains of volume, which would be a magnum charge. In most deer hunting situations, two pellets are plenty.

Although loose Pyrodex provides excellent ignition, the Pyrodex Pellet, to ensure super ignition, has a base impregnated with black powder. In tests, ignition was 100 percent. Incidentally, laboratory tests of the pellet without the blackpowder base still revealed excellent ignition.

To test ignition, a shooter properly loaded two pellets with the blackpowder bases down. The three shots averaged 1,426 feet per second, with a high of 1,432 fps and low of 1,422 fps. Another test resulted in an average of 1,433 fps, with a 1,454 fps high and 1,411 fps low.

A third test had the shooter load the pellets incorrectly, with the blackpowder bases up. The three shots averaged 1,411 fps, with a high of 1,449 fps and a low of 1,375 fps.

As the numbers show, the Pyrodex Pellet, when loaded properly, provides consistent and impressive results.

— The Complete Blackpowder Handbook, Krause Publications

.50 Cal. Ballistics - Lead Conicals with Black Powder or Pyrodex

Bullet	Black Powder or Pyrodex®	Range in Yards	Impact from line of Sight	Velocity f.p.s	Energy ft./lbs.
350 Grain Maxi-Hunter® or 370 Grain Maxi-Ball®	100 Grains	50	+1.9	1383	1572
	100 Grains	100	0.0	1176	1137
	100 Grains	150	-8.1	1041	891
	100 Grains	200	-21.8	951	743
350 Grain Maxi-Hunter® or 370 Grain Maxi-Ball®	150 Grains	50	+1.5	1574	2036
	150 Grains	100	0.0	1326	1445
	150 Grains	150	-4.6	1142	1072
	150 Grains	200	-15.2	1016	848

.50 Cal. Ballistics - Mag Express Sabots with Black Powder or Pyrodex

Bullet	Black Powder or Pyrodex	Range in Yards	Impact from line of Sight	Velocity f.p.s	Energy ft./lbs.
240 Grain XTP™	100 Grains	50	+1.1	1696	1532
	100 Grains	100	0.0	1539	1261
	100 Grains	150	-4.8	1399	1043
	100 Grains	200	-14.1	1276	867
240 Grain XTP™	150 Grains	50	+.7	2006	2143
	150 Grains	100	0.0	1830	1783
	150 Grains	150	-3.2	1660	1468
	150 Grains	200	-9.6	1507	1210
275 Grain XTP™	100 Grains	50	+1.4	1571	1506
	100 Grains	100	0.0	1420	1232
	100 Grains	150	-5.7	1289	1014
	100 Grains	200	-16.6	1177	846
275 Grain XTP™	150 Grains	50	+.8	1887	2175
	150 Grains	100	0.0	1705	1775
	150 Grains	150	-3.8	1540	1447
	150 Grains	200	-11.4	1393	1185
300 Grain XTP™	100 Grains	50	+1.4	1573	1649
	100 Grains	100	0.0	1452	1404
	100 Grains	150	-5.6	1343	1200
	100 Grains	200	-15.9	1244	1030
300 Grain XTP™	150 Grains	50	+.8	1862	2310
	150 Grains	100	0.0	1718	1965
	150 Grains	150	-3.8	1583	1669
	150 Grains	200	-11.1	1461	1421

THE INFORMATION PROVIDED HERE is based on testing done by Thompson/Center Arms with 26-inch barrels and components specified in the chart. Caution: 150-grain magnum loads of FFG black powder or the Pyrodex equivalent should be used only in guns approved by the manufacturer for use with magnum charges.

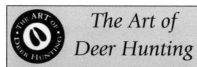

The Art of Deer Hunting

BY TOM CARPENTER

Invite a Deer to Lunch

For most of us, the amount of time we can spend in the deer woods is limited and precious. Despite this, many hunters leave the woods at noon, only to eat lunch while sitting in their vehicle or, worse yet, at the local diner. This is a mistake, because lunch-hour hunts sometimes yield big rewards. My hunting group, for example, has killed many bucks at midday during the past two decades.

Why are such hunts so effective? It's a combination of factors. Aside from the fact you're in the woods, midday hunts are productive because, contrary to popular belief, deer move at noon. This is especially true during gun season, when deer use lulls in hunting pressure to return to their core range.

Knowing this, take the time to pack a lunch and stay in your stand through lunch hour.

These midday hunts don't need to be solo endeavors to be successful. This past opening day, for example, my father, brother, friend and I were having opening-day lunch together when a buck emerged from the thick cover 30 yards away. I don't know who was more surprised — the buck or us — but we capitalized on the situation.

Nobody invited that buck to lunch, but it sure was welcome!

Cleaning Your Muzzleloader

After you've fired your muzzleloader, the real work begins — cleaning. That's because Pyrodex and blackpowder leave a much thicker, more corrosive residue than smokeless powder. As a result, cleaning is not only more difficult, it's vital for preventing rust.

The simplest and most common way to clean a muzzleloader is to fill a bathtub or large bucket with hot, soapy water. Stand the barrel in the water nipple-end-down and run a patch back and forth down the bore. The scrubbing action will suck water up the bore through the nipple, rinsing out residue.

When the water coming out of the bore is clean, remove the barrel from the soap solution and rinse it with clean hot water. This removes any loose residue and heats the steel, speeding drying.

Next, run dry patches down the bore until they come out clean. Then, dry all parts and apply a coat of oil-displacing lubricant.

During the following days, inspect the barrel and bore for any signs of rusting.

Preparing for Long Shots

Long-range accuracy with scoped muzzleloaders entails two things — knowledge and ability. You must know the bullet drop or trajectory, distance to the target and the effect of any wind that might be present. You must also refine some of the former, and obtain the shooting skills to ensure that your shot will strike the vitals of a deer. Here are some key tools that hunters should use for long shots.

1. Drop chart — Memorize or write a drop chart on the side of your rifle.

2. Laser range-finder — These items are crucial for determining distances.

3. Shooting rest — Underwood shooting sticks, Harris bipods, Snipe Pods or any handy rest can be helpful.

4. Back-up — If possible, have your buddy ready to help put down a wounded animal.

5. Practice — Take shots at a variety of distances and learn what effect wind has on your bullet.

6. Be prepared to pass on shots — Only take ideal shots within your ability. Wishing to undo a shot is no way to end a hunt.

Today's Hot New Muzzleloaders

■ **Knight** Rifle's DISC Extreme offers superior power, accuracy and dependability. The rifle features Knight's innovative Full Plastic Jacket ignition system, which provides a virtually weatherproof seal for the 209 shotgun primer. The rifle also has a Green Mountain action and barrel, allowing it to handle up to 150 grains of powder. The DISC Extreme weighs 7.5 pounds and is available in .45- and .50-caliber models, with several stock options.

■ **Winchester's** X-150 bolt-action muzzleloader offers reliable long-range performance. The rifle features fiber-optic sights, 1-in-28-inch-twist rifling, stainless steel bolt assembly, ergonomic composite stock, Winchester's 209 breech plug ignition system and a one-piece, 26-inch fluted barrel. Winchester offers the X-150 in .45 and .50 caliber.

■ **Thompson/Center Arms** introduces the Omega 50, a .50-caliber muzzleloader with a pivoting breech. The unique action uses the forward motion of the trigger guard to pivot the breech block downward, allowing easy access to the 209 primer pocket. When the primer is in place, the trigger guard is pulled back, sealing the breech and protecting the 209 primer from weather and moisture. The closed-breech ignition system eliminates blow back and allows for breech plug removal. The Omega 50 sports fiber-optic sights and a 28-inch blued or stainless steel barrel. The gun is available with a composite, gray laminated or Realtree Hardwoods stock.

■ **Traditions** Lightning LD Muzzleloader provides reliable ignition and long-distance accuracy. The bolt-action rifle features a 26-inch fluted barrel, Thunder Dome removable stainless steel breech plug and adjustable Tru-Glo fiber-optic sights. The Lightning's 209 shotgun primer ignition system ensures reliable shooting, and its magnum receiver handles up to 150 grains of powder or Pyrodex pellets, providing downrange power. Traditions offers the rifle with a blued or stainless barrel, and with a black, Mossy Oak Break-Up or High Definition Advantage Timber stock.

SAMANTHA HELING, 14, of Shawano, Wis., was making a drive on Day 2 of Wisconsin's 2001 firearms season when she saw a pair of deer legs protruding from a hollow log. Her grim discovery shows the tenacity — and unpredictability — of whitetails.

5

The Weird World of the Whitetail

Even in a Scientific Age, Deer Surprise and Baffle Us

As most experienced hunters know, in nature, anything goes. Despite extensive research on their behavior, white-tailed deer always seem to be doing things that leave people looking for explanations.

Take, for example, what a first-time Wisconsin hunter discovered on Day 2 of the state's 2001 firearms season. Her bizarre discovery, shown on the opposite page, shows just how far some whitetails might go to evade danger — or perhaps satisfy curiosity.

Fourteen-year-old Samantha Heling, of Shawano, Wis., and her hunting party were making a drive when she noticed something strange protruding from the uprooted stump of a hollow tree. A closer examination of the tree revealed the unthinkable: a deer's hind legs and tail were sticking out of the trunk! Heling quickly gathered her hunting party and led them to her find.

Signs indicated the deer, struggled to get out of — or farther into — the tree. The soft mud at the trunk's base was scored with deep hoof marks, suggesting the deer had been kicking frantically while inside the tree, and the deer's body was outstretched within the trunk, as if it had been trying to crawl deeper within the log. Eerily, Heling and her party could see the deer's still-open eye shining through a crack in the tree while they examined the unusual scene.

The deer — a buck fawn — appeared to have been dead about a day. This is especially interesting, considering the firearms deer season had been open only one day and Heling's party and their neighbors hadn't shot at any antlerless deer.

Because of how tightly the deer was sandwiched within the tree, Heling and her party were unable to remove it from the stump and therefore couldn't determine its cause of death. Although they theorized the buck might have been shot by a hunter and then crawled within the stump for protection, the baffled hunters saw no bullet wounds on the deer.

Although no one will ever know what transpired during the fawn's final moments, the incident is a potent reminder of whitetails' off-the-wall behavior.

Editor's note: *If you have encountered bizarre situations in the deer woods and would like to see them in print, we want to hear from you! If we publish your item, we will send you a free copy of the* 2003 Deer Hunters' Almanac. *Send your unusual stories and photos to:* Deer & Deer Hunting, *attn: Ryan Gilligan, 700 E. State St., Iola, WI 54990-0001.*

Browse Lines

News and Notes from Whitetail Country

Bridge-Running Buck Commits Suicide

In Fall 2001, my brother and I were invited to go pheasant hunting with our friend Tim near the Black River in west-central Wisconsin.

As we drove to the hunting area, a small buck jumped in front of Tim's truck and began running in front of us down the road, eventually venturing out onto a bridge that crossed the Black River. We stopped at the start of the bridge and watched the deer. Our headlights seemed to make the deer nervous, no vehicles were coming from the opposite direction. While we watched, the deer continued making his way across the bridge. He made it about half way down the bridge, then stopped and looked back at us. He then looked over the concrete barrier on the right side of the bridge and jumped. It was still dark when this happened and we didn't know if he jumped into the river or if there was land below.

Dismissing the odd encounter, we continued driving to our pheasant hunting area. On our way home, however, we stopped at the bridge to see where the deer might have gone earlier that morning. The view afforded us by the daylight revealed the buck's bizarre fate.

Although there was land below where the buck had jumped, it was

WISCONSIN'S MIKE JAMES couldn't believe it when he saw this yearling buck jump off a bridge and fall 25 feet to its death. Although the fall broke the buck's neck, it caused little other damage to its body.

25 feet below the bridge! As we peered off the edge of the bridge, we spotted the buck lying dead on the ground below.

My brother and I snapped a quick photo, called the sheriff's office and received a special permit to keep the deer. The 5-pointer had only slight bruising on his left front shoulder and a broken neck.

— Mike James

Minnesota Buck Suffers Gruesome Injury

Ron Morris didn't notice anything unusual about the 8-point buck he had centered in his riflescope. After he pulled the trigger, however, things changed. When Morris approached the fallen buck, he immediately noticed it had a large gouge-type wound at the base of its neck.

Morris initially thought the wound had been caused by an arrow or bullet, but after considering the wound's size — about 7 inches wide, 5 inches long and about 2 inches deep — he began to think a predator might have inflicted the wound.

This theory is especially convincing because Morris killed the buck in north-central Minnesota, an area home to wolves, bears, bobcats and a few cougars. These predators ususally attack large prey like white-

THIS MINNESOTA buck likely survived an encounter with a bear, wolf or cougar, as evidenced by the large wound on its neck, above.

tails by biting the animal's neck and throat, killing them through trauma or suffocation.

— RYAN GILLIGAN

First-Time Fishermen Rescue Trapped Fawn

When Gary Klavon of Port Byron, Ill., headed to the Mississippi River one morning in Summer 2001, he knew he was in for a memorable day. After all, he was accompanied by his two young grandsons, who had never been fishing. Although, Klavon had

GARY KLAVON pulled this fawn from the streamside mud while fishing with his young grandsons.

hoped the boys would get their first taste of fishing, they were in for a much different experience.

Soon after arriving at his fishing spot, Klavon and his grandsons spotted movement along the river bank. A closer look revealed a small fawn trapped in a pool of thick mud.

As his curious grandsons watched, Klavon freed the fawn and set it on dry ground above the river bank. After a few-minute rest, the fawn recovered from its ordeal and bounded into the nearby woods, where its mother had been watching.

Although they didn't catch any fish, it was an experience Klavon and his grandsons would never forget.

— RYAN GILLIGAN

New York Hunter Completes Quest For Piebald Buck

To some hunters, tall times and long, thick beams alone make a white-tailed buck a trophy. However, the season Charles Baechtle of Lake Katrine, N.Y., experienced in Fall 2000 proved a buck doesn't need a big rack to deserve a trip to the taxidermist.

While sitting in his tree stand on the second day of New York's 2000 archery season, Baechtle glimpsed a flash of white that would shape his season. As his eyes focused on the distant white-and-brown figure, Baechtle realized he was looking at a piebald buck — the first one he had seen in 49 years of avid deer hunting! Although the buck never came within range that day, Baechtle's season was forever changed, as he vowed to hunt the unusual whitetail exclusively.

After spending many days in his stand and passing up two large bucks, Baechtle hadn't seen the piebald. Then on Oct. 20, 2000, he spotted the piebald's tell-tale white flank moving past his stand at 50 yards. Unfortunately, the buck's path was leading him toward a large bedding area and out of range of Baechtle's stand.

Disappointed, Baechtle settled back in his seat. Suddenly, he spotted the buck again. The buck had turned around and was quickly closing the distance to Baechtle's tree stand. As the 5-point piebald stepped in an opening 15 yards away, Baechtle drew his bow and

CHARLES BAECHTLE killed this New York piebald on Oct. 20, 2000, after spotting the buck on opening weekend of the state's archery season.

released, sending his arrow through the buck's chest. The buck ran about 75 yards, and then crashed into a cedar stand.

After recovering the buck, Baechtle had a long-awaited chance to examine the buck that had consumed his hunting season. The buck's sides and legs were mostly white, while the buck's head retained more normal coloration. To better preserve his trophy and honor the rare buck, Baechtle had his taxidermist make a full-body mount of the piebald.

According to *Deer & Deer Hunting* research editor John Ozoga's book *Whitetail Intrigue,* although rare, piebald deer are much more common than albinos. In addition to bizarre coloration, piebalds generally have short legs, arched noses and goat-like ears.

— RYAN GILLIGAN

Wisconsin Whitetail Gets 'Wired'

Soon after rattling on opening morning of Wisconsin's 2001 gun season, I spotted four does walking through a nearby clearing. Because the season was only minutes old, I refrained from shooting. Plus, I suspected a mature buck was using the area.

My patience was rewarded when I spotted a decent buck marching toward the does. As I settled my sights behind its shoulder, I noticed something was entwined in the buck's antlers. Dismissing it as dried grass, I squeezed the trigger, killing the buck instantly.

However, when I approached the fallen deer, I realized it was anything but grass. Several yards of barbwire were wound in figure-eights around the buck's beams. Interestingly, the wire was so tight my hunting partners and I used it as a handle to drag the buck from the woods.

— PAT TRATZ

WHEN PAT TRATZ shot this buck, he believed grass was entangled in its antlers. A closer examination revealed the buck had wound several yards of barbwire in its rack.

Confused Buck 'Breeds' Archery Target

A BACKYARD ARCHERY TARGET was a more-than-convincing decoy for this rut-crazed yearling.

Despite the whitetail's abundance, many avid deer hunters and wildlife photographers never witness a deer breeding sequence. Those who do usually consider themselves fortunate to have seen a brief event that usually occurs at night. However, Michael Vander Velden of Suamico, Wis., witnessed a perhaps rarer event when a spike buck wandered into his neighbor's yard on a rainy morning in November 2000.

After Vander Velden noticed the young buck, it approached a 3-D whitetail target staked behind his neighbor's house. The spike then attempted to mount the foam deer, struggling to postion his front legs atop the slippery target. The buck persisted for about five minutes, giving Vander Velden time to snap several photos of the unusual encounter.

— RYAN GILLIGAN

Hunter Reunites with Buck, Then its Antler

In Fall 2001, Massachusetts bow-hunter Gerry Bennett learned the best things *do* come to those who wait

Bennett and his brother, Peter, had drawn Iowa archery tags for the 2001 hunt. The brothers hooked up with Dick Paul, a friend and southwestern Iowa guide whom they'd met two years earlier.

On Day 1, Paul's son, Travis, escorted Bennett to a ladder stand. Bennett saw action early, as a 120-class buck chased a doe past his stand, and several more does and bucks passed within 40 yards.

As two small bucks strode through, Bennett noticed a sapling violently rocking. A quick inspection through binoculars revealed a buck with a massive left beam and a stunted right beam was rubbing the tree. Fifteen minutes later, the buck and another smaller buck approached, eventually walking right under Bennett's stand.

Although the larger buck had what appeared to be a 9-point, Boone and Crockett-class left beam, its small right beam convinced Bennett to let the buck walk.

However, by the time the buck had left his sight, Bennett was already second-guessing his decision. With the shot opportunity gone, the

GERRY BENNETT passed up this incredible buck on Day 1 of his 2001 Iowa bow-hunt, because of its seemingly stunted right beam. A few days later, Bennett saw the buck again and shot it. As he walked back to camp for tracking help, Bennett found a broken antler. After Bennett and his party retrieved the unusual buck, they discovered the broken antler matched a missing part of the buck's right beam.

memory would have to be reward enough.

Bennett passed on several smaller bucks in subsequent days and eventually decided to again hunt the area where he'd seen the lop-sided buck.

A few small bucks showed the morning Bennett moved back to the lop-sided buck's territory. During a lull, Bennett pulled out a Bible and began to read. Almost immediately, he heard something coming through the leaves. Bennett soon spotted a large buck working behind his stand. He quickly set down the Bible, picked up his bow and rose for the shot. As the buck stepped into his shooting lane, Bennett confirmed the buck's size and released, hitting it perfectly. Everything had happened so quickly Bennett didn't have time to get excited. Although he thought he had hit the buck well, Bennett wanted to give the buck time to lay down, so he sat and resumed reading.

After about 20 minutes, Bennett descended from his tree stand and looked for blood. He didn't find any, so he went back to Paul's place for help.

While walking back, Bennett encountered an area where the leaves had been scuffled. In the middle of the area was a large, 4-point antler that appeared to have broken off just above the brow tine. Bennett pocketed the find and resumed his walk.

After breakfast, Bennett and his companions returned to Bennett's stand, and Travis located the buck almost immediately. Upon his discovery, Travis was a bit disappointed, as he thought it was only a 2½-year-old buck. However, he soon realized the right beam was much smaller than the left. Bennett had unknowingly shot the same buck he'd seen earlier!

Amazingly, the hunters had transported the deer all of the way back to Paul's truck before they thought to see if the antler Bennett had found fit the rack. As Bennett lined up the broken antler with his buck's right beam, he was shocked. Suddenly, the right antler was no longer a disproportionate 3-point beam, but a 7-point, double-beamed trophy.

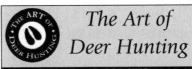

The Art of Deer Hunting

BY TOM CARPENTER

Twist-Ties:
Essential Field-Dressing Tools

There's no disputing it: Efficient field dressing cools a deer carcass quickly and is the secret to good-tasting venison. However, few hunters take care of one easy but imperative detail in this fairly standard process: They don't close the deer's anus, allowing bacteria-rich contaminants to reach the meat.

The solution? Carry an extra-long twist-tie — like the kind you use to close garbage bags — in your pocket while hunting. When you kill a deer, cut around the anus, freeing it from the pelvic walls. After you detach it, close it off with the twist-tie, then pull it back through the pelvic opening when removing the rest of the entrails.

Closing off the anus with a twist-tie adds only about 17 seconds to field dressing and is easier than using a string. It's part of the deer hunting art.

The left antler sported 9 points, making the deer a 16-pointer. Although the rack cannot be officially scored because of the broken antler, the buck unofficially grossed 187⁴/₈ nontypical, and netted 175²/₈.

Bennett said he was glad he'd passed on the buck the first time. If he hadn't, he'd have never found the amazing broken beam.

— JOE SHEAD

Virginian's First Buck Sports Unusual Tumor

Menieka Kline-Garber made an unusual discovery when she approached the buck she killed in Fall 2001. Aside from it being her first buck and sporting an impressive 11-point rack, the buck was also memorable because it had a melon-sized tumor growing from its belly. Cuts and scratches on the tumor suggested the tumor hung so low that it caught on fences the deer crossed. Despite this, Kline-Garber said the deer seemed unaffected by the growth before she shot it.

— Ryan Gilligan

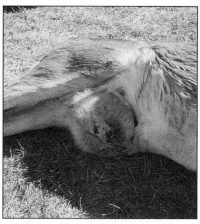

AN 11-POINT RACK wasn't the only amazing feature of this Virginia buck. A melon-sized tumor hung from the deer's belly.

Hunter Follows Family of Albino Whitetails

Albino deer are extremely rare. As such, any hunter who has seen one can count himself part of a fortunate few. However, Terry Weier of Mascoutah, Ill., has developed an especially close link with albinos.

In Spring 1998, while scouting a southern Illinois farm, Weier spotted an amazing sight: three albino fawns with their normally colored mother.

That chance encounter began an ongoing relationship with an extraordinary whitetail.

In the following months, Weier kept close tabs on the unusual family and soon realized each fawn was a buck.

Each fawn survived its first year. However, at age 1½, one of the bucks was killed by a poacher. The following year, another one of albinos was killed, this time by a car. Despite the dwindling litter, Weier maintained his watch over the remaining albino.

In Fall 2001, Weier again spotted the easily recognizable buck, which then sported an impressive rack. Amazingly, the buck was sparring with normal bucks and tending does.

In December 2001, Weier snapped a photo of the big albino as it walked by his tree stand (albino deer are protected in Illinois). As far as Weier knows, the unique buck is still roaming his hunting area.

— Ryan Gilligan

TERRY WEIER first photographed this albino buck when it was a fawn in 1998. The buck was one of three albino buck fawns born to a normal doe.

Buck Invades College Student's Apartment

Whether they live in big cities or in the big woods, Wisconsinites are accustomed to sharing their backyards with deer. However, on Aug. 26, 2001, Adam Bauer, a student from the University of Wisconsin at Stevens Point, received a much closer encounter than he'd experienced.

That afternoon, while watching television in his apartment, Bauer heard glass shatter outside. As he ran outside to investigate the sound, he saw students standing outside, pointing at his shattered bedroom window.

Still unsure of what had happened, Bauer charged back into his apartment and down the hallway. As he reached the bedroom, an 8-point buck ran past him, crashed into the bathroom and kicked the door shut behind it. As the agitated buck thrashed around the bathroom, Bauer called the police.

Although police were soon on the scene, the officers lacked the equipment and training to tranquilize the buck. After two hours of unsuccessful attempts to contact an animal-control specialist, Bauer called UWSP wildlife-management professor James Hardin for advice.

In an amazing coincidence, Hardin said that Safe-Capture International Inc., a group specializing in wildlife immobilization, was in town teaching a weekend workshop.

With the buck still trapped, the officers rushed to campus, pulled Safe Capture International instructor Keith Amass out of the class and brought him to Bauer's apartment. Using mirrors to monitor the buck through the partially opened door, Amass and the officers tranquilized the buck and

Ohio Doe Gives Birth in October

The whitetail's birthing cycle is finely honed to ensure species survival in an environment where predation and harsh winters are common. However, even this evolutionally perfected system sometimes hiccups. Take, for example, what a Seneca County, Ohio, farmer found in October 2001.

Frank Bugner was harvesting his cornfield at night when the combine's lights illuminated a doe laying ahead of him. Although he initially thought he had hit the deer with his machinery, he realized otherwise when the doe stood and walked out of sight. When it did, Bugner saw a fawn protruding from the doe, which had presumably been giving birth!

Amazingly, the doe must have been bred in April!

pulled it outside.

Although the buck had sustained only minor cuts from its ordeal, the officers were forced to kill it, because the immobilization chemicals would have remained in the buck's system until after the bow-hunting opener, making the buck a risk to hunters.

Ironically, the buck's demise might have been unintentionally caused by animal-rightists. According to witnesses, the buck sprinted toward the apartment after students — in an apparent attempt to have fun — chased it from a nature preserve. Witnesses said several of those students were notorious animal-rights activists.

— RYAN GILLIGAN

Saskatchewan Whitetail Gets Unwelcome Eyeful

When Mike Stachewicz of Eagle River, Wis., spotted a glint of antler moving through the timber near his stand, he knew he might be looking at the buck of a lifetime. Although he was right, the circumstances were anything but predictable.

It was Nov. 20, 2001, and Stachewicz and his wife, Sharon, were hunting near Porcupine Plain, Saskatchewan. Stachewicz had watched several deer filter through the funnel near his stand when he spotted the big buck.

As it stepped into a shooting lane, Stachewicz centered the deer in his scope and squeezed the trigger. At the shot, the buck flinched and fled into the nearby brush.

THIS SASKATCHEWAN buck sported a third beam, which sprouted from beneath its right eye. The growing beam had apparently damaged the buck's eye and the buck's cape indicated the beam had grown during previous years.

Minutes later, Stachewicz picked up the buck's blood trail, and soon found the 8-pointer laying on its right side.

Although he was happy about filling his tag, Stachewicz couldn't help but feel slightly disappointed, because the buck was smaller than he had anticipated. However, he changed his tune when he lifted the buck's head for a closer look. Stachewicz immediately noticed the buck had a short antler growing from beneath its right eye. The buck's eye was scarred over and it seemed as though the buck couldn't see through it.

When Stachewicz caped out the buck, he made another fascinating discovery: the unusual antler's pedicel sprouted from the bone mass below the buck's eye. What's more, judging from the cape's condition and the bone structure, it seemed like the buck had grown and shed the third antler the previous year.

Although buck's like Stachewicz's are rare, they've been found throughout the whitetail's range. For example, the September 2001 issue of *Deer & Deer Hunting* featured a story about a Texas whitetail with four separate beams — one of which grew from its jawbone.

— RYAN GILLIGAN

Illinois Gun-Hunter Fools Record-Class Piebald

After awaking in the pre-dawn darkness Nov. 18, 2000, it seemed the elements were conspiring against Dan Kittle of Winnebago, Ill. Kittle was looking forward to his morning gun-hunt, but the trees rocked in a strong west wind and temperatures hovered at about freezing. Although he was anxious to spend a day in the woods, he knew doing so while perched 18 feet up a tree would be physically punishing.

Despite the conditions, Kittle and friends Brent Timmer and Rick Sneath headed to the the farm-country woods near Kittle's home, and were soon settled in their stands.

DAN KITTLE killed this huge piebald buck while gun-hunting a Winnebago, County, Ill., farm on Nov. 18, 2000. When Kittle initially spotted the buck, he thought its white coloration was snow that had collected on the buck's coat the previous night.

Kittle's stand was positioned along the edge of a 5-acre woodlot and a harvested beanfield. As he struggled to stay warm while waiting for daybreak, Kittle heard deer moving through the overgrown woods behind him. However, as daylight seeped across the field, Kittle saw no deer. Without deer sightings to keep his mind off the cold, he was in for a grueling day.

With the cold quickly sapping his desire to hunt, Kittle began anxiously awaiting the sound of a truck horn. He had arranged that when Sneath left his stand, he would honk his truck horn, then begin walking toward Kittle's location. The pair hoped Sneath would push any bedded deer out of the tangled woodlot and past Kittle's stand.

Sneath's signal finally came at 8:30 a.m. With renewed alertness, Kittle began scanning the woods for movement and soon spotted three does bounding through the woods. However, they never passed within range of his 12-gauge.

Moments later, Sneath arrived at Kittle's stand, and the two hunters

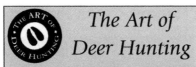

The Art of Deer Hunting

BY TOM CARPENTER

The Art of Deer Driving Part 2: Handling 'Hangers'

Although today's whitetails are adept at evading drivers by squirting out at unexpected places, they sometimes choose a much different escape tactic. They occasionally stay put or sneak behind the drivers.

I call these deer "hangers" because that's what they do — hang around where they know they are safe, instead of scampering across a field, clear-cut or other opening.

To outsmart these wary deer while drive-hunting, have at least one hunter remain behind the drivers and away from the posters, in the opposite direction the hunt is moving. Deer know which way the action is heading, and they have every reason to go the opposite direction.

When using this tactic, keep safety in mind. Never shoot toward the drivers and standers.

began planning their next move. They decided Kittle would stay in his stand while Sneath circled the woodlot and worked toward the stand from a different direction.

Knowing his scent had been blowing into that area all morning, Kittle held little hope that the plan would pay off. Plus, he wasn't thrilled about spending another half-hour in the biting wind. However, he hoped persistence would pay off.

Soon after Sneath circled behind the downwind side of the woodlot, Kittle snapped to attention.

"Coming at you!" echoed Sneath from the far end of the woods.

Kittle spotted a large doe crashing through the brush, heading toward the beanfield. As Kittle watched the doe bound into the open, another deer caught his eye. A wide-racked, large-bodied buck was following the doe. However, size wasn't the buck's most amazing attribute. Much of its head and neck seemed to be covered with snow, and the bizarre coloration extended down the buck's back.

To Kittle's dismay, the buck changed direction, taking a trail that would lead it downwind of the stand and eventually out of shotgun range. Meanwhile, the mature doe stepped into the harvested beanfield and stood broadside at 70 yards.

Although he was torn, Kittle decided to pass up the doe, hoping the buck would step within range, but when he turned to face the approaching buck, it walked downwind and out of sight. Kittle was about to give up on the buck when the doe snorted loudly. Seemingly interested by the sound, the buck turned and began trotting toward the doe.

Kittle prepared for the shot of a lifetime. As the big buck stepped into the beanfield near the doe, Kittle squeezed the trigger, sending a slug into the buck's vitals. Amazingly, the hard-hit buck turned to the right and started walking away. Kittle fired again, squarely hitting the buck.

However, the buck continued walking and disappeared into the brush before Kittle could take another shot.

As Sneath reached the edge of the woods, Kittle descended from his stand. Anxious to find the buck, the two hunters walked to where Kittle had last seen the buck and soon found the fallen deer mere feet from where it stepped out of sight. To their amazement, the massive 12-pointer had mottled white-and-brown hair on its face and shoulders. Although Kittle initially though the white might have been snow built up on the buck's coat, a closer look revealed the unbelievable: Kittle had shot a piebald buck!

After hauling the wide-racked buck out of the woods, Kittle, Sneath and Timmer showed the buck to the landowner. Although the landowner observed deer on the property year-round, he had never seen the big piebald.

According to an employee of the Illinois Department of Natural Resources, Kittle's buck was $3\frac{1}{2}$ years old and is likely the biggest piebald buck ever killed in Illinois.

— Ryan Gilligan

Gun-Hunter Bags Mysterious 8-Point Doe

An evening hunt on his parents' 5-acre Wisconsin property turned out to be one Matt Gruennert of Mukwonago, Wis., will never forget. Gruennert was sitting in his stand near a large marsh on the third day of Wisconsin's 2001 firearms season when six deer appeared and started walking toward him. The deer stopped for about five minutes to loaf among some trees about 40 yards away. At first, Gruennert was unable to determine if any of the deer were bucks, but after looking through his binoculars, he spotted a rack. Just then, two of the deer, including the buck, began moving closer to Gruennert, cutting the distance in half. The pair now stood only 20 yards away, but the deer that had grabbed Gruennert's attention was standing behind a tree.

Moments later, the deer stepped in front of the tree, and Gruennert raised his binoculars to confirm the

MATT GRUENERT shot this velvet-antlered during Wisconsin's 2001 firearms season. Much to his surprise, the "buck" had female anatomy.

antlers. The movement startled the deer, and five of them bounded for cover. However, the antlered deer froze. Gruennert shouldered his 12-gauge and fired. After the shot, all six deer bolted for the marsh.

Deer Found Trapped in a Car

Deer that live in and around large cities often surprise their human neighbors. After all, they crash through office windows, trot down sidewalks, destroy backyard gardens and jump into traffic. However, in January 2001, one Madison, Wis., deer recieved an unusual amount of attention because of its involvement with a vehicle — that is, *in* a vehicle.

Early one morning, Madison police received a call that a yearling buck was trapped inside a parked car.

When police arrived on the scene, they pulled the frantic buck from the 1991 Hyundai. However, they had to kill the deer because one of its front legs was broken.

After getting the situation under control, the police officers surmised the buck had been hit by the car. The drivers, who abandoned the vehicle, presumably wanted the venison, so they stowed the deer in the back seat and continued driving. However, the deer then regained consciousness and began thrashing around the car, sending the drivers fleeing the scene.

Gruennert unloaded his shotgun and descended from his stand. It was getting dark and Gruennert wanted to maximize the remaining daylight.

Five minutes of searching the area where the deer had stood revealed no blood. Gruennert made a bigger sweep of the area and found a blood trail. He left his hat where the trail started, then took his gear back to his parents' house, where he also got some flashlights. At the house, Gruennert met his neighbor, Wayne Morro, who had heard the shot and offered to assist Gruennert.

The two men returned to the blood trail. After 20 yards of trailing, the blood trail petered out. Equipped with flashlights, the hunters continued to search the area. After an hour or so, Morro found the dead deer.

The hunters immediately noticed the deer's 8-point rack was covered in velvet, and thought it unusual that late in the season. However, that wasn't the only surprise in store for them. After tagging the deer, Gruennert rolled it over to gut it and noticed that the deer was "missing parts." In fact, the deer had doe anatomy instead of buck anatomy.

Morro decided this was extremely rare and decided he and Gruennert should take the deer to a Department of Natural Resources field station before gutting it. After dragging the 8-point deer out of the marsh, Gruennert called the DNR, but only got an answering machine. Fearing the meat would spoil in the warm weather, Gruennert field dressed the deer, but kept the reproductive organs intact.

The next day, Gruennert took the deer to the DNR where a game warden confirmed the deer as an 8-point doe and gave Gruennert a special tag.

Although Gruennert didn't tag a true buck during the 2001 gun season, it's safe to say he wasn't disappointed.

— JOE SHEAD

Big-City Buck Visits Saskatchewan Hunter's Home

When most hunters think of Saskatchewan, they picture endless Northern forests inhabited by cagey wilderness bucks. Stephen Gerwing of suburban Saskatoon was among that group until returning from a morning of back-country deer hunting with his friends in early October 2000.

Gerwing had seen little deer activity that morning, and was busy making phone calls and planning his hunting party's next trip when he noticed an out-of-place shape on his front lawn. As he turned for a better look, he saw a mature white-tailed buck standing stone-still mere feet from his front door. Too still, it seemed.

STEPHEN GERWING had just returned from an unsuccessful deer hunt when this mature whitetail wandered into his suburban Saskatoon, Saskatchewan lawn. The displaced buck eventually wandered into Gerwing's open garage.

Gerwing was certain his buddies had planned a trick for him while he had been talking on the phone. He thought the deer was a fake. However, those suspicions fell apart when the buck turned its head and started panting, as if it were out of breath.

Gerwing found a camera and snapped several photos of the buck while it stood in his front yard. Then, the buck turned and walked toward Gerwing's neighbor's house. Gerwing thought the buck was gone. However, when he opened his front door and stepped outside, he found the deer standing in his garage! Gerwing quickly snapped another picture, sending the startled buck out of the garage and into a neighbor's yard.

By then, the buck had caught the attention of several neighbors and the local police. Officers considered shooting the out-of-place whitetail, but the gathering crowd decided it would be best to to drive the buck from the subdivision and into a wooded area almost a half-mile from Gerwing's house.

Amazingly, the plan worked. After being pushed five city blocks, the buck fled into a woodlot and out of sight.

After the ordeal, area residents reported they saw the buck being chased into town by a large dog moments before it sought shelter in Gerwing's yard — and garage!

— RYAN GILLIGAN

DEER & DEER HUNTING MAGAZINE CELEBRATES 25TH ANIVERSARY

It's hard to believe, but a quarter-century has passed since two Wisconsin men made their dream of "deer hunting for a living" come true.

In the mid-1970s, Jack Brauer, an insurance salesman, and Al Hofacker, a teacher, decided they loved white-tailed deer hunting so much that they'd quit their jobs and start a club — and later a magazine — devoted to their hobby. The magazine, *Deer & Deer Hunting*, was not only an instant success, it helped build one of today's most successful North American industries.

When the first issue of *D&DH* rolled off the press in 1977, skeptics said it would never last. White-tailed deer hunting was too small of a niche, claimed the naysayers.

How wrong they were. Today, economists estimate that people spend more than $15 billion a year to hunt white-tailed deer.

Today, *D&DH* is headed by publisher Hugh McAloon, an avid whitetail hunter from Oshkosh, Wis., who joined Krause in 1984. Although he worked primarily with the company's sports collecting division for many years, McAloon

MUCH HAS changed about *Deer & Deer Hunting's* appearance since its first issues hit newsstands in 1977. However, it has continued offering whitetail enthusiasts the same quality of hard-core deer information.

helped convince Krause executives to pull the trigger on purchasing the magazine from Brauer, Hofacker and Rob Wegner in 1992.

"We thought it would be a natural extension to our business," McAloon said. "Besides, in the publishing business, it's not often that you get a chance to acquire the No. 1 publication in its field."

Krause didn't hesitate, and the

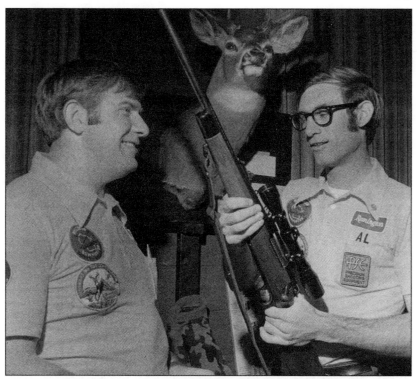

A QUARTER-CENTURY AGO, Wisconsin's Jack Brauer, an insurance salesman, and Al Hofacker, an electrician, decided to quit their jobs and use their passion for deer hunting to forge new careers. Brauer, left, and Hofacker, right, soon started an innovative, research-based hunting club, The Stump Sitters, and later *Deer & Deer Hunting* magazine. From its humble beginnings, *D&DH* developed quickly. Today, the magazine is published nine times annually and is read by about 464,000 hunters.

rest, as they say, is history. Now printed nine times per year, *D&DH* attracts 464,000 readers per issue (includes readers who share copies with family and friends).

As they did in the beginning, readers absorb every issue. According to an independent research study, the average *D&DH* reader spends more than three hours reading each issue. Now that's hard-core!

From its inception, *D&DH*

always attempted to provide deer hunters with a diverse blend of articles about white-tailed deer and hunting them. Here's to hoping the next quarter-century brings equal prosperity for the future of white-tailed deer and deer hunting.

— DANIEL E. SCHMIDT
EDITOR, *DEER & DEER HUNTING*

WE HAVE ALL HEARD hunters comment how hunting was better in the "good ol' days." However, even a casual glance at the latest harvest statistics proves hunters are more successful now than ever. In addition, today's herds offer unprecedented opportunities for record-class bucks like this.

6
National Whitetail Trends

Taking Advantage of Today's Deer Herds

I t's inappropriately romantic to look at a picture of hunters standing beside the sagging buck pole at a turn-of-the-century deer camp and let yourself believe those were deer hunting's glory days.

That's not to say deer hunting wasn't a tremendous experience a century ago — it probably was. However, images from such deer camps often gloss over the potent reality of early deer hunting.

First, successful camps from that period were the exception, not the rule. After all, by 1900, market hunting and habitat loss had brought whitetail numbers — and those of most North American big game — to an all-time low of about 500,000. Plus, the best hunting was isolated in pockets of the species' former strongholds, such as Michigan and Wisconsin.

Even at their best, early hunts were still iffy. Deer densities were low, the country was rugged, equipment was poor and hunters usually logged countless hours afield before seeing, much less killing, a deer.

Fast forward 100 years. Deer populations have grown so high

	All-Time Single-Season Whitetail Harvests		
Rank	State	Year	Total Harvest
1.	Wisconsin	2000	618,274
2.	Michigan	1999	544,895
3.	Michigan	2001	541,701
4.	Texas	1987	504,953
5.	Pennsylvania	2000	504,600
6.	Wisconsin	1999	494,116
7.	Pennsylvania	2001	486,014
8.	Michigan	1995	478,960
9.	Alabama	2001	478,700
10.	Texas	1989	477,491
11.	Texas	1988	474,968
12.	Texas	1991	474,047
13.	Texas	1992	468,893
14.	Wisconsin	1995	467,100
15.	Wisconsin	1996	460,524
16.	Texas	1993	452,509
17.	Michigan	1989	452,490
18.	Texas	1995	450,593
19.	Michigan	1998	450,000
20.	Wisconsin	2001	446,957
21.	Georgia	2001	446,000
22.	Texas	1986	445,119
23.	Texas	1999	438,627
24.	Michigan	1991	434,340
25.	Michigan	1990	432,690
26.	Pennsylvania	1995	430,583
27.	Texas	1990	429,532
28.	Georgia	1998	427,000
29.	Georgia	1999	426,000
30.	Texas	2000	424,000
31.	Alabama	1997	423,400
32.	Texas	1994	421,423

Statistics compiled by:
Deer hunters' 2003 Almanac, Krause Publications.

Single-Season Record Whitetail Harvests by State

State	Year	Harvest
Alabama	2001	478,700
Arizona	1984	7,181
Arkansas	1999	194,687
Connecticut	1995	13,740
Delaware	2001	12,200
Florida	2001	140,000
Georgia	2000	446,000
Illinois	2000	149,063
Indiana	1996	123,086
Iowa	2001	130,959
Kansas	2000	108,000
Kentucky	2000	157,321
Louisiana	2000	276,000
Maine	1959	41,735
Maryland	1998	93,570
Massachusetts	2000	11,096
Michigan	1999	544,895
Minnesota	1992	243,068
Mississippi	1995	334,962
Missouri	2001	257,910
Nebraska	2001	59,518
New Hampshire	1967	14,186
New Jersey	2000	77,444
New York	2000	306,679
North Carolina	1992	217,743
North Dakota	1995	70,764
Ohio	1995	179,543
Oklahoma	2000	101,935
Oregon	2000	1,013
Pennsylvania	2000	504,600
Rhode Island	2000	2,307
South Carolina	2001	308,828
South Dakota	1997	49,943
Tennessee	2001	156,356
Texas	1987	504,953
Vermont	1980	25,932
Virginia	1995	218,476
Washington	1991	18,000
West Virginia	1997	235,305
Wisconsin	2000	618,274
Wyoming	1992	14,749

Editor's note: Several Western states, including Idaho, Colorado and Montana, do not distinguish between white-tailed deer and other deer species in their annual harvest statistics. The whitetail harvests in those states are marginal and, therefore, are not represented in this chart.

Statistics compiled by: *Deer Hunters' 2003 Almanac*, Krause Publications.

whitetails have become a nuisance across much of their range.

This population explosion has ensured that most hunters — even city-dwellers — live near excellent hunting. In addition, burgeoning herds have prompted most whitetail states to prescribe unprecedented antlerless quotas, letting even casual hunters kill multiple deer annually.

Want proof that hunting today is better than ever? Consider this: From 1970 to 1979 — a period many Wisconsin hunters consider the "good ol' days" of deer hunting — Badger State hunters killed 1,168,472 deer. At an average of more than 116,000 deer per year, that figure dwarfs many states' modern deer harvests. However, that's only the beginning. From 1980 to 1984, Wisconsin hunters killed 1,095,000 deer, and from 2000 to 2001, they killed 1,062,000.

In other words, 30 years ago, it took Wisconsinites 10 years to kill 1 million deer. In recent seasons, however, Wisconsin hunters have been breaking the 1 million mark every two years — five times faster than in the 1970s.

Of course, Wisconsin isn't alone. For example, recent harvests in leading whitetail states like Michigan, Georgia, Pennsylvania and Alabama are more than three times higher than those states' 1980 harvests. And some states, such as Kentucky, Kansas and Rhode Island, have made even more dramatic comebacks, achieving harvests more than 10 times larger than those from 1980.

If those figures don't convince

you, check out the state-by-state deer harvest information on the following pages. Aside from illustrating the incredible size of some states' deer harvests, the numbers confirm that virtually every states' harvest has been steadily rising since modern deer seasons were established. What's more, you'll probably find that your state achieved a record harvest within the past five years.

The statistics found on these pages were compiled by our editorial staff through annual surveys of deer managers from each state. No two states have the same reporting systems, therefore, recent harvest figures are subject to minor changes from year to year. For example, a state that reports an overall deer harvest of 350,000 most likely submitted an estimate based on early harvest reports. Final figures would then be reported in next year's *Almanac*.

The totals on this page are five-year averages. Some states compile harvest figures at various times of the year. Some averages are from 1996 to 2000, and some are from 1995 to 1999. Use this chart to see how your home state ranks, then flip through the chapter to learn more interesting facts on deer hunting in other parts of the country.

Editor's note — *This chapter is designed to educate hunters on various aspects of deer hunting in the United States. Regulations are provided in general terms.*

Annual White-tailed Deer Harvests in the U.S.

5-Year Averages: 1997 through 2001

(Last year's rankings in parenthesis)

1. Wisconsin (1)	465,253
2. Michigan (2)	455,029
3. Pennsylvania (4)	428,824
4. Alabama (6)	412,280
5. Texas (5)	392,070
6. Georgia (3)	338,672
7. Mississippi (7)	314,468
8. Louisiana (8)	259,880
9. New York (9)	258,436
10. S. Carolina (11)	243,906
11. Missouri (10)	232,812
12. West Virginia (12)	213,868
13. Virginia (13)	193,752
14. Minnesota (15)	181,724
15. Arkansas (16)	172,987
16. N. Carolina (14)	161,451
17. Illinois (19)	139,723
18. Tennessee (17)	123,050
19. Iowa (20)	120,513
20. Kentucky (21)	113,880
21. Ohio (18)	112,561
22. Indiana (22)	101,380
23. Florida (23)	98,327
24. Kansas (28)	89,648
25. Oklahoma (24)	84,310
26. Maryland (25)	80,766
27. Montana (27)	68,640
28. New Jersey (26)	68,215
29. North Dakota (29)	62,118
30. South Dakota (30)	46,523
31. Nebraska (31)	46,416
32. Washington (38)	35,714
33. Maine (32)	31,104
34. Idaho (33)	25,502
35. Vermont (34)	18,330
36. Connecticut (35)	11,731
37. Delaware (37)	10,802
38. N. Hampshire (36)	10,458
39. Massachusetts (39)	10,025
40. Arizona (40)	4,103
41. Rhode Island (41)	1,966
42. Oregon (42)	857

Editor's note: Several Western states do not distinguish between whitetails and other deer species in their harvest statistics. Those states are not represented in this chart.

Statistics compiled by: *Deer Hunters' 2003 Almanac*, Krause Publications.

ALABAMA

Camellia State

Harvest Ranking: #4

For more information, contact:

Dept. of Wildlife and Freshwater Fisheries
64 N. Union St.
Montgomery, AL 36130
(334) 242-3469   www.dcnr.state.al.us

HISTORY OF ALABAMA'S WHITETAIL HARVEST

Year	Firearms	Bow	Total
1963-64	NA	NA	31,123
1964-65	NA	NA	59,230
1965-66	NA	NA	37,819
1966-67	NA	NA	47,842
1967-68	NA	NA	68,406
1968-69	NA	NA	63,674
1969-70	NA	NA	74,239
1970-71	NA	NA	63,502
1971-72	NA	NA	80,184
1972-73	NA	NA	82,555
1973-74	NA	NA	121,953
1974-75	NA	NA	120,727
1975-76	NA	NA	125,625
1976-77	NA	NA	144,155
1977-78	NA	NA	147,113
1978-79	NA	NA	152,733
1979-80	NA	NA	140,685
1980-81	NA	NA	130,532
1981-82	NA	NA	202,449
1982-83	NA	NA	141,281
1983-84	NA	NA	192,231
1984-85	NA	NA	237,378
1985-86	NA	NA	280,436
1986-87	288,487	17,653	306,140
1987-88	309,517	15,683	325,200
1988-89	257,734	18,854	276,588
1990-91	263,100	31,300	294,400
1991-92	269,500	25,500	295,000
1992-93	261,500	31,600	293,100
1993-94	305,300	45,200	350,500
1994-95	353,000	45,100	398,100
1995-96	334,200	32,600	366,800
1996-97	310,000	40,000	350,000
1997-98	367,900	55,500	423,400
1998-99	349,000	41,300	390,300
1999-2000	372,000	47,000	419,000
2000-2001	435,100	43,600	478,700

Alabama's High Deer Density

According to recent studies by the Alabama Department of Wildlife and Freshwater Fisheries, about half of the state's counties have more than 30 deer per square mile.

ALABAMA WHITETAIL RECORDS

•**Record harvest:** 478,700 (2000-01)
•**Record low harvest:** 31,123 (1963-64)
•**Bow-hunting record:** 55,500 (1997-98)
•**Gun-hunting record:** 435,100 (2001)

•**Season to remember:** 2000-2001. Alabama hunters kill 478,700 deer, setting a new state record and surpassing the 400,000 mark for the third time in Alabama history.

Alabama Strives to Control its Deer Herd

Not long ago, a deer track was a rare sight in the Camellia State. Today, thanks to the work of conservationists, Alabama whitetails have rebounded. However, with a herd surpassing 1.5 million, the state might have too much of a good thing.

To deal with this tremendous population, Alabama's Division of Wildlife and Freshwater Fisheries implemented a 75-day either-sex season for 32 of Alabama's 67 counties. The DWFF also added either-sex hunting days to the season to promote doe harvests.

The DWFF plans also address buck management. In the past, Alabama's liberal buck season, coupled with low doe harvest quotas, has resulted in unbalanced adult doe-to-antlered buck ratios, and has prevented relatively few bucks from reaching maturity. In addition, these hunting practices have caused extended breeding and fawning periods, virtually eliminating buck sign and natural breeding behaviors.

To combat this, the DWFF and private groups have urged Alabama hunters to pass up yearling bucks and kill more does. This change has greatly increased buck hunting opportunities and herd health.

ALABAMA SNAPSHOT

Deer Population: 1.6 million, 4th in U.S.

Average Harvest: 412,280, 4th in U.S.

Harvest Calculation Method: Surveys

Does State Predict Annual Harvest? No

How Close is Annual Prediction? NA

Gun-Hunters: 225,000

Bow-Hunters: 60,000

Muzzleloading Hunters: 18,180

Hunter Education: Required for persons born on or after Aug. 1, 1977. Bow-hunter education is not required.

Orange Required for Gun-Hunting? Yes.

ARIZONA
Grand Canyon State

Harvest Ranking: #40

For more information, contact:

Game & Fish Department
2221 W. Greenway Road
Phoenix, AZ 85023

(602) 942-3000   www.gf.state.az.us

HISTORY OF ARIZONA'S WHITETAIL HARVEST

Year	Firearms	Bow	Total
1958	5,096	NA	5,096
1959	5,421	NA	5,421
1960	4,982	NA	4,982
1961	4,734	NA	4,734
1962	4,194	NA	4,194
1963	4,343	NA	4,343
1964	4,339	NA	4,339
1965	3,612	NA	3,612
1966	2,993	NA	2,993
1967	2,662	NA	2,662
1968	2,927	NA	2,927
1969	2,202	NA	2,202
1970	2,232	NA	2,232
1971	1,535	NA	1,535
1972	1,673	NA	1,673
1973	2,097	NA	2,097
1974	3,248	NA	3,248
1975	2,870	NA	2,870
1976	2,662	NA	2,662
1977	2,319	NA	2,319
1978	2,287	NA	2,287
1979	3,264	NA	3,264
1980	3,523	NA	3,523
1981	3,504	NA	3,504
1982	4,002	60	4,062
1983	4,221	71	4,292
1984	7,116	65	7,181
1985	6,902	138	7,040
1986	5,934	94	6,028
1987	4,895	115	5,010
1988	4,600	108	4,708
1989	4,387	189	4,576
1990	4,449	100	4,549
1991	5,375	129	5,504
1992	5,737	95	5,832
1993	5,556	152	5,772
1994	5,363	1,315	6,678
1995	4,899	239	5,138
1996	4,126	178	4,304
1997	4,229	175	4,404
1998	4,160	204	4,364
1999	3,339	255	3,594
2000 (estimated)	4,250	214	4,500
2001	3,440	225 (estimated)	3,654

ARIZONA WHITETAIL RECORDS

•**Record whitetail harvest:** 7,181 (1984)
•**Record low deer harvest:** 1,535 (1971)
•**Bow-hunting record:** 1,315 (1994)
•**Gun-hunting record:** 7,116 (1984)

•**Season to remember:** 1984. Arizona hunters kill 7,181 deer — a 60 percent increase from 1983.

Arizona Hunters Make a Big Economic Impact

Although whitetails aren't plentiful in the Grand Canyon State, Arizona hunters still have a positive impact on the state's economy. Each year, Arizona's 167,000 hunters spend more than $505 million, generating $14 million in tax revenue ad creating 7,300 jobs.

Arizona Offers Opportunities for Coues Deer

Although a deer scoring 65 inches might not even warrant a photo to hunters in most of the whitetail's range, it's a monster in the arid country of southeastern Arizona.

That's because the Grand Canyon State is home to the Coues deer, a rare, diminutive whitetail subspecies whose tiny proportions are perfectly suited to survival in the desert Southwest.

Coues deer have white bellies, white "halos" around their eyes and grayish-brown, salt-and-pepper coats. With Coues bucks standing just higher than 30 inches at the shoulder and rarely weighing more than 100 pounds, they are much smaller than most other whitetail subspecies.

ARIZONA SNAPSHOT

Deer Population: 182,000 (all species)

Average Harvest: 4,103, 40th in U.S.

Does State Predict Annual Harvest? No

How Close is Annual Prediction? NA

Gun-Hunters: 46,430

Bow-Hunters: 22,775

Muzzleloading Hunters: 1,120

Hunter Education: Required for ages 10 to 14. Bow-hunter education is not required.

Orange Required for Gun-Hunting? No.

ARKANSAS
Land of Opportunity
Harvest Ranking: #15

For more information, contact:
Game & Fish Commission
#2 Natural Resources Drive
Little Rock, AR 72205

(800) 364-4263   www.agfc.state.ar.us

HISTORY OF ARKANSAS' WHITETAIL HARVEST

Year	Firearm	Bow	Total
1938-39	203	NA	203
1941-42	433	NA	433
1944-45	1,606	NA	1,606
1947-48	2,016	NA	2,016
1950-51	4,122	NA	4,122
1953-54	6,245	NA	6,245
1956-57	8,249	NA	8,249
1960-61	15,000	NA	15,000
1963-64	25,148	NA	25,148
1966-67	20,028	NA	20,028
1968-69	20,063	NA	20,063
1969-70	24,018	1,678	25,696

THIRTY-YEAR HISTORY

Year	Firearm	Bow	Total
1970-71	24,784	1,233	26,017
1971-72	23,375	1,345	24,720
1972-73	31,415	672	32,087
1973-74	32,292	1,502	33,794
1974-75	32,168	1,595	33,763
1975-76	32,210	1,112	33,322
1976-77	27,249	540	27,789
1977-78	27,862	1,247	29,109
1978-79	41,018	2,434	43,452
1979-80	32,841	3,233	36,074
1980-81	41,693	3,509	45,202
1981-82	41,567	3,024	44,591
1982-83	35,051	7,822	42,873
1983-84	42,709	17,539	60,248
1984-85	53,679	12,360	66,039
1985-86	48,027	12,049	60,076
1986-87	67,941	11,939	79,880
1987-88	89,422	16,970	106,392
1988-89	94,193	16,014	110,207
1989-90	97,031	16,048	113,079
1990-91	70,498	20,412	90,910
1991-92	NA	NA	110,896
1992-93	NA	NA	110,401
1993-94	106,119	15,944	122,063
1994-95	104,061	16,433	120,494
1995-96	144,932	18,992	163,924
1996-97	133,704	18,756	152,460
1997-98	164,132	15,093	179,225
1998-99	NA	NA	156,431
1999-2000	179,601	15,086	194,687
2000-2001	167,328	14,804	182,132

ARKANSAS WHITETAIL RECORDS

•**Record harvest:** 194,687 (1999-2000)
•**Record low harvest:** 203 (1938-39)
•**Bow-hunting record:** 21,190 (1997-98)
•**Gun-hunting record:** 167,328 (2000-2001)

•**Season to remember:** 1997-98. Decades of trap-and-transplant programs and tightened hunting regulations pay off, as Arkansas hunters kill 179,225 deer.

Arkansas Whitetails Have Overcome Adversity

White-tailed deer played an important role in Arkansas history. In 1539, for example, Spanish explorer Hernando de Soto found Caddo Indians depending heavily on the state's abundant whitetail herd for venison and hides.

As European settlers moved into the area, they too relied on deer. However, the settler's unrestricted hunting and land clearing took its toll on Arkansas' deer, and by the early 1900s, numbers were low throughout the state.

In 1919, the newly created Game and Fish Commission attempted to reverse the downward trend by creating a law that required hunters to shoot only bucks. However, deer numbers continued to decrease, prompting the state to establish deer refuges in 1926-27. By 1930, only a few hundred deer remained.

With hunting tightly restricted by the 1940s, the Arkansas GFC bought more than 1,800 deer from neighboring states and relocated them throughout Arkansas.

These restoration efforts, along with increased public awareness and restrictive regulations, was a complete success. Today Arkansas is home to about 1 million whitetails.

ARKANSAS SNAPSHOT

Deer Population: 1 million, 7th in U.S.

Average Harvest: 172,987, 15th in U.S.

Harvest Calculation Method: Mandatory registration

Does State Predict Annual Harvest? Yes

How Close is Annual Prediction? 10%

Gun-Hunters: 161,298

Bow-Hunters: 70,700

Muzzleloading Hunters: 78,956

Hunter Education: Required for persons born on or after Dec. 31, 1968. Bow-hunter education not required.

Orange Required for Gun-Hunting? Yes.

COLORADO
Colorful Colorado

Harvest Ranking: Not ranked

For more information, contact:
Colorado Division of Wildlife
6060 Broadway
Denver, CO 80216

(303) 297-1192   www.dnr.state.co.us/

Hunting is Valued Part of Colorado Culture

Colorado Governor Bill Owens recently addressed the importance of hunting.

"Hunting and angling are valued traditions in Colorado," Owens said. "License fees support wildlife management and protection. Hunters and anglers pump almost $2 billion dollars into Colorado's economy each year. Their spending is vital to the social and economic stability of many rural communities. But, just as important, hunting and angling bring families and friends together, foster a special understanding of our natural world and build strong community ties.

"The legal and ethical pursuit of game and fish in the wild is a powerful teacher for youth and adults," Owens continued. "I invite all Coloradans to appreciate our state's rich wildlife legacy and support our hunting and angling traditions."

Poaching Penalties Increase

Colorado is one of several states that is part of a consortium that seeks to crack down on poachers. Violators whose hunting and fishing licenses are revoked in one state will have those same licenses revoked in nine others states. Also participating are Arizona, Idaho, Minnesota, Montana, Nevada, Oregon, Utah, Washington and Wyoming.

The law went into effect in 2000. It is the result of an incident where a Minnesota man poached an elk in Montana. The man lost his hunting, fishing and trapping privileges in Montana, but he was still allowed to hunt in his home state. Under the new law, he would have lost the same privileges in Minnesota and the other states.

Editor's note: Colorado does not distinguish between white-tailed deer and mule deer in its harvest statistics. Biologists there estimate that about 1,000 whitetails are taken each year. Most of these deer come from the river bottoms of the eastern plains of Colorado.

Colorado Researchers Developing Live-Test for Chronic Wasting Disease

In response to increasing cases of chronic wasting disease, a fatal illness that attacks the brains of deer and elk, the Colorado Division of Wildlife is working on a test for diagnosing the disease among live deer.

The test, which analyzes a deer's tonsil tissue, finds warped proteins called prions, which researchers believe cause the disease.

Aside from letting biologist test live animals, the method is more sensitive than conventional brain-tissue tests because prions congregate in the tonsils early in the disease's development.

Raffles for Big-Game Tags Help Fund Colorado Wildlife

Deer and other Colorado big game reap big benefits each year when the Colorado Division of Wildife and nonprofit and conservation groups auction and raffle off deer, elk, moose, antelope, mountain goat and bighorn sheep licenses. Money generated by such programs funds hunter education, wildlife research and habitat improvement projects.

In 2001, auctions and raffles for Colorado tags raised about $195,000 for these programs. In 1999, a Wisconsinite set the record for the highest amount paid — $93,000 for a bighorn sheep tag.

— COLORADO DIVISION OF WILDLIFE

COLORADO SNAPSHOT

Deer Population: 516,458 (all species)

Average Harvest: Not available

Gun-Hunters: 90,551

Bow-Hunters: 20,650

Muzzleloading Hunters: 6,300

Hunter Education: Required for persons born after Jan. 1, 1949. Bow-hunter education is not required.

Orange Required for Gun-Hunting? Yes.

CONNECTICUT
Constitution State
Harvest Ranking: #36

For more information, contact:

Dept. of Environmental Protection
391 Route 32
N. Franklin, CT 06254

(860) 424-3105   www.dep.state.ct.us

HISTORY OF CONNECTICUT'S DEER HARVEST

Year	Firearms	Bow	Total
1975	475	75	550
1976	530	100	630
1977	780	125	905
1978	805	125	930
1979	870	140	1,010
1980	2,189	376	2,565
1981	2,463	393	2,856
1982	2,233	391	2,624
1983	3,152	639	3,791
1984	3,742	596	4,338
1985	3,817	722	4,539
1986	4,575	819	5,394
1987	5,618	854	6,472
1988	6,843	799	7,642
1989	7,837	926	8,763
1990	NA	NA	9,896
1991	NA	NA	11,311
1992	NA	NA	12,486
1993	NA	NA	10,360
1994	NA	NA	10,438
1995	11,039	2,701	13,740
1996	9,323	2,691	12,014
1997	9,537	2,300	11,837
1998	7,958	2,186	10,144
1999	8,791	2,561	11,352
2000	10,586	2,687	13,273
2001	9,424	2,262	12,050

Connecticut Deer Prove Resilient

Over-harvesting and habitat loss caused by extensive land clearing, made white-tailed deer uncommon in Connecticut from 1700 to about 1900. Numerous laws enacted during this period to protect the dwindling deer resource, plus the improvement in deer habitat contributed to a slow but steady rebound in deer numbers.

In 1974, Connecticut passed the Deer Management Act and, in 1975, held its first gun-hunting season.

CONNECTICUT WHITETAIL RECORDS

• **Record harvest:** 13,740 (1995)
• **Record low harvest:** 550 (1975)
• **Bow-hunting record:** 2,701 (1995)
• **Gun-hunting record:** 11,039 (1995)

• **Season to remember:** 1975. After centuries of unrestricted hunting, habitat loss and encroachment by civilization, Connecticut deer numbers grow high enough to support the state's first modern firearms season.

Suburban Deer Are Difficult to Control

Although encroaching civilization once cursed Connecticut's whitetails, it has recently created a paradise for them. The Constitution State's deer herd continues to expand, as deer benefit from light hunting pressure, land clearing and manicured suburban environments.

The state's growing herd is testament to Connecticut's sound management and the work of conservationists. However, it also causes extensive property damage and increased vehicle-deer collisions.

To deal with nuisance deer, Connecticut farmers and landowners often surround their property with 8- to 10-foot electrified fences and use scent repellents, such as human hair and bone meal. Landowners also foil hungry deer by planting high-value crops away from woods and other deer cover. However, these methods are only somewhat successful.

According to the Connecticut Department of Environmental Protection, the most practical way to keep deer populations in balance with cultural and habitat carrying capacities is through hunting.

CONNECTICUT SNAPSHOT

Deer Population: 75,000, 32nd in U.S.

Average Harvest: 11,731, 36th in U.S.

Harvest Calculation Method: Mandatory registration.

Does State Predict Annual Harvest? No

How Close is Annual Prediction? NA

Gun-Hunters: 32,261

Bow-Hunters: 11,039

Muzzleloading Hunters: 2,651

Hunter Education: Required for first-time hunters. Bow-hunter education not required.

Orange Required for Gun-Hunting? Yes.

DELAWARE
First State
Harvest Ranking: #37

For more information, contact:

Department of Natural Resources
89 Kings Hwy., Box 1401
Dover, DE 19903

(302) 739-5295   www.dnrec.state.de.us

HISTORY OF DELAWARE'S WHITETAIL HARVEST

Year	Firearms	Bow	Total
1976-77	1,475	19	1,494
1977-78	1,630	22	1,652
1978-79	1,679	20	1,699
1979-80	1,783	20	1,803
1980-81	1,737	17	1,754
1981-82	2,080	31	2,111
1982-83	2,046	48	2,094
1983-84	2,210	21	2,231
1984-85	2,473	41	2,514
1985-86	2,383	58	2,439
1986-87	2,772	78	2,850
1987-88	3,420	121	3,541
1988-89	3,844	154	3,998
1990-91	4,814	252	5,066
1991-92	4,970	362	5,332
1992-93	6,721	524	7,245
1993-94	6,917	548	7,465
1994-95	7,151	673	7,824
1995-96	8,050	728	8,778
1996-97	9,034	786	9,820
1997-98	9,073	930	10,003
1998-99	9,386	926	10,312
1999-00	9,921	835	10,756
2000-01	9,907	834	10,741
2001-2002	10,945	1,037	12,200

*estimated

Delaware Hunting License Sales

Year	Resident	Nonresident	Total
1972	23,713	1,357	25,070
1978	25,411	2,443	27,854
1981	23,811	2,600	26,411
1984	23,644	3,516	27,160
1987	23,378	4,320	27,698
1990	21,157	3,848	25,005
1991	21,674	2,995	24,669
1992	21,863	2,362	24,225
1993	21,664	2,184	23,848
1994	21,769	2,042	23,811
1995	19,518	1,945	21,463
1996	19,914	1,693	21,607
1997	20,257	1,731	21,988

DELAWARE WHITETAIL RECORDS

•**Record harvest:** 12,200 (2001-02)
•**Record low harvest:** 1,494 (1976)
•**Bow-hunting record:** 1,037 (2001-02)
•**Gun-hunting record:** 10,945 (2001-02)

•**Season to remember:** 1997-98. Delaware bow-hunters kill a record 930 deer. Although diminutive compared to other states' archery harvests, this figure is amazing considering Delaware bow-hunters killed only 22 deer just 10 years earlier.

State Lands Offer Some of Delaware's Best Opportunities

Covering little area and containing even less rural land, Delaware is hardly a deer-hunting destination. However, Delaware hunters can find some opportunities on state parks.

If you'd like to hunt on state park lands, register for the Delaware State Parks Hunting Program. If you receive a permit, you must carry your state parks hunting registration and valid Delaware hunting license whenever hunting on state park lands. There is no charge for registration.

Some parks have additional pre-registration requirements. or complete information.

Each state park has its unique set of hunting rules. You can obtain a copy of these rules and park hunting maps at each park's headquarters or at 89 Kings Highway, Dover, Del.

The Delaware Department of Natural Resources reminds hunters that state parks are multiple-use areas. Hunters will be share the parks with other hikers, campers, bikers, boaters and horseback riders. Therefore, hunters must use extreme caution when hunting state park lands.

— DELAWARE DEPARTMENT OF NATURAL RESOURCES

DELAWARE SNAPSHOT

Deer Population: 30,000, 33rd in U.S.

Average Harvest: 10,802, 37th in U.S.

Harvest Calculation Method: Mandatory registration.

Does State Predict Annual Harvest? No

How Close is Annual Prediction? NA

Gun-Hunters: 17,000

Bow-Hunters: 6,900

Muzzleloading Hunters: 8,500

Hunter Education: Required for persons born after Jan. 1, 1967. Bow-hunter education is not required

Orange Required for Gun-Hunting? Yes.

FLORIDA
Sunshine State
Harvest Ranking: #23

For more information, contact:
Fish & Game Commission
620 S. Meridian Farris Bryant Blvd.
Tallahassee, FL 32399
(850) 488-3641   www.state.fl.us/gfc

HISTORY OF FLORIDA'S WHITETAIL HARVEST

Year	Firearms	Bow	Total
1971	NA	NA	48,900
1972	NA	NA	58,500
1973	NA	NA	57,122
1974	NA	NA	54,102
1975	NA	NA	54,380
1976	NA	NA	60,805
1977	NA	NA	85,744
1978	NA	NA	NA
1979	NA	NA	54,765
1980	NA	NA	72,039
1981	NA	NA	66,489
1982	NA	NA	64,557
1983	NA	NA	77,146
1984	NA	NA	73,895
1985	NA	NA	80,947
1986	NA	NA	89,212
1987	NA	NA	105,917
1988	NA	NA	107,240
1989	NA	NA	85,753
1990	NA	NA	79,170
1991	NA	NA	81,255
1992	NA	NA	81,942
1993	NA	NA	104,178
1994	NA	NA	84,408
1995	NA	NA	81,891
1996	NA	NA	78,446
1997	NA	NA	80,000
1998	NA	NA	80,000
1999	NA	NA	80,000
2000	93,319	18,317	111,636
2001	117,000	23,000	140,000

Florida Harbors Big Bucks

Several Florida hunters bagged trophy bucks during the 2000-2001 season. Among the biggest was a Jefferson County buck killed by Carl Joiner. His buck scored 149⅝ inches.

Two other bucks entered into Florida's big-buck registry included a 138-inch 8-pointer taken by Tom Price in Clay County, and a 136-inch 11-pointer taken by Mark Johnson in Calhoun County.

FLORIDA WHITETAIL RECORDS

•**Record harvest:** 140,000 (2001)
•**Record low harvest:** 48,900(1971)
•**Bow-hunting record:** 23,000 (2001)
•**Gun-hunting record:** 117,000 (2001)

•**Season to remember:** 2001. Florida hunters kill an estimated 140,000 deer, surpassing the 1999 harvest by about 60,000.

Florida Deer Faced A Rough Road to Recovery

Although Florida now supports one of the highest deer populations in the nation, Sunshine State whitetails were nearly wiped out less than a century ago.

Historical records indicate European settlers were overhunting deer in Florida as early as the mid-1700s. This trend continued through the early 20th century, when the population was about to collapse.

To prevent the whitetail's extirpation, Florida established wildlife sanctuaries. The Pittman-Robertson Act of 1937 also helped, funding deer management projects and habitat improvements.

By the 1960's, Florida's deer herd was expanding significantly, thanks to ever-improving management and habitat. In addition, poaching decreased drastically, primarily because of increased law enforcement

This trend continued though the following decades, and in 1985, Florida hunters killed more than 100,000 animals for the first time in recorded history.

Today, Florida biologists face the opposite challenge: keeping deer herds in check with the habitat's ability to support them.

FLORIDA SNAPSHOT

Deer Population: 820,000, 14th in U.S.

Average Harvest: 98,327, 23rd in U.S.

Harvest Calculation Method: Surveys and voluntary registration.

Does State Predict Annual Harvest? No

How Close is Annual Prediction? NA

Gun-Hunters: 117,509

Bow-Hunters: 27,878

Muzzleloading Hunters: 19,949

Hunter Education: Required for persons born on or after June 1, 1975. Bow-hunter education is not required.

Orange Required for Gun-Hunting? Yes.

GEORGIA
Peach State
Harvest Ranking: #6

For more information, contact:
Wildlife Resources
2070 U.S. Hwy. 278 SE
Social Circle, GA 30025
(770) 414-3333   www.dnr.state.ga.us

HISTORY OF GEORGIA'S WHITETAIL HARVEST

Year	Firearm	Bow	Total
1980-81	NA	NA	135,500
1981-82	NA	NA	134,000
1982-83	NA	NA	144,000
1983-84	NA	NA	164,000
1984-85	NA	NA	177,000
1985-86	NA	NA	189,600
1986-87	NA	NA	226,000
1987-88	NA	NA	280,536
1988-89	NA	NA	300,624
1989-90	NA	NA	293,167
1990-91	NA	NA	351,652
1991-92	265,352	15,708	281,060
1992-93	284,412	21,841	306,253
1993-94	309,522	37,331	346,853
1994-95	345,869	35,687	381,556
1995-96	355,267	36,328	391,595
1996-97	351,990	49,368	401,358
1997-98	350,000	45,000	395,000
1998-99	383,000	44,000	427,000
1999-2000	380,000	46,000	426,000
2000-2001 (estimated)	401,400	44,600	446,000

Understanding Doe Productivity

A healthy herd of 50 mature does will out-produce an unhealthy herd of 100 mature does. For example:

✓ 50 healthy does give birth to two fawns each.

✓ 95 percent of the fawns survive, meaning the herd increases by 95 deer.

On the other hand:

✓ 100 unhealthy does give birth to one fawn each.

✓ 50 percent of the fawns survive, meaning the herd, at best, increases by 50 deer. Healthy does will reproduce every year until they die. "Barren does" occur mostly in poor-health herds.

GEORGIA WHITETAIL RECORDS

•**Record harvest:** 446,000 (2000-01)
•**Record low harvest:** 134,000 (1981-82)
•**Bow-hunting record:** 49,368 (1996-97)
•**Gun-hunting record:** 401,100 (2000-2001)

•**Season to remember:** 1993-94. Georgia bow-hunters experience a banner season, killing 37,331 deer — 15,490 more deer than the previous year.

Roll Up Your Sleeves To Enhance Hunting

Georgia landowners often take pride in managing deer herds on their properties. To produce large numbers of mature, quality bucks, the Georgia Wildlife Resources Division advises hunters to shift hunting pressure from immature bucks to does. This increases the odds that bucks will reach maturity. In addition, an increased doe harvest ensures a balanced sex ratio and prevents overbrowsing.

Along with regulating the harvest on their properties, landowners should manage the habitat to improve nutrition. Manage forest openings with mowing and planting. Mowing native vegetation every two to three years encourages growth in browse species, such as blackberry, greenbriar and honeysuckle.

Planting wheat, rye, ryegrass and clover provides good winter food. Corn, grain, sorghum and joint vetch are good food-plot crops from summer through fall.

To provide Georgia hunters more information on managing whitetails on their property, the Georgia Wildlife Resources Division offers "Deer Herd Management For Georgia Hunters," an instructional booklet available at Game Management offices throughout the state.

GEORGIA SNAPSHOT

Deer Population: 1.3 million, 6th in U.S.

Average Harvest: 338,672, 6th in U.S.

Harvest Calculation Method: Surveys

Does State Predict Annual Harvest? No

How Close is Annual Prediction? NA

Gun-Hunters: 279,382

Bow-Hunters: 96,844

Muzzleloading Hunters: 42,259

Hunter Education: Required for persons born after Jan. 1, 1961. Bow-hunter education is not required.

Orange Required for Gun-Hunting? Yes.

IDAHO
Gem State
Harvest Ranking: #34

For more information, contact:
Fish & Game Department
Box 25
Boise, ID 83707
(208) 334-3717
www.state.id.us/fishgame/fishgame.html

HISTORY OF IDAHO'S DEER HARVEST

Year	Firearm	Bow	Total
1980	NA	NA	45,988
1981	NA	NA	50,580
1982	NA	NA	48,670
1983	NA	NA	50,600
1984	NA	NA	42,600
1985	NA	NA	48,950
1986	NA	NA	59,800
1987	NA	NA	66,400
1988	NA	NA	82,200
1989	NA	NA	95,200
1990	NA	NA	72,100
1991	16,721	364	17,085
1992	NA	NA	23,633
1993	23,251	303	23,554
1994	29,760	595	30,355
1995	28,180	320	28,500
1996	NA	NA	22,600
1997	37,450	1,100	38,550
1998	38,162	880	39,042
1999	17,070	310	17,380
2000	15,850	390	16,240
2001 (estimated)	15,850	450	16,300

Editor's note — The figures before 1991 include white-tailed deer and mule deer.

Feeding Often Harms Whitetails

Although well-meaning individuals attempt to help deer by providing supplemental foods in winter, such efforts can be detrimental. Eye and respiratory infections are common at feeding sites, and the change from natural to supplemental feed often causes diarrhea in fawns.

Research shows that animals in good condition can survive winter with little nutrition. Supplemental feeding is virtually irrelevant to survival, and it is not an adequate way to make up for loss of habitat. There is no substitute for healthy habitat.

IDAHO WHITETAIL RECORDS

•**Record harvest:** 39,042 (1998)
•**Record low harvest:** 16,240 (2000)
•**Bow-hunting record:** 1,312 (1999)
•**Gun-hunting record:** 41,972 (1999)

•**Season to remember:** 1991. For the first time in state history, Idaho recognizes white-tailed deer separately. Of the 17,085 deer killed, 97.9 percent were taken by gun-hunters.

Idaho Hunters Are Extremely Safe

Many people assume hunting is dangerous. However, National Safety Council statistics show hunting is one of the country's safest forms of recreation.

Need proof? Every year, NSC statistics show that every year, more people are injured playing ping-pong or shooting pool than hunting. In the study, for every 100,000 hunters, seven were injured in hunting incidents. If you remove ammunition reloading accidents and other related events from the equation, the number drops to less than two accidents per 100,000 participants.

For perspective, football caused 3,313 injuries, cycling caused 1,189, golf caused 185 and bowling caused 60 injuries. In other words, you're about eight times more likely to hurt yourself while bowling than while hunting. Admittedly, however, bowling accidents are much less traumatic and almost never fatal, unlike hunting accidents.

Even so, hunting accidents aren't nearly as common as often believed, and statistics show Idaho hunters are no exception.

In 2001, for example, Idaho hunter were involved in 11 hunting accidents. Careless gun handling caused six. Incidentally, one of those accidents was fatal, the first since 1999.

IDAHO SNAPSHOT

Deer Population: 255,000, 24th in U.S.

Average Harvest: 25,502, 34th in U.S.

Harvest Calculation Method: Surveys

Does State Predict Annual Harvest? No

How Close is Annual Prediction? NA

Gun-Hunters: 130,000

Bow-Hunters: 12,800

Muzzleloading Hunters: 3,300

Hunter Education: Required for persons born after Jan. 1, 1975. Bow-hunter education is required for first-time bow-hunters.

Orange Required for Gun-Hunting? No.

ILLINOIS

Prairie State

Harvest Ranking: #17

For more information, contact:

Department of Conservation
524 S. Second St.
Springfield, IL 62701

(217) 782-7305 www.dnr.state.il.us

HISTORY OF ILLINOIS' WHITETAIL HARVEST

Year	Firearm	Bow	Total
1957	1,709	NA	1,709
1958	2,493	NA	2,493
1959	2,604	NA	2,604
1960	2,438	NA	2,438
1961	4,313	NA	4,313
1962	6,289	NA	6,289
1963	6,785	NA	6,785
1964	9,975	NA	9,975
1965	7,651	NA	7,651
1966	7,357	NA	7,357
1967	6,588	NA	6,588
1968	8,202	NA	8,202
1969	8,345	NA	8,345
1970	8,889	590	9,479
1971	10,359	566	10,925
1972	10,100	552	10,652
1973	12,902	960	13,862
1974	12,853	1,425	14,278
1975	15,614	1,608	17,222
1976	15,308	1,600	16,908
1977	16,231	2,810	19,041
1979	20,058	1,074	21,132
1980	20,825	1,463	22,288
1981	20,800	1,766	22,566
1982	22,657	2,205	24,862
1983	26,112	2,554	28,666
1984	29,212	3,023	32,235
1985	31,769	3,746	35,515
1986	36,056	4,357	40,413
1987	42,932	6,646	49,578
1988	47,786	7,820	55,606
1989	56,143	10,000	66,143
1990	NA	NA	81,000
1991	83,191	18,099	101,290
1992	84,537	19,564	104,101
1993	92,276	23,215	115,491
1994	97,723	25,607	123,330
1995	107,742	34,491	22,288
1996	97,498	35,239	132,737
1997	96,511	36,763	133,274
1998	99,008	36,280	135,288
1999	95,222	41,310	136,532
2000	106,433	42,630	149,063
2001	101,566	42,900	144,460

ILLINOIS WHITETAIL RECORDS

- **Record harvest:** 149,063 (2000)
- **Record low harvest:** 1,709 (1957)
- **Bow-hunting record:** 42,900 (2001)
- **Gun-hunting record:** 107,742 (1995)

•**Season to remember:** 2000. Illinois hunters kill 149,063 deer, surpassing the previous record of 142,233, set in 1995. That figure is especially amazing considering that 20 years earlier, the harvest was only 22,288.

Big-Buck Program Celebrates Illinois Whitetails

In the early 1980s, the Illinois Department of Natural Resources unveiled its Big Buck Recognition Program. The program, patterned after the standards of the Boone & Crockett Club, promotes deer hunting while recognizing hunters who take big bucks. Here's a look at some of the top bucks:

Firearm — Typical

Hunter	Score	Date	County
Larry Shaw	$188\frac{7}{8}$	1998	Clark
Daniel Lincoln	$187\frac{7}{8}$	1998	Mercer
Bernard Emat	$183\frac{3}{8}$	1996	La Salle

Firearm — Nontypical

Hunter	Score	Date	County
William Seidel	$239\frac{1}{8}$	1987	Unknown
John Boshears	$220\frac{1}{8}$	1998	Iroquois
Chris Schweigert	$219\frac{3}{8}$	1998	Fulton

Archery — Typical

Hunter	Score	Date	County
Gary Adcock	$177\frac{0}{8}$	1998	Hamilton
Mark Simon	$176\frac{4}{8}$	1998	Will
Mike Foote	$176\frac{1}{8}$	1998	Adams

Archery — Nontypical

Hunter	Score	Date	County
Walter Baker	$216\frac{3}{8}$	1998	Jersey
Ronald Okonek	$205\frac{7}{8}$	1998	Greene

Editor's note — These are Illinois BBRP listings. They do not reflect official records of the Boone and Crockett Club.

ILLINOIS SNAPSHOT

Deer Population: 700,000, 15th in U.S.

Average Harvest: 139,723, 17th in U.S.

Harvest Calculation Method: Mandatory registration.

Does State Predict Annual Harvest? Yes

How Close is Annual Prediction? 5%

Gun-Hunters: 190,000

Bow-Hunters: 110,000

Muzzleloading Hunters: 7,050

Hunter Education: Required for persons born after Jan. 1, 1980. Bow-hunter education is not required.

Orange Required for Gun-Hunting? Yes.

144

INDIANA
Hoosier State
Harvest Ranking: #22

For more information, contact:
Division of Wildlife
553 E. Miller Drive
Bloomington, IN 47401
(317) 232-4080   www.state.in.us/dnr

HISTORY OF INDIANA'S WHITETAIL HARVEST

Year	Firearm	Bow	Total
1951	NA	NA	1,590
1953	NA	NA	83
1955	NA	NA	149
1957	NA	NA	NA
1959	NA	NA	800
1961	NA	NA	2,293
1963	NA	NA	4,634
1965	NA	NA	4,155
1967	NA	NA	6,560
1969	NA	NA	7,323
THIRTY-YEAR HISTORY			
1970	NA	NA	5,175
1971	NA	NA	5,099
1972	NA	NA	NA
1973	NA	NA	8,244
1974	NA	NA	9,461
1975	NA	NA	8,758
1976	NA	NA	11,344
1977	NA	NA	12,476
1978	NA	NA	9,896
1979	NA	NA	13,718
1980	NA	NA	19,780
1981	12,600	5,527	18,127
1982	16,267	4,651	20,918
1983	21,244	3,988	25,232
1984	21,944	5,640	27,584
1985	25,768	6,371	32,139
1986	33,837	9,621	43,458
1987	38,937	12,841	51,778
1988	46567	13,667	60,234
1989	62,901	16,417	79,318
1990	70,928	17,775	88,703
1991	77,102	21,581	98,683
1992	73,396	21,918	95,314
1993	77,226	23,988	101,214
1994	89,037	23,379	112,416
1995	92,496	25,233	117,729
1996	99,886	23,200	123,086
1997	84,637	20,300	104,937
1998	82,101	18,360	100,461
1999	79,384	20,234	99,618
2000	76,313	22,412	98,725
2001	79,047	24,116	103,163

INDIANA WHITETAIL RECORDS

•**Record harvest:** 123,086 (1996)
•**Record low harvest:** 68 (1954)
•**Bow-hunting record:** 25,233 (1995)
•**Gun-hunting record:** 99,886 (1996)

•**Season to remember:** 1996. Indiana hunters break the firearms and overall harvest records, killing 123,086 whitetails. Amazingly, just eight years earlier, Indiana hunters killed just 60,234 deer — less than half as many as in 1996.

Indiana Offers On-Line Hunting Licensing

Like many states, Indiana is making getting into the woods faster and easier with on-line licensing.

The Indiana Department of Natural Resources and accessIndiana, the state's official Web site, have teamed up to offer all Indiana resident and non-resident hunting licenses online.

As home computers become more common, this system promises to save hunters and anglers time, money and inconvenience, because they will be able to purchase licenses wherever they can access the Internet.

Indiana's on-line licensing system is simple. Hunters need only provide basic personal information, such as their name, address and date of birth, and then select which license they wish to purchase. To fund the innovative program, on-line license buyers must pay a $1 convenience charge in addition to the standard license fee, plus a small processing fee.

To learn more about the hunting licenses available on accessIndiana, visit the Indiana Department of Natural Resources Web site, www.wildlife.IN.gov.

INDIANA SNAPSHOT

Deer Population: 450,000, 18th in U.S.

Average Harvest: 101,380, 22nd in U.S.

Harvest Calculation Method: Mandatory registration.

Does State Predict Annual Harvest? No

How Close is Annual Prediction? NA

Gun-Hunters: 211,767

Bow-Hunters: 122,617

Muzzleloading Hunters: 93,015

Hunter Education: Required for persons born after Dec. 31, 1986. Bow-hunter education is not required.

Orange Required for Gun-Hunting? Yes.

IOWA
Hawkeye State
Harvest Ranking: #19

For more information, contact:
Department of Natural Resources
Wallace State Office Bldg.
Des Moines, IA 50319-0034

(515) 281-4687   www.state.ia.us/wildlife/

HISTORY OF IOWA'S WHITETAIL HARVEST

Year	Firearm	Bow	Total
1953	4,007	1	4,008
1954	2,413	10	2,423
1955	3,006	58	3,064
1956	2,561	117	2,678
1957	2,667	138	2,805
1958	2,729	162	2,891
1959	2,476	255	2,731
1960	3,992	277	4,269
1961	4,997	367	5,364
1962	5,299	404	5,703
1963	6,612	538	7,151
1964	9,024	670	9,694
1965	7,910	710	8,620
1966	10,742	579	11,321
1967	10,392	791	11,183
1968	12,941	830	13,771
1969	10,731	851	11,582
1970	12,743	1,037	13,780
1971	10,459	1,232	11,691
1972	10,485	1,328	11,813
1973	12,208	1,822	14,030
1974	15,817	2,173	17,990
1975	18,948	2,219	21,167
1976	14,257	2,350	16,607
1977	12,788	2,400	15,188
1978	15,168	2,957	18,125
1979	16,149	3,305	19,454
1980	18,857	3,803	22,660
1981	21,578	4,368	25,946
1982	21,741	4,720	26,461
1983	30,375	5,244	35,619
1984	33,756	5,599	39,355
1985	38,414	5,805	44,219
1986	52,807	9,895	62,702
1987	66,036	9,722	75,758
1988	83,184	9,897	93,756
1989	87,300	11,857	99,712
1990	87,856	10,146	98,002
1991	74,828	8,807	83,635
1992	68,227	8,814	77,684
1993	67,139	9,291	76,430
1994	75,191	12,040	87,231
1995	83,884	13,372	97,256
1996	90,000	16,000	106,000
1997	104,091	14,313	118,404
1998	102,000	13,000	115,000
1999 (estimated)	NA	NA	115,000
2000	107,934	15,266	123,200
2001	112,161	18,798	130,959

IOWA WHITETAIL RECORDS

•**Record harvest:** 130,959 (2001)
•**Record low harvest:** 2,423 (1954)
•**Bow-hunting record:** 18,798 (2001)
•**Gun-hunting record:** 112,161 (2001)

•**Season to remember:** 2001. Iowa hunters kill a record 130,959 whitetails. Just 15 years earlier, Hawkeye hunters killed only 44,219.

Iowa Deer Benefit from Pittman-Robertson Funds

Iowa whitetails have it good, largely thanks to funds generated through the Pittman-Robertson Act of 1937. The act, which was signed into law by President Franklin Delano Roosevelt, acquired the 10 percent excise tax on hunting and fishing equipment and directed it toward wildlife management and habitat improvement. Half of the Iowa Wildlife Bureau's $4 million budget comes from Pittman-Robertson funding.

Much of this money helps maintain and improve Iowa's more than 250,000 acres of wildlife management areas. It also lets the Iowa Department of Natural Resources help private landowners, who control most of the state's land, improve habitat on their properties through food plots, prairie grasses, shelterbelts and sound land-use.

The results have been surprisingly good. For example, 30 years ago, deer hunting opportunities were limited in Iowa. Today, however, Iowa is a leading destination for big-buck hunters

Without Pittman-Robertson funding, the wildlife programs that maintain Iowa's quality herd would be impossible.

IOWA SNAPSHOT

Deer Population: 350,000, 21st in U.S.

Average Harvest: 120,513, 19th in U.S.

Harvest Calculation Method: Surveys

Does State Predict Annual Harvest? Yes

How Close is Annual Prediction? 5%

Gun-Hunters: 173,497

Bow-Hunters: 45,787

Muzzleloading Hunters: 23,862

Hunter Education: Required for persons born after Jan. 1, 1967. Bow-hunter education is not required.

Orange Required for Gun-Hunting? Yes.

KANSAS
Sunflower State

Harvest Ranking: #24

For more information, contact:

Department of Wildlife
Box 1525
Emporia, KS 66801

(620) 672-5911   www.kdwp.state.ks.us

HISTORY OF KANSAS' WHITETAIL HARVEST

Year	Firearm	Bow	Total
1965	1,340	164	1,504
1966	2,139	376	2,515
1967	1,542	434	1,976
1968	1,648	614	2,262
1969	1,668	583	2,251
1970	2,418	793	3,211
1971	2,569	578	3,147
1972	2,318	664	2,982
1973	3,220	892	4,112
1974	4,347	1,130	5,477
1975	4,352	1,136	5,488
1976	3,955	1,114	5,069
1977	3,766	1,174	4,940
1978	4,942	1,738	6,680
1979	5,810	2,259	8,069
1980	7,296	3,007	10,303
1981	9,413	2,939	12,352
1982	11,446	3,441	14,887
1983	13,640	3,918	17,558
1984	19,446	4,167	23,613
1985	21,296	4,230	25,526
1986	24,123	4,358	28,481
1987	31,664	4,329	35,993
1988	35,236	5,118	40,354
1989	34,000	5,550	39,550
1990	40,800	5,000	45,800
1991	41,803	NA	41,803
1992	31,750	NA	31,750
1993	33,590	NA	33,590
1994	36,040	7,800	43,840
1995	39,390	7,200	46,590
1996	43,550	8,500	52,050
1997	53,440	9,700	63,140
1998	73,100	8,000	81,100
1999	84,230	11,770	96,000
2000	NA	NA	108,000
2001 (estimated)	92,500	7,500	100,000

Kansas Encourages Hunting

The Kansas Department of Wildlife offers a hunting recruitment and retention plan.

For more information, call (316) 672-5911 or send e-mail to mikegm@wp.state.ks.us

KANSAS WHITETAIL RECORDS

•**Record harvest:** 108,000 (2000)
•**Record low harvest:** 1,504 (1965)
•**Bow-hunting record:** 11,770 (1999)
•**Gun-hunting record:** 92,500 (2001)

•**Season to remember:** 1999. Kansas bow-hunters kill 11,770 deer, doubling the archery harvest from just 10 years earlier.

Kansas Offers Bow-Hunter Education

Although most states have required general hunter education for many years, bow-hunter education is relatively new. Despite this, many states and provinces, including Maine, Idaho, Alaska, Kentucky, Louisiana, Washington, Connecticut, Montana, Nebraska, New York, New Jersey, Rhode Island, South Dakota and Nova Scotia require bow-hunter education for at least some of their bow-hunters.

Despite the fact Kansas doesn't require bow-hunter education for hunters older than 13, it is helping its hunters become safer, more effective archers through the International Bowhunter Education Program . The standardized education course covers bow-hunter responsibilities, game laws, equipment, safety, conservation, survival, first aid, methods, scouting, deer anatomy and more.

Bow-hunter education in Kansas is administered by the Kansas Department of Wildlife and Parks. Thanks to the program, about 230 students are certified each year. To date more than 2,000 students have completed the Kansas bow-hunter education course.

To learn more about Kansas' bow-hunter education opportunities, contact the Kansas Department of Wildlife & Parks, bow-hunting education coordinator Gene Brehm, 512 SE 25th Ave., Pratt, KS 67124, or call (620) 672-5911.

— KANSAS DEPARTMENT OF WILDLIFE

KANSAS SNAPSHOT

Deer Population: 250,000, 25th in U.S.

Average Harvest: 89,648, 24th in U.S.

Gun-Hunters: 74,126

Bow-Hunters: 21,508

Muzzleloading Hunters: 4,909

Hunter Education: Required for persons born after July 1, 1957. Bow-hunter education is not required.

Orange Required for Gun-Hunting? Yes.

KENTUCKY
Bluegrass State
Harvest Ranking: #20

For more information, contact:

Department of Wildlife
#1 Game Farm Road
Frankfort, KY 40601

(800) 858-1549   www.state.ky.us

HISTORY OF KENTUCKY'S WHITETAIL HARVEST

Year	Firearm	Bow	Total
1976	3,476	NA	3,476
1977	5,682	NA	5,682
1978	6,012	421	6,433
1979	7,442	620	8,062
1980	7,988	1,714	9,702
1981	13,134	1,849	14,983
1982	15,804	2,165	17,969
1983	16,027	2,705	18,732
1984	20,344	2,668	23,012
1985	26,024	4,051	30,075
1986	34,657	4,863	39,520
1987	54,372	6,000	60,372
1988	57,553	6,707	64,260
1989	62,667	7,482	70,149
1990	66,151	7,767	73,918
1991	84,918	8,016	92,934
1992	73,664	8,274	81,938
1993	64,598	8,680	73,278
1994	93,444	12,672	106,116
1995	98,033	12,900	110,933
1996	98,430	13,010	111,440
1997	NA	NA	109,496
1998	94,299	9,771	104,070
1999	83,309	11,920	95,229
2000	138,821	18,500	157,321
2001	90,278	13,006	103,284

Kentucky's Top Deer Counties

Where's the best place to hunt deer in Kentucky? Well, if sheer numbers are what you're after, it's hard to beat Owen, Crittenden, Lawrence, Shelby and Christian counties.

In 2000, Owen County hunters bagged a state-high 3,098 whitetails, including 1,374 bucks. In Crittenden County, hunters bagged 2,597 deer (1,069 bucks). Rounding out the Top 5 were Lawrence, 2,368, (993); Shelby, 2,057, (938); and Christian, 2,027, (911).

KENTUCKY WHITETAIL RECORDS

•**Record harvest:** 157,321 (2000)
•**Record low harvest:** 3,476 (1976)
•**Bow-hunting record:** 18,500 (2000)
•**Gun-hunting record:** 138,821 (2000)

•**Season to remember:** 2001. Kentucky hunters kill 103,284 deer. Although that harvest is the seventh-highest in state history, it's about 35 percent lower than the record-breaking 2000 harvest.

Understanding Kentucky's New Deer-Tagging System

The 2002 hunting season marks the first year in which all Kentucky hunters must fill out a hunter harvest log for every deer they kill.

After killing a deer, document the date, county of kill, and sex of the animal on the hunter log, which should be supplied with your hunting license.

By 9 a.m. the day following the day you killed the deer, call (877) 245-4263 to check in the kill. The call is free and can be made from any touch-tone phone. When you call, you will be given a confirmation number. Write the number in the blank provided on the hunter log, and keep the log with you whenever you're afield during hunting season.

Tagging procedures also changed for the 2002 season. Deer tagging is only required when your deer leaves your immediate possession, such as during transport or while giving the deer to a butcher or taxidermist.

The tag must be attached so it remains fixed to the carcass until processing begins.

— KENTUCKY DEPARTMENT OF WILDLIFE

KENTUCKY SNAPSHOT

Deer Population: 611,191, 16th in U.S.

Average Harvest: 113,880, 20th in U.S.

Harvest Calculation Method: Mandatory registration.

Does State Predict Annual Harvest? Yes

How Close is Annual Prediction? 5%

Gun-Hunters: 199,500

Bow-Hunters: 72,450

Muzzleloading Hunters: 89,890

Hunter Education: Required for persons born after Jan. 1, 1975. Bow-hunter education is also required.

Orange Required for Gun-Hunting? Yes.

LOUISIANA
Pelican State
Harvest Ranking: #8

For more information, contact:
Department of Wildlife
Box 98000
Baton Rouge, LA 70898
(225) 765-2887   www.wlf.state.la.us

HISTORY OF LOUISIANA'S WHITETAIL HARVEST

Year	Firearm	Bow	Total
1960-61	16,500	NA	16,500
1961-62	NA	NA	NA
1962-63	NA	NA	NA
1963-64	24,000	NA	24,000
1964-65	23,000	NA	23,000
1965-66	26,000	NA	26,000
1966-67	32,500	NA	32,500
1967-68	36,000	NA	36,000
1968-69	50,000	NA	50,000
1969-70	53,000	NA	53,000
1970-71	53,500	NA	53,500
1971-72	61,000	NA	61,000
1972-73	65,000	NA	65,000
1973-74	74,500	NA	74,500
1974-75	82,000	NA	82,000
1975-76	77,000	NA	77,000
1976-77	84,500	NA	84,500
1977-78	82,500	NA	82,500
1978-79	85,000	NA	85,000
1979-80	90,000	5,000	95,000
1980-81	105,500	5,000	110,500
1981-82	115,000	5,500	120,500
1982-83	132,000	5,500	137,500
1983-84	131,000	6,000	137,000
1984-85	128,000	6,500	134,500
1985-86	139,000	7,500	146,500
1986-87	149,000	8,750	157,750
1987-88	164,000	9,500	173,500
1988-89	161,000	10,500	171,500
1989-90	162,000	11,000	173,000
1990-91	176,200	18,200	194,300
1991-92	186,400	17,700	204,100
1992-93	192,300	22,600	214,900
1993-94	193,000	20,100	213,100
1994-95	210,200	27,200	237,400
1995-96	208,500	26,200	234,700
1996-97	220,000	25,000	245,000
1997-98	243,400	24,200	267,600
1998-99	222,300	21,100	243,400
1999-00	246,900	20,500	267,400
2000-01 (estimated)	256,000	20,000	276,000

Hunter-Education Program Improves Hunting's Image

Every year, Louisiana hosts more than 600 hunter-education courses. State officials hope the extensive education program will continue to reduce hunting accidents, promote shooting sports and improve hunting's image through ethical and responsible conduct.

Anyone 10 and older can participate in the 10-hour course, which requires classroom attendance, passing a written test and completing a live-fire exercise.

After completing the course, students receive a Louisiana hunter-education certification card, which all other states recognize and is required for anyone born on or after Sept. 1, 1969, to purchase a Louisiana hunting license.

Most of the courses Louisiana offers are taught by volunteers recruited from schools, law-enforcement agencies, sportsmen's groups and other conservation organizations.

For information on a Hunter Safety Course or a duplicate card, contact an education coordinator in your area. For contact information, call (225) 765-2932.

LOUISIANA WHITETAIL RECORDS

- **Record harvest:** 276,000 (2000-01)
- **Record low harvest:** 16,500 (1960-61)
- **Bow-hunting record:** 27,200 (1994-95)
- **Gun-hunting record:** 256,000 (2000-01)

- **Season to remember:** 2000-01. Louisiana bow- and gun-hunters kill an estimated 276,000 whitetails, breaking the previous record harvest of 267,600, set in 1997-98.

LOUISIANA SNAPSHOT

Deer Population: 1 million, 7th in U.S.

Average Harvest: 259,880, 8th in U.S.

Harvest Calculation Method: Surveys

Does State Predict Annual Harvest? Yes

How Close is Annual Prediction? 10%

Gun-Hunters: 182,529

Bow-Hunters: 51,342

Muzzleloading Hunters: 51,494

Hunter Education: Required for persons born after Sept. 1, 1969. Bow-hunter education is not required.

Orange Required for Gun-Hunting? Yes.

MAINE
Pine Tree State
Harvest Ranking: #33

For more information, contact:
Department of Inland Fisheries and Wildlife
284 State St., State House Station 41
Augusta, ME 04333
(207) 287-2571   www.state.me.us/ifw

HISTORY OF MAINE'S DEER HARVEST

Year	Firearm	Bow	Total
1919	5,784	NA	5,784
1929	11,708	NA	11,708
1939	19,187	NA	19,187
1949	35,051	NA	35,051
1959	41,720	15	41,735
1969	30,388	21	30,409

THIRTY-YEAR HISTORY

Year	Firearm	Bow	Total
1970	31,738	12	31,750
1971	18,873	30	18,903
1972	28,664	34	28,698
1973	24,681	39	24,720
1974	34,602	65	34,667
1975	34,625	50	34,675
1976	29,918	47	29,965
1977	31,354	76	31,430
1978	28,905	97	29,002
1979	26,720	101	26,821
1980	37,148	107	37,255
1981	32,027	140	32,167
1982	28,709	125	28,834
1983	23,699	100	23,799
1984	19,225	133	19,358
1985	21,242	182	21,424
1986	19,290	302	19,592
1987	23,435	294	23,729
1988	27,754	302	28,056
1989	29,844	416	30,260
1990	25,658	319	25,977
1991	26,236	500	26,736
1992	28,126	694	28,820
1993	26,608	682	27,402
1994	23,967	716	24,683
1995	26,233	1,151	27,384
1996	27,601	774	28,375
1997	30,149	1,003	31,152
1998	26,996	1,245	28,241
1999	29,361	2,112	31,473
2000	34,724	2,161	36,885
2001	25,558	2,211	27,769

MAINE WHITETAIL RECORDS

•**Record harvest:** 41,735 (1959)
•**Record low harvest:** 5,784 (1919)
•**Bow-hunting record:** 2,211 (2001)
•**Gun-hunting record:** 41,730 (1951)

•**Season to remember:** 1999. After decades of relatively low deer harvests, Maine bow-hunters kill a record 2,112 whitetails.

Maine Whitetails Peaked When Other Herds Faltered

The whitetail's story is relatively similar throughout North America: Deer populations were exploited during the 19th century, dwindled to all-time lows in the early 20th century, then grew steadily to all-time highs by the late 1990s. Maine, however, has followed a different trend. There, peak deer populations and harvests occurred in the 1950s, when harvests averaged 38,000 deer. What's more, Maine hunters killed a record 41,735 deer in 1959, a time when most state's deer harvests were a fraction of today's levels.

During recent times, however, Maine's deer harvests have been lower, ranging from 19,500 to 31,000 since 1984. In fact, Maine's Department of Inland Fisheries and Wildlife has recently limited antlerless harvests to increase the deer population.

Despite today's lower harvests and deer populations, Maine hunters have some of the best opportunities in history to kill big bucks. For example, recent buck harvests are 50 percent higher than those from 1978-82. Plus, about one out of five bucks killed by Maine hunters is at least 4½ years old.

— MAINE DEPT. OF INLAND FISHERIES AND WILDLIFE

MAINE SNAPSHOT

Deer Population: 342,000, 22nd in U.S.

Average Harvest: 31,104, 33rd in U.S.

Harvest Calculation Method: Mandatory registration.

Does State Predict Annual Harvest? Yes

How Close is Annual Prediction? 5%

Gun-Hunters: 175,200

Bow-Hunters: 9,250

Muzzleloading Hunters: 11,000

Hunter Education: Required for all first-time hunters. Bow-hunter education is also required.

Orange Required for Gun-Hunting? Yes.

MARYLAND
Old Line State

Harvest Ranking: #26

For more information, contact:

Division of Wildlife
4220 Steele Neck Road
Vienna, MD 21869

(410) 260-8200   www.dnr.state.md.us

HISTORY OF MARYLAND'S WHITETAIL HARVEST

Year	Firearm	Bow	Total
1983	16,239	2,181	18,420
1984	17,324	2,501	19,825
1985	17,241	2,549	19,790
1986	22,411	3,404	25,815
1987	24,846	4,216	29,062
1988	27,625	5,983	33,608
1989	38,305	7,988	46,293
1990	37,712	8,605	46,317
1991	36,169	10,454	46,623
1992	39,858	11,240	51,098
1993	39,429	11,251	51,234
1994	39,547	11,324	50,871
1995	49,237	12,397	61,634
1996	39,048	13,588	52,636
1997	52,600	12,919	65,519
1998	57,270	16,300	93,570
1999	59,963	16,214	76,177
2000	66,535	18,241	84,776
2001	65,431	18,356	83,787

Maryland Recognizes Outstanding Bucks

Each year, the Maryland Bowhunters Society and the DNR co-sponsor the *Maryland Trophy Deer Contest*. This contest recognizes hunters who have killed big bucks and promotes Quality Deer Management in Maryland.

The contest is open only for deer taken legally in Maryland. A possession tag is required. Deer taken with crop damage permits and road-killed deer are not eligible.

For more information, contact the Maryland Department of Natural Resources at the address/phone number listed at the top of this page.

MARYLAND WHITETAIL RECORDS

•**Record harvest:** 93,570 (1998)
•**Record low harvest:** 18,420 (1983)
•**Bow-hunting record:** 18,356 (2001)
•**Gun-hunting record:** 66,535 (2000)

•**Season to remember:** 2001. Maryland bow-hunters kill a record 18,356 deer — about 22 percent of the total harvest.

Maryland Laws Protect Sportsmen from Anti-Hunters

Despite Maryland's largely urban, nonhunting public, the state's recently adopted regulations protect hunters from animal-rightists' meddling.

If Maryland's Division of Wildlife believes hunters in a given area might encounter significant interference by anti-hunters, it may adopt regulations to prohibit that disruption.

For example, if a hunter is on private land or in a state hunting area managed by the Division of Wildlife, another person may not intentionally disrupt the hunter's lawful killing of wildlife, or harass, drive or disturb game animals to prevent a successful hunt.

To combat such activities, a natural resources officer or other Delaware police officer may order the violator to desist or to leave the area. If the person resists, the officers arrest the person.

Of course, these regulations do not apply to incidental interference, which arises from lawful activity, such as mining, farming, logging or outdoor recreation.

— MARYLAND DIVISION OF WILDLIFE

MARYLAND SNAPSHOT

Deer Population: 224,000, 27th in U.S.

Average Harvest: 80,766, 26th in U.S.

Harvest Calculation Method: Mandatory registration.

Does State Predict Annual Harvest? No

How Close is Annual Prediction? NA

Gun-Hunters: 69,400

Bow-Hunters: 35,770

Muzzleloading Hunters: 37,200

Hunter Education: Required for persons born after July 1, 1977. Bow-hunter education is not required.

Orange Required for Gun-Hunting? Yes.

MASSACHUSETTS
Bay State
Harvest Ranking: #39

For more information, contact:
Massachusetts Wildlife
Westborough, MA 01581
(617) 727-1614
www.state.ma.us/dfwele

HISTORY OF MASSACHUSETTS' DEER HARVEST

Year	Firearm	Bow	Total
1989	5,818	890	6,708
1990	5,829	1,061	6,890
1991	8,085	1,378	9,463
1992	8,470	1,570	10,040
1993	6,514	1,387	8,345
1994	7,545	1,587	9,132
1995	9,158	1,901	11,059
1996	7,029	1,687	8,714
1997	8,473	1,813	10,286
1998	7,501	1,803	9,304
1999	7,042	2,466	9,508
2000	8,297	2,765	11,096
2001	6,915	2,914	9,930*

*includes 101 tribal deer-kills

Massachusetts Encourages Women Hunters

In an effort to attract more women to outdoor sports, Massachusetts holds several "Becoming an Outdoor Woman" programs each year.

This program focuses on outdoor skills — skills traditionally passed from father to son — but valuable to anyone wishing to enjoy outdoor pursuits. A sampling of workshop offerings can include fishing, shooting, kayaking, orienteering, reading the woods, archery, pond and stream adventures, nature photography and game cooking. Designed primarily for women, it is an opportunity for anyone 18 or older who want an opportunity to learn outdoor skills. The program is co-sponsored by the Massachusetts Sportsmen's Council.

For more information, contact the Massachusetts Division of Wildlife at the address/phone number listed at the top of this page, or visit the Web site: www.magnet.state.ma.us

MASSACHUSETTS DEER RECORDS

•**Record harvest:** 11,096 (2000)
•**Record low harvest:** 6,708 (1989)
•**Bow-hunting record:** 2,914 (2001)
•**Gun-hunting record:** 9,158 (1995)

•**Season to remember:** 2000. Massachusetts bow- and gun-hunters kill a record 11,096 whitetails, about 25 percent of which were bow-kills.

Hunters Experience Near-Record Season

The 2001 Massachusetts deer harvest will likely rank as the fourth-highest in state history. Preliminary figures, which were generated by phone calls to 73 deer-check stations around the state, suggest bow-hunters killed 2,886 deer, gun-hunters killed 6,014 and muzzleloaders tagged 846. Paraplegic hunters killed four deer during the special hunt for disabled sportsmen.

The 9,750 deer total places 2001 behind only the 2000 (11,096), 1995 (11,059) and 1997 (10,286) seasons. Hunters also killed another 101 deer as part of the Quabbin Reservation controlled hunt.

Although the harvest was one of Massachusetts' highest, state wildlife officials believe it could have been much higher. Biologists blame the slightly lower harvest on lower hunter numbers, an abundant mast crop, unseasonably warm temperatures during the firearms season and less hunter access caused by development. In coming seasons, Massachusetts hopes to maintain its deer harvest levels, thus balancing deer populations with habitat and social carrying capacity. This task will likely become more difficult as hunter deterrents worsen.

— MASSACHUSETTS WILDLIFE

MASSACHUSETTS SNAPSHOT

Deer Population: 90,000, 31st in U.S.

Average Harvest: 10,025, 39th in U.S.

Harvest Calculation Method: Mandatory registration.

Does State Predict Annual Harvest? No

How Close is Annual Prediction? NA

Gun-Hunters: 61,500

Bow-Hunters: 25,500

Muzzleloading Hunters: 18,150

Hunter Education: Required for first-time hunters and hunters ages 15 to 18. Bow-hunter education is not required.

Orange Required for Gun-Hunting? Yes.

MICHIGAN
Wolverine State
Harvest Ranking: #2

For more information, contact:
Department of Natural Resources
Box 30028
Lansing, MI 48909
www.dnr.state.mi.us

HISTORY OF MICHIGAN'S WHITETAIL HARVEST

Year	Firearm	Bow	Total
1878	NA	NA	21,000
1899	NA	NA	12,000
1911	NA	NA	12,000
1920	NA	NA	25,000
1929	NA	NA	28,710
1939	44,770	6	44,776
1949	77,750	780	78,530
1959	115,400	1,840	117,240
1969	106,698	2,582	109,280

THIRTY-YEAR HISTORY

Year	Firearms	Bow	Total
1970	68,843	3,187	72,030
1971	62,076	3,354	65,430
1972	55,796	3,694	59,490
1973	66,359	4,631	70,990
1974	92,111	7,969	100,080
1975	106,800	8,790	115,590
1976	107,625	10,365	117,990
1977	137,110	21,250	158,360
1978	145,710	25,140	170,850
1979	119,790	25,640	145,430
1980	137,380	28,110	165,490
1981	175,090	33,320	208,410
1982	163,520	38,420	201,940
1983	127,770	30,640	158,410
1984	131,280	32,630	163,910
1985	197,370	42,050	239,420
1986	219,260	57,960	277,220
1987	265,860	72,820	338,680
1988	311,770	72,020	383,790
1989	355,410	97,080	452,490
1990	338,890	93,800	432,690
1991	318,460	115,880	434,340
1992	274,650	99,990	374,640
1993	232,820	98,160	330,980
1994	251,420	112,490	363,910
1995	346,830	132,130	478,960
1996	319,289	100,000	419,289
1997	282,000	100,000	382,000
1998	329,000	121,000	450,000
1999	402,280	142,615	544,895
2000	412,775	128,926	541,701

MICHIGAN WHITETAIL RECORDS

- **Record harvest:** 544,895 (1999)
- **Record low harvest:** 8,000 (1916)
- **Bow-hunting record:** 142,615 (1999)
- **Gun-hunting record:** 412,775 (2000)

- **Season to remember:** 1999. Michigan hunters break several state records, including the all-time harvest. The overall harvest is second only to Wisconsin's 2000 harvest of 618,274 whitetails.

Special Seasons Encourage Michigan's Young Deer Hunters

The Michigan Department of Natural Resources goes the extra mile to encourage parents, guardians and other adult hunters to take young people hunting. The DNR stresses that passing on the hunting heritage to hunting's next generation also helps youngsters learn valuable lessons about responsibility, ethics and conservation.

Michigan holds a youth firearms deer season in late September on all lands in the state. Youths 12 to 16 may kill one deer during this special two-day season. Twelve- and 13-year-olds are restricted to archery-only hunting.

To participate in Michigan's youth deer season, young hunters must be accompanied by an adult 18 or older. The accompanying adult cannot carry a firearm or bow and does not need a deer hunting license.

Hunters Contribute to Michigan's Economy

As renewable resources, hunting and fishing are important to Michigan's economy. Hunters spend more than $800 million each year, and anglers, including 334,000 nonresidents, spend nearly $1 billion annually.

MICHIGAN SNAPSHOT

Deer Population: 1.9 million, 2nd in U.S.

Average Harvest: 455,029, 2nd in U.S.

Harvest Calculation Method: Surveys

Does State Predict Annual Harvest? No

How Close is Annual Prediction? NA

Gun-Hunters: 721,980

Bow-Hunters: 351,077

Muzzleloading Hunters: 174,505

Hunter Education: Required for persons born after Jan. 1, 1969. Bow-hunter education is not required.

Orange Required for Gun-Hunting? Yes.

MINNESOTA
Gopher State
Harvest Ranking: #14

For more information, contact:
Department of Natural Resources
Box 7, 500 Lafayette Road
St. Paul, MN 55155
(651) 296-4506   www.dnr.state.mn.us

HISTORY OF MINNESOTA'S WHITETAIL HARVEST

Year	Firearm	Bow	Total
1918	9,000	NA	9,000
1928	27,300	NA	27,300
1938	44,500	NA	44,500
1948	61,600	NA	61,600
1958	75,000	403	75,403
1968	103,000	819	103,819
1978	57,800	2,608	60,408
1988	138,900	8,262	147,162

THIRTY-YEAR HISTORY

Year	Firearms	Bow	Total
1970	50,000	453	50,453
1971	closed	1,279	1,279
1972	73,400	1,601	75,001
1973	67,100	1,935	69,035
1974	65,000	2,176	67,176
1975	63,600	2,265	65,865
1976	36,200	1,167	37,367
1977	58,100	2,609	60,709
1978	57,800	2,608	60,408
1979	55,400	2,578	57,978
1980	77,100	3,641	80,741
1981	108,100	5,535	113,635
1982	107,000	5,566	112,566
1983	NA	5,977	NA
1984	132,000	6,390	138,390
1985	138,000	7,575	145,575
1986	129,800	7,610	137,410
1987	135,000	7,535	142,535
1988	138,900	8,262	147,162
1989	129,600	9,307	138,907
1990	166,600	11,106	177,706
1991	206,300	12,964	219,264
1992	230,064	13,004	243,068
1993	188,109	13,722	202,928
1994	180,008	13,818	193,826
1995	200,645	14,521	215,166
1996	142,979	14,338	157,317
1997	130,069	13,258	143,327
1998	146,548	12,306	158,854
1999	166,487	13,000	179,487
2000	193,754	15,746	209,500
2001	201,557	15,895	217,452

MINNESOTA WHITETAIL RECORDS

•**Record harvest:** 243,068 (1992)
•**Record low harvest:** 1,279 (1971)
•**Bow-hunting record:** 15,895 (2001)
•**Gun-hunting record:** 230,064 (1992)

•**Season to remember:** 1928. In an era when most states' deer herds were all but nonexistent, Minnesota hunters kill 27,300 whitetails.

Minnesotans Are Confident in Their Hunting Prospects

The Minnesota Department of Natural Resources recently completed one of the most comprehensive deer hunter surveys in state history. The survey asked hunters about their views on a variety of deer issues, including population status, regulation complexity, season structure and quality deer management. Here's a look at a few of the survey's most interesting findings.

✓ 91 percent of hunters were very or somewhat satisfied with their hunting experiences.

✓ 68 percent of hunters disagreed that there were too many hunters in the area they hunt.

✓ 73 percent of firearms hunters support the current season timing — 74 percent approve of the current season length.

✓ 72 percent of Minnesota deer hunters hunt private land — this is especially interesting because 23 percent of the state, more than 11 million acres, is publicly owned.

✓ 82 percent of hunters strongly or moderately believe there are enough deer where they hunt, which is surprising considering that Minnesota's average harvest is almost 300,000 less than neighboring Wisconsin's.

✓ 53 percent of respondents were not familiar with quality deer management.

MINNESOTA SNAPSHOT

Deer Population: 960,000, 10th in U.S.

Average Harvest: 181,724, 14th in U.S.

Harvest Calculation Method: Mandatory registration.

Does State Predict Annual Harvest? No

How Close is Annual Prediction? NA

Gun-Hunters: 460,300

Bow-Hunters: 70,218

Muzzleloading Hunters: 11,037

Hunter Education: Required for persons born after Jan. 1, 1980. Bow-hunter education is not required.

Orange Required for Gun-Hunting? Yes.

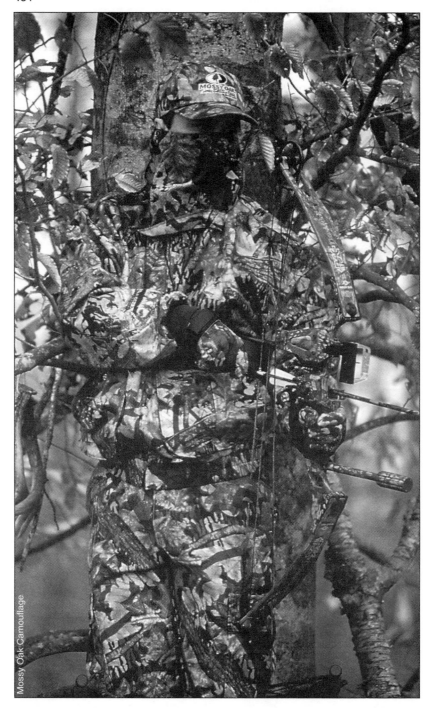

Mossy Oak Camouflage

MISSISSIPPI
Magnolia State
Harvest Ranking: #7

For more information, contact:
Department of Conservation
Southport Mall, Box 451
Jackson, MS 39205

(800) 546-4868   www.mdwfp.com

HISTORY OF MISSISSIPPI'S WHITETAIL HARVEST

Year	Firearm	Bow	Total
1971	580	39	619
1972	816	53	869
1973	919	57	976
1974	NA	NA	NA
1975	NA	NA	NA
1976	2,529	975	3,504
1977	NA	NA	NA
1978	NA	NA	NA
1979	NA	NA	NA
1980	184,163	17,437	201,600
1981	196,856	14,860	211,716
1982	227,432	16,222	243,654
1983	176,400	19,747	196,147
1984	209,574	17,815	227,389
1985	216,959	18,120	235,079
1986	237,075	19,209	256,284
1987	240,337	24,662	264,999
1988	236,012	28,744	264,756
1989	236,012	28,744	262,386
1990	218,347	29,982	249,572
1991	243,175	33,940	277,714
1992	260,093	40,886	300,980
1993	229,425	32,971	262,409
1994	262,342	47,345	309,687
1995	286,293	48,669	334,962
1996	289,399	44,574	333,973
1997	284,190	48,119	332,309
1998	256,692	38,406	295,098
2000	243,000	33,000	276,000
2001	NA	NA	NA

Ample Land and Deer Make Mississippi a Hunting Leader

Mississippi has more than 800,000 acres of public hunting lands held in 38 intensively managed wildlife management areas. Mississippi also has one of the country's largest deer populations, making the state a prime hunting destination.

MISSISSIPPI WHITETAIL RECORDS

•**Record harvest:** 334,962 (1995-96)
•**Record low harvest:** 619 (1971)
•**Bow-hunting record:** 48,669 (1995-96)
•**Gun-hunting record:** 289,399 (1996-97)

•**Season to remember:** 1995-96. Mississippi bow- and gun-hunters kill a record 334,962 deer. Less than 20 years earlier, the harvest was 3,504 — almost 99 percent less.

Management Has Changed Mississippi Deer Hunting

In many ways, the history of deer management in Mississippi mirrors that of other states. Namely, the state experienced some of its lowest deer numbers at the beginning of the 20th century, and those numbers gradually grew to all-time highs less than 100 years later. By then, hunters were putting excessive pressure on yearling bucks and neglecting doe harvests, resulting in an unbalanced herd with few big bucks.

To combat this, Southern hunters began the Deer Management Assistance Program in 1978. The program advocated killing more antlerless deer and sparing young bucks.

However, change was slow to come in Mississippi. Harvest data indicate 60 percent to 70 percent of the state's 1987-88 harvest was 1½-year-old bucks. To change these trends, Mississippi increased public-educational efforts.

It worked.

Doe harvests became more accepted, and in 1995, the state changed the bag limit and instituted the "Four Points or Better" law, which stipulated that hunters may only kill bucks with four or more points per side. Today, more than 40 percent of the state's buck harvest is composed of mature animals.

— MISSISSIPPI WILDLIFE, FISHERIES & PARKS

MISSISSIPPI SNAPSHOT

Deer Population: 1.5 million, 5th in U.S.

Average Harvest: 314,468, 7th in U.S.

Harvest Calculation Method: Surveys

Does State Predict Annual Harvest? No

How Close is Annual Prediction? NA

Gun-Hunters: 182,000

Bow-Hunters: 49,500

Muzzleloading Hunters: 49,000

Hunter Education: Required for persons born after Jan. 1, 1972. Bow-hunter education is not required.

Orange Required for Gun-Hunting? Yes.

MISSOURI
Show-Me State
Harvest Ranking: #11

For more information, contact:

Department of Conservation
Box 180
Jefferson City, MO 65102-0180
(573) 751-4115
www.conservation.state.mo.us

HISTORY OF MISSOURI'S WHITETAIL HARVEST

Year	Firearm	Bow	Total
1944	583	NA	583
1948	1,432	NA	1,432
1952	7,466	2	7,468
1956	7,864	33	7,897
1960	17,418	263	17,681
1964	20,619	316	20,935
1968	22,090	559	22,649

THIRTY-YEAR HISTORY

Year	Firearm	Bow	Total
1970	28,400	828	29,228
1971	31,722	962	32,684
1972	30,084	1,130	31,214
1973	33,438	1,285	34,723
1974	29,262	1,437	30,699
1975	51,823	1,850	53,673
1976	40,683	1,973	42,656
1977	36,562	2,199	38,761
1978	40,261	2,781	43,042
1979	53,164	3,327	56,491
1980	49,426	3,661	53,087
1981	50,183	3,495	53,678
1982	55,852	4,191	60,043
1983	57,801	4,626	62,427
1984	71,569	5,134	76,703
1985	80,792	5,621	86,413
1986	102,879	5,832	108,711
1987	132,500	8,077	140,577
1988	139,726	10,183	149,909
1989	157,506	10,970	168,476
1990	161,857	11,118	172,975
1991	149,112	14,096	164,384
1992	150,873	15,029	166,929
1993	156,704	14,696	172,120
1994	164,624	17,136	181,760
1995	187,406	20,077	207,483
1996	190,770	23,566	214,336
1997	196,283	20,915	217,198
1998	207,764	20,000	227,764
1999	193,720	23,414	217,134
2000	220,495	23,558	244,053
2001	234,752	26,165	257,910

MISSOURI WHITETAIL RECORDS

• **Record harvest:** 257,910 (2001)
• **Record low harvest:** 583 (1944)
• **Bow-hunting record:** 23,566 (1996)
• **Gun-hunting record:** 236,143 (2001)

• **Season to remember:** 2001. Missouri bow- and gun-hunters kill 257,910 deer, surpassing the previous record of 244,053, set in 2000. In addition, a regulations change that allowed muzzleloaders to purchase a muzzleloading tag and a modern firearms tag spurred an 80 percent higher muzzleloading harvest.

A Missouri Success Story

The history of white-tailed deer in Missouri parallels that of many states. Pre-settlement populations were sizable and well-distributed with largest concentrations occurring on the more fertile soils and diversified habitats found in northern Missouri. The actual size of the Missouri deer population during pre-settlement times is unknown, but was estimated to be in excess of 700,000.

By 1890, deer had disappeared from northern and western counties. Extensive logging, overgrazing by domestic livestock and annual burning, coupled with uncontrolled market hunting almost led to the extirpation of white-tailed deer from Missouri by the early 1900s.

The first effective conservation legislation was passed in 1905 when a 2-month bucks-only season was established. By 1925, deer season was closed. For the first time, deer management began to progress beyond the mere passage and enforcement of legislation. Land was acquired and established as wildlife refuges, and Michigan deer were imported and released on these areas. A 4-day season was restored in 1931, but deer restocking continued until 1957.

— MISSOURI DEPT. OF CONSERVATION

MISSOURI SNAPSHOT

Deer Population: 850,000, 13th in U.S.

Average Harvest: 232,812, 11th in U.S.

Harvest Calculation Method: Mandatory registration.

Does State Predict Annual Harvest? Yes

How Close is Annual Prediction? 10%

Gun-Hunters: 435,448

Bow-Hunters: 96,982

Muzzleloading Hunters: 15,500

Hunter Education: Required for persons born after Jan. 1, 1967. Bow-hunter education is not required.

Orange Required for Gun-Hunting? Yes.

MONTANA
Treasure State
Harvest Ranking: #27

For more information, contact:
Department of Fish and Wildlife
1420 E. Sixth Ave.
Helena, MT 59620
(900) 225-5397   www.fwp.state.mt.us

HISTORY OF MONTANA'S ANNUAL DEER HARVEST

Year	Firearm	Bow	Total
1984	NA	NA	56,760
1985	NA	NA	43,019
1986	NA	NA	44,733
1987	NA	NA	40,675
1988	NA	NA	43,971
1989	NA	NA	44,261
1990	NA	NA	49,419
1991	NA	NA	56,789
1992	58,565	2,067	60,632
1993	60,369	2,038	62,407
1994	67,577	1,857	69,434
1995	60,907	1,636	62,543
1996	76,487	1,800	78,287
1997	70,000	1,600	71,600
1998	84,445	1,500	85,945
1999	41,798	3,031	44,809
2000	45,242	6,212	51,454

*Totals before 1998 include mule deer harvest figures.

Montana Harbors Big Whitetails

Montana has a reputation as a top-notch elk hunting state, but its deer hunting opportunities are what lure most hunters.

Known for record-class whitetails and mule deer, Montana attracts more than 160,000 deer hunters annually. In fact, 70 percent of all big-game hunters in Montana hunt strictly for deer.

Including elk hunters and small-game hunters, Montana hunters spend more than $215 million each year to hunt the Treasure State. That's an average of $954 per hunter.

In 1996, Montana hunters spent more than $116 million on hunting equipment, according to a survey by the United States Fish & Wildlife Service.

MONTANA WHITETAIL RECORDS

•**Record harvest:** 85,945 (1998)
•**Record low harvest:** 40,675 (1987)
•**Bow-hunting record:** 6,212 (2000)
•**Gun-hunting record:** 84,445 (1998)

•**Season to remember:** 1999. For the first time in state history, Montana segregate mule deer and whitetail harvest figures. Montana hunters kill 44,809 whitetails.

Block Management Areas Offer Hunting Opportunities

Do you think private land is out of reach? If so, consider Montana. Through a unique arrangement between private landowners and Montana's Fish Wildlife and Parks, Block Management provides the public with free hunting access to certain private and isolated public lands.

There is no charge to hunt on block management lands — referred to as Block Management Areas or BMAs. Program funding comes from the sale of nonresident upland gamebird licenses and nonresident variable-priced, outfitter-sponsored combination deer/elk licenses.

Landowner participation is voluntary. Contracts are negotiated annually in the spring and summer, and some fluctuations in enrolled acreage occur from year to year. After enrollment is complete, each FWP administrative region publishes a Block Management Hunting Guide, which lists the block management opportunities available to you for the current season.

In 2001, approximately 1,100 landowners enrolled nearly 8.3 million acres in the program.
— MONTANA DEPT. OF FISH AND WILDLIFE

MONTANA SNAPSHOT

Deer Population: 400,000, 19th in U.S.

Average Harvest: 68,640, 27th in U.S.

Harvest Calculation Method: Surveys and automobile checks.

Does State Predict Annual Harvest? Yes

How Close is Annual Prediction? 20%

Gun-Hunters: 157,090

Bow-Hunters: 27,011

Muzzleloading Hunters: 2,020

Hunter Education: Required for persons 12-17. Bow-hunter education is required for all first-time bow-hunters.

Orange Required for Gun-Hunting? Yes.

NEBRASKA
Cornhusker State
Harvest Ranking: #31

For more information, contact:
Nebraska Game and Parks
Box 508
Bassett, NE 68714-0508
(402) 471-0641   www.ngpc.state.ne.us

HISTORY OF NEBRASKA'S WHITETAIL HARVEST

Year	Firearm	Bow	Total
1945	2	0	2
1949	0	0	0
1952	7	0	7
1955	189	0	189
1958	340	103	443
1961	1,443	198	1,641
1964	5,138	326	5,464
1969	5,440	524	5,964

THIRTY-YEAR HISTORY

Year	Firearms	Bow	Total
1970	6,460	654	7,114
1971	6,343	662	7,005
1972	5,635	624	6,259
1973	7,090	865	7,955
1974	7,894	1,032	8,926
1975	8,404	1,155	9,559
1976	7,595	831	8,426
1977	5,921	769	6,690
1978	6,164	958	7,122
1979	7,899	1,151	9,050
1980	9,939	1,639	11,578
1981	11,364	2,025	13,389
1982	12,957	2,049	15,006
1983	15,980	2,781	18,761
1984	19,679	2,471	22,150
1985	20,930	2,593	23,523
1986	22,859	2,291	25,150
1987	24,266	2,812	27,078
1988	24,938	2,951	27,889
1989	24,359	2,847	27,206
1990	21,973	2,716	24,689
1991	20,820	2,931	23,751
1992	20,125	3,141	23,266
1993	23,377	3,282	26,683
1994	26,050	3,830	29,880
1995	26,000	4,000	34,160
1996	30,400	4,500	34,560
1997	41,700	3,900	45,600
1998	38,085	3,887	41,972
1999	37,263	4,254	41,490
2000	39,200	4,300	43,500
2001	55,377	4,141	59,518

NEBRASKA WHITETAIL RECORDS

•**Record harvest:** 59,518 (2001)
•**Record low harvest:** 0 (1949)
•**Bow-hunting record:** 4,500 (1996)
•**Gun-hunting record:** 55,377 (2001)

•**Season to remember:** 1949. With Nebraska's modern deer season in its infancy, the state's hunters experienced a trying season, failing to kill any deer.

Chronic Wasting Disease Taking Heavy Toll in Nebraska

Nebraska biologists made an ominous discovery in Fall 2001, when a wild mule deer killed by a hunter tested positive for chronic wasting disease, the fatal brain disease spreading through wild cervid populations in Colorado, Wyoming, South Dakota, Saskatchewan and Wisconsin.

After the discovery, state biologists faced a paradox: they had to decimate the deer population in Sioux County, Neb., to save the herd.

To stop the disease's spread, the state instituted an unlimited-bag, antlerless-only deer season in northern Sioux County, running from Oct. 28 to the Friday nearest Feb. 15.

Biologists hope the season will lower deer densities 50 percent. After hunters accomplish this goal, the season will be structured to indefinitely maintain the area's deer density at about 10 deer per square mile.

Researchers have found no evidence that CWD can infect human. However, hunters should not eat venison from deer that appear sick.

— RYAN GILLIGAN

NEBRASKA SNAPSHOT

Deer Population: 300,000, 23rd in U.S.

Average Harvest: 46,416, 31st in U.S.

Harvest Calculation Method: Mandatory registration.

Does State Predict Annual Harvest? No

How Close is Annual Prediction? NA

Gun-Hunters: 86,400

Bow-Hunters: 15,760

Muzzleloading Hunters: 17,800

Hunter Education: Required for persons born after Jan. 1, 1977. Bow-hunter education is required.

Orange Required for Gun-Hunting? Yes.

NEW HAMPSHIRE
Granite State
Harvest Ranking: #38

For more information, contact:
New Hampshire Fish & Game
Region 1, Rt. 2, Box 241
Lancaster, NH 03584
(603) 271-3422
www.wildlife.state.nh.us

HISTORY OF NEW HAMPSHIRE'S DEER HARVEST

Year	Firearm	Bow	Total
1922	1,896	NA	1,896
1932	1,687	NA	1,687
1942	4,844	NA	4,844
1952	6,932	NA	6,932
1962	7,917	5	7,922

TEN-YEAR HISTORY

Year	Firearm	Bow	Total
1970	7,214	17	7,231
1971	7,263	12	7,275
1972	6,923	20	6,943
1973	5,440	22	5,462
1974	6,875	20	6,895
1975	8,308	24	8,332
1976	9,076	14	9,090
1977	6,877	62	6,939
1978	5,545	57	5,602
1979	4,939	42	4,981
1980	5,353	31	5,384
1981	6,028	125	6,153
1982	4,577	97	4,674
1983	3,156	124	3,280
1984	4,169	120	4,289
1985	5,523	148	5,671
1986	6,557	263	6,820
1987	5,864	257	6,121
1988	5,900	225	6,125
1989	6,749	489	7,238
1990	6,466	482	7,872
1991	8,060	732	8,792
1992	9,013	1,202	10,215
1993	9,012	877	9,889
1994	7,478	901	8,379
1995	9,627	1,580	11,207
1996	8,901	1,462	10,363
1997	10,042	1,758	11,800
1998	8,236	1,549	9,785
1999	8,722	1,981	10,703
2000	8,889	1,970	10,859
2001	7,566	1,577	9,143

NEW HAMPSHIRE DEER RECORDS

•**Record harvest:** 14,186 (1967)
•**Record low harvest:** 1,402 (1923)
•**Bow-hunting record:** 1,981 (1999)
•**Gun-hunting record:** 14,153 (1967)

•**Season to remember:** 1962. Five deer fall to New Hampshire bow-hunters — the first bow-killed deer in recorded history. By 1995, bow-hunters were killing about 15 percent of the state's total harvest.

Deer Herd is Rebounding

Although recent winters have been mild, Winter 2000-01 proved hard on New Hampshire whitetails.

To compensate for winter-killed deer, the 2001 season featured regulations that protected does to allow for herd recovery and continued growth. Although New Hampshire hunters killed fewer antlerless deer in Fall 2001, hunters took advantage of the state's quality buck population. Hunters set a state record in 2000 by harvesting 6,554 adult bucks — several of which were trophy-class animals.

The 2000 harvest of 10,859 deer was the third highest in the past decade. The harvest included 7,472 bucks and 3,387 does.

New Hampshire has a long history of deer hunting with attractive hunting seasons. The 92-day archery season offers opportunities over the course of 4 months. The early muzzleloader season is unique to New Hampshire and is often viewed as the premiere time of the year to be deer hunting. Finally, the 26-day firearms season often sees significant snow, helping hunters see and kill more deer.

— KIP ADAMS

NEW HAMPSHIRE SNAPSHOT

Deer Population: 75,000, 32nd in U.S.

Average Harvest: 10,458, 38th in U.S.

Harvest Calculation Method: Mandatory registration.

Does State Predict Annual Harvest? No
How Close is Annual Prediction? NA

Gun-Hunters: 68,833
Bow-Hunters: 22,353
Muzzleloading Hunters: 30,564

Hunter Education: Required for persons born after 1971. Bow-hunter education is not required.

Orange Required for Gun-Hunting? No.

NEW JERSEY
Garden State
Harvest Ranking: #28

For more information, contact:
Division of Fish & Wildlife
Box 418
Port Republic, NJ 08241
(609) 748-2044   www.state.nj.us/dep/fgw

HISTORY OF NEW JERSEY'S WHITETAIL HARVEST

Year	Firearm	Bow	Total
1909	86	NA	86
1919	353	NA	353
1929	1,331	NA	1,331
1939	2,336	NA	2,336
1949	3,618	9	3,627
1959	9,612	1,230	10,842
1969	7,121	1,356	8,477

THIRTY-YEAR HISTORY

Year	Firearm	Bow	Total
1970	6,866	1,387	8,253
1971	6,111	1,434	7,545
1972	9,557	1,464	11,021
1973	9,629	1,689	11,318
1974	11,429	1,717	13,146
1975	10,675	2,013	12,688
1976	10,908	2,110	13,018
1977	11,828	2,591	14,419
1978	13,177	2,641	15,818
1979	13,843	2,263	16,106
1980	16,030	5,161	21,191
1981	16,291	5,846	22,137
1982	16,817	6,928	23,745
1983	16,403	6,902	23,305
1984	17,920	7,699	25,619
1985	21,480	7,971	29,451
1986	23,590	10,187	33,777
1987	27,415	11,813	39,228
1988	33,140	12,760	45,900
1989	34,812	13,714	48,526
1990	34,372	13,850	48,222
1991	29,936	15,480	45,416
1992	31,257	16,418	47,675
1993	32,936	17,006	49,942
1994	32,602	18,840	51,442
1995	39,176	20,593	59,769
1996	36,709	19,995	56,704
1997	39,290	20,261	59,551
1998	39,039	20,975	60,014
1999	50,266	25,132	75,398
2000	52,602	24,842	77,444
2001	45,153	23,516	68,669

NEW JERSEY WHITETAIL RECORDS

•**Record harvest:** 77,444 (2000)
•**Record low harvest:** 86 (1909)
•**Bow-hunting record:** 25,132 (1999)
•**Gun-hunting record:** 52,602 (2000)

•**Season to remember:** 1949. New Jersey
bow-hunters kill nine whitetails — the first
recorded bow-kills in state history.
Amazingly, by 2001, bow kills constituted
more than half of the New Jersey's harvest.

New Jersey Recognizes Outstanding Whitetails

Although heavily populated by humans,
New Jersey produces some bruiser white-
tails. To better recognize New Jersey's
bucks, the Division of Fish and Wildlife, the
New Jersey State Federation of Sportsmen's
Clubs, the United Bowhunters of New
Jersey and the Atlantic County Federation of
Sportsmen's Clubs, formed the The
Outstanding White-tailed Deer Program,.
The program was initiated in 1964 and
includes categories for the heaviest deer and
those with the highest-scoring rack.

Typical and nontypical racks are judged
separately. The minimum score is 125 for
typicals and 135 for nontypicals.

Weight categories for the heaviest deer
taken are also subdivided: bucks 200 pounds
and above taken by shotgun, bow and
muzzleloader and does 135 and above taken
by shotgun , bow and muzzleloader. Does
may be weighed on an official deer check
station scale, however, bucks must be
weighed on a certified scale.

Age, health, genetics and nutrition are
the major factors contributing to deer reaching trophy status.

NEW JERSEY SNAPSHOT

Deer Population: 165,500, 28th in U.S.
Average Harvest: 68,215, 28th in U.S.
Harvest Calculation Method: Mandatory
registration.
Does State Predict Annual Harvest? Yes
How Close is Annual Prediction? 5%
Gun-Hunters: 94,900
Bow-Hunters: 45,350
Muzzleloading Hunters: 24,240
Hunter Education: Required for first-time
hunters. Bow-hunter education is also
required.
Orange Required for Gun-Hunting? Yes.

NEW YORK

Empire State

Harvest Ranking: #9

For more information, contact:

Department of Conservation
50 Wolf Road
Albany, NY 12233

(518) 402-8985
www.dec.state.ny.us/website/outdoors

HISTORY OF NEW YORK'S WHITETAIL HARVEST

Year	Firearm	Bow	Total
1941	18,566	NA	18,566
1951	31,049	75	31,124
1961	57,723	731	58,454

THIRTY-YEAR HISTORY

Year	Firearm	Bow	Total
1970	63,865	1,148	65,013
1971	47,039	1,243	48,282
1972	54,041	1,596	55,637
1973	73,191	2,002	75,193
1974	100,097	3,206	103,303
1975	99,835	3,288	103,323
1976	86,421	3,794	90,215
1977	79,035	4,169	83,204
1978	81,749	3,810	85,559
1979	90,691	3,368	94,059
1980	131,606	4,649	136,255
1981	161,593	3,792	165,385
1982	178,825	6,175	185,000
1983	161,640	5,466	167,106
1984	124,244	5,400	129,644
1985	142,802	9,705	152,507
1986	168,366	9,705	178,071
1987	192,867	11,325	204,192
1988	181,186	11,644	192,830
1989	167,558	12,770	180,328
1990	175,544	14,664	190,208
1991	192,812	19,008	211,820
1992	212,988	18,947	231,935
1993	200,240	20,048	220,288
1994	146,255	19,428	165,683
1995	166,430	21,854	188,284
1996	180,082	22,683	202,765
1997	194,684	22,152	216,836
1998	205,074	25,684	230,758
1999	225,524	30,435	255,959
2000	276,867	29,812	306,679
2001	252,939	28,931	281,870

New York Hunters Share Venison

In 2001, New York deer hunters again proved their generosity, donating almost 30,000 pounds of ground venison to state food pantries.

NEW YORK WHITETAIL RECORDS

•**Record harvest:** 306,679 (2000)
•**Record low harvest:** 15,136 (1945)
•**Bow-hunting record:** 30,435 (1999)
•**Gun-hunting record:** 276,867 (2000)

•**Season to remember:** 2000. New York hunters accomplish kill 306,679 deer, setting a new state record and surpassing the 300,000 mark for the first time in state history.

New York Struggles to Control Deer Numbers

Despite steadily decreasing hunter numbers, New York has experienced several record and near-record seasons in the past few years. For example, in 2000 New York hunters killed a record 306,679 deer — the first time the harvest has ever surpassed 300,000. The total included about 141,000 bucks and a record 154,000 antlerless deer.

Although less successful than 2000, the 2001 season was also one of New York's most productive. Despite record high temperatures, hunters killed an estimated 280,000 deer.

Firearms seasons account for most of New York's deer harvests, though archery seasons add to the overall totals. In 2000, New York bow-hunters killed almost 30,000 deer and muzzleloaders killed about 11,000 deer.

Despite recent harvests' size, New York wildlife biologists believe deer numbers remain above population objectives in about 60 percent of the state's wildlife management units.

Biologists are concerned that New York's growing deer herd, which numbers more than 1 million, might exert an increasing toll on habitats and human activities, such as farming, gardening and logging.

NEW YORK SNAPSHOT

Deer Population: 975,000, 9th in U.S.
Average Harvest: 258,436, 9th in U.S.
Harvest Calculation Method: Mandatory registration.
Does State Predict Annual Harvest? Yes
How Close is Annual Prediction? 3%
Gun-Hunters: 719,696
Bow-Hunters: 177,762
Muzzleloading Hunters: 80,356
Hunter Education: Required for all first-time hunters. Bow-hunter education is also required.
Orange Required for Gun-Hunting? Yes.

NORTH CAROLINA
Tar Heel State
Harvest Ranking: #16

For more information, contact:
North Carolina Wildlife
512 N. Salisburg St.
Raleigh, NC 27604-1188
(919) 733-3393
www.state.nc.us/Wildlife

HISTORY OF NORTH CAROLINA'S DEER HARVEST

Year	Firearm	Bow	Total
1949	NA	NA	14,616
1951	NA	NA	17,739
1952	NA	NA	15,572
1953	NA	NA	18,598
1954	NA	NA	20,084
1955	NA	NA	20,114
1962	NA	NA	28,808
1964	NA	NA	39,793
1967	NA	NA	38,688

THIRTY-YEAR HISTORY

Year	Firearm	Bow	Total
1970	NA	NA	38,405
1972	NA	NA	47,469
1974	NA	NA	53,079
1976	22,645	539	23,184
1977	28,182	679	28,861
1978	29,193	781	29,974
1979	29,246	841	30,087
1980	27,792	1,142	28,934
1981	33,644	1,400	35,044
1982	35,840	2,092	37,932
1983	45,316	2,543	47,859
1984	47,565	2,355	49,920
1985	52,315	2,759	55,074
1986	59,767	2,924	62,691
1987	74,767	3,498	78,265
1988	79,694	3,405	83,099
1989	85,030	4,660	148,208
1992	NA	NA	217,743
1993	107,669	8,727	118,638
1994	116,462	8,235	124,697
1995	202,000	14,000	216,000
1996	177,500	13,500	191,000
1997	181,000	14,000	195,000
1998	110,352	8,095	132,372
1999	116,023	8,258	124,281
2000	198,920	13,560	212,480
2001	134,501	8,268	143,122

* *North Carolina's harvest statistics are calculated from mail-survey estimates.*

NORTH CAROLINA DEER RECORDS

•**Record harvest:** 217,743 (1992)
•**Record low harvest:** 14,616 (1949)
•**Bow-hunting record:** 14,000 (1995, 1997)
•**Gun-hunting record:** 202,000 (1995)

•**Season to remember:** 2000. North Carolina hunters kill 212,480 deer, 88,119 more than the previous year. However, the harvest dropped to 143,122 in 2001.

Tar Heel Hunters Excel in Venison Donation

Hunters for the Hungry has provided over 150,000 pounds of ground venison to North Carolina's hungry population since its formation in 1996. This program is funded through contributions from industry, conservation organizations and private citizens. HFTH has recently become affiliated with the national organization, Farmers and Hunters Feeding the Hungry.

First Laws Protected Deer

When it comes to whitetails, North Carolina has one of the most storied histories in North America. The state enacted its first game laws in 1738, in which deer were prominently mentioned.

At the time, deer-protection laws were much needed because deer had become an important medium of exchange. For example, traders on the French Broad River gave one quart of inferior grade brandy for two deer skins.

The deer hide trade took its toll. For example, in 1753 alone, traders shipped more than 30,000 deer skins from the colony.

NORTH CAROLINA SNAPSHOT

Deer Population: 1 million, 7th in U.S.

Average Harvest: 161,451, 16th in U.S.

Harvest Calculation Method: Surveys and mandatory registration.

Does State Predict Annual Harvest? No

How Close is Annual Prediction? NA

Gun-Hunters: 178,571

Bow-Hunters: 45,450

Muzzleloading Hunters: 60,600

Hunter Education: Required for first-time hunters. Bow-hunter education is not required.

Orange Required for Gun-Hunting? Yes.

NORTH DAKOTA
Peace Garden State
Harvest Ranking: #29

For more information, contact:
North Dakota Game Department
100 N. Bismarck Expy.
Bismarck, ND 58501
(701) 328-6300
www.state.nd.us/gnf

HISTORY OF NORTH DAKOTA'S DEER HARVEST

Year	Firearm	Bow	Total
1941	NA	NA	2,665
1950	NA	NA	13,933
1954	NA	NA	22,705
1958	NA	NA	9,828
1962	NA	NA	23,429
1966	NA	NA	26,469
1967	NA	NA	26,524

THIRTY-YEAR HISTORY

Year	Firearm	Bow	Total
1970	NA	NA	22,882
1971	NA	NA	28,673
1972	NA	NA	25,424
1973	NA	NA	27,780
1974	NA	NA	23,445
1975	NA	NA	20,666
1976	NA	NA	19,969
1977	NA	NA	17,201
1978	NA	NA	17,120
1979	NA	NA	18,118
1980	NA	NA	24,179
1981	NA	NA	27,006
1982	NA	NA	31,210
1983	NA	NA	35,709
1984	NA	NA	41,582
1985	NA	NA	43,074
1986	NA	NA	60,122
1987	NA	NA	47,157
1988	NA	NA	41,190
1989	47,025	2,934	49,959
1990	42,347	2,862	45,209
1991	46,980	3,299	50,279
1992	54,144	3,996	58,142
1993	58,246	4,006	62,252
1994	56,462	3,946	60,408
1995	66,686	4,078	70,764
1996	65,303	4,861	70,164
1997	52,971	2,894	55,865
1998	55,405	3,200	58,605
1999	55,980	3,400	59,380
2000	63,275	3,300	66,575
2001	81,000	NA	NA

NORTH DAKOTA DEER RECORDS

•**Record harvest:** 70,764 (1995)
•**Record low harvest:** 2,665 (1941)
•**Bow-hunting record:** 4,861 (1996)
•**Gun-hunting record:** 81,000 (2001)

•**Season to remember:** 1995. North Dakota hunters kill a record 70,764 deer. What's more, the harvest was 10,356 higher than the previous year's — the second-highest increase since 1986.

Did You Know ...

✓ North Dakota hunters may hunt deer with their bow during the regular firearms season. However, they must wear at least 400 square inches of hunter orange.

✓ While hunting North Dakota whitetails, you may use your bow to fill a firearms tag. Furthermore, if you are seeking to fill a firearms tag, you can bring a gun and bow afield. However, the same is not true in reverse. Hunters seeking to fill their bow tag may not bring a firearm afield, nor may they fill their bow tag with a firearm.

✓ In North Dakota, if you shoot a deer on property you have permission and/or legal right to hunt, and that deer runs onto adjacent posted property, you are legally entitled to track and retrieve the deer from the posted land. However, you cannot bring a weapon without the landowner's consent.

✓ Like many states, North Dakota provides young hunters special opportunities to hunt deer. These early seasons typically occur in late September and are only open to residents. Contact the North Dakota Game Department for application deadlines.

NORTH DAKOTA SNAPSHOT

Deer Population: 243,750, 26th in U.S.
Average Harvest: 62,118, 29th in U.S.
Harvest Calculation Method: Surveys
Does State Predict Annual Harvest? Yes
How Close is Annual Prediction? 5%
Gun-Hunters: 80,000
Bow-Hunters: 11,000
Muzzleloading Hunters: 1,700
Hunter Education: Required for all persons born after Dec. 31, 1961. Bowhunter education is not required.
Orange Required for Gun-Hunting? Yes.

OHIO

Buckeye State

Harvest Ranking: #21

For more information, contact:

Division of Wildlife
1840 Belcher Drive
Columbus, OH 43224

(614) 265-6300   www.dnr.state.oh.us

HISTORY OF OHIO'S WHITETAIL HARVEST

Year	Firearm	Bow	Total
1952	NA	NA	450
1954	NA	NA	closed
1956	NA	NA	3,911
1958	NA	NA	4,415
1960	NA	NA	2,584
1962	NA	NA	2,114
1964	NA	NA	1,326
1966	NA	NA	1,073
1968	NA	NA	1,396

THIRTY-YEAR HISTORY

Year	Firearm	Bow	Total
1970	NA	NA	2,387
1971	NA	NA	3,831
1972	NA	NA	5,074
1973	NA	NA	7,594
1974	NA	NA	10,747
1975	NA	NA	14,972
1976	NA	NA	23,431
1977	NA	NA	22,319
1978	NA	NA	22,967
1979	NA	NA	34,874
1980	NA	NA	40,499
1981	NA	NA	47,634
1982	NA	NA	52,885
1983	NA	NA	59,812
1984	NA	NA	66,860
1985	NA	NA	64,263
1986	NA	NA	67,626
1987	NA	NA	79,355
1988	NA	NA	100,674
1989	NA	NA	91,236
1990	80,109	12,087	92,196
1991	94,342	17,109	111,451
1992	97,676	19,577	117,253
1993	104,540	23,160	138,752
1994	141,137	29,390	170,527
1995	149,413	27,299	179,543
1996	130,237	26,305	158,000
1997	125,504	26,639	153,159
1998	92,722	25,548	118,270
1999	96,701	29,319	126,020
2000	115,291	34,333	149,624
2001	116,092	34,340	150,432

OHIO WHITETAIL RECORDS

• **Record harvest:** 179,543 (1995)
• **Record low harvest:** 406 (1965)
• **Bow-hunting record:** 34,340 (2001)
• **Gun-hunting record:** 149,413 (1995)

• **Season to remember:** 2001. Ohio bow-hunters kill a record 34,340 deer, surpassing the 30,000 mark for just the second time in state history.

Deer Hunting in Ohio

✓ Legislation passed in late 1997 made it legal to hunt deer on Sunday. While no formal surveys have been conducted to assess Sunday hunting participation rates, an analysis of the 2000 deer harvest suggests it's relatively low — less than 3 percent of deer killed during the gun-hunting season were killed on Sunday.

✓ In 2000, Ohio bow-hunters killed 34,333 deer, shattering 1994's record harvest of 29,390. Muzzleloading hunters also had a record-setting year, killing 18,346 whitetails. The record harvest for crossbow hunters is now 19,945, set in 2000. The old crossbow harvest record of 16,946 was set in 1999.

✓ Saturdays are the most popular day for bow-hunting in Ohio. About 30 percent of the total bow-hunting harvest occurs on Saturdays. The next most popular days are Monday and Thursday. Each day accounts for about 11 percent of the annual harvest.

✓ The opportunity to kill a mature buck is greatest in southeast Ohio, not only because bucks tend to live longer there, but also because the area has more deer than anywhere else in the state.

OHIO SNAPSHOT

Deer Population: 475,000, 17th in U.S.

Average Harvest: 112,561, 21st in U.S.

Harvest Calculation Method: Mandatory registration.

Does State Predict Annual Harvest? Yes

How Close is Annual Prediction? 10%

Gun-Hunters: 481,000

Bow-Hunters: 287,700

Muzzleloading Hunters: 111,500

Hunter Education: Required for first-time hunters. Bow-hunter education is not required.

Orange Required for Gun-Hunting? Yes.

OKLAHOMA
Sooner State
Harvest Ranking: #25

Fore more information, contact:
Department of Wildlife
1801 N. Lincoln, Box 53465
Oklahoma City, OK 73105
(405) 521-3851   www.state.ok.us

HISTORY OF OKLAHOMA'S DEER HARVEST

Year	Firearms	Bow	Total
1964	3,368	140	3,508
1965	4,090	213	4,303
1966	4,925	275	5,200
1967	4,976	259	5,235
1968	5,490	260	5,750
1969	6,069	304	6,373

THIRTY-YEAR HISTORY

Year	Firearms	Bow	Total
1970	6,895	331	7,226
1971	6,587	465	7,052
1972	7,714	508	8,222
1973	7,140	427	7,567
1974	7,821	489	8,310
1975	9,028	649	9,677
1976	10,544	1,004	11,548
1977	10,192	680	10,872
1978	13,080	1,028	14,108
1979	13,023	1,185	14,208
1980	12,800	1,497	14,297
1981	11,446	1,964	13,410
1982	17,006	2,249	19,255
1983	19,222	2,698	21,920
1984	20,041	2,568	23,609
1985	16,664	3,523	20,187
1986	25,096	3,320	28,416
1987	29,239	4,115	33,354
1988	34,436	4,414	38,850
1989	33,752	4,589	38,341
1990	38,545	5,525	44,070
1991	40,197	7,079	47,286
1992	42,620	7,792	50,412
1993	49,978	7,853	57,831
1994	51,145	9,054	60,199
1995	56,770	9,116	65,886
1996	52,826	11,430	64,256
1997	60,277	10,930	71,207
1998	67,788	12,220	80,008
1999	70,967	11,757	82,724
2000	87,663	14,272	101,935
2001	75,711	9,964	85,675

OKLAHOMA WHITETAIL RECORDS

•**Record harvest:** 101,935 (2000)
•**Record low harvest:** 3,508 (1964)
•**Bow-hunting record:** 14,272 (2000)
•**Gun-hunting record:** 87,663 (2000)

•**Season to remember:** 1990. Oklahoma deer and deer hunting show amazing progress. Although the harvest of 44,070 deer pales compared to more recent harvests, it's huge compared to the harvest from 20 years earlier, when Oklahoma hunters killed only 7,226 deer.

Oklahoma Whitetail Timeline

✓ 1900 — State deer population bottoms out after decades of unregulated hunting.

✓ 1933 — Oklahoma holds first modern deer season in seven southeastern counties. Hunters kill 235 bucks.

✓ 1943 — State begins deer restoration program by trapping and transplanting 22 deer.

✓ 1946 — Oklahoma's first modern archery season. Hunters kill no deer.

✓ 1949 — During the state's fourth archery season, a hunter achieves Oklahoma's first bow-kill.

✓ 1954 — In Oklahoma's first statewide firearms season, hunters kill 1,487 bucks.

✓ 1969 — First primitive firearms season yields two deer in LeFlore County.

✓ 1972 — Oklahoma holds nine-day gun season with a two-day antlerless season. Hunters kill 7,670 deer.

✓ 1976 — State increases antlerless harvest in 19 counties. Total harvest increases to 11,548 — 26 percent of which were does.

✓ 1990 — Deer population estimated at 250,000. Hunters kill 44,070 deer.

✓ 1999 — Statewide deer population estimated at 425,000 deer. Hunters kill 82,500 deer.

— OKLAHOMA DEPT. OF WILDLIFE

OKLAHOMA SNAPSHOT

Deer Population: 397,000, 20th in U.S.

Average Harvest: 84,310, 25th in U.S.

Harvest Calculation Method: Mandatory registration.

Does State Predict Annual Harvest? Yes

How Close is Annual Prediction? 5%

Gun-Hunters: 163,671

Bow-Hunters: 86,893

Muzzleloading Hunters: 106,978

Hunter Education: Required for all persons born after Jan. 1, 1972. Bow-hunter education is not required.

Orange Required for Gun-Hunting? Yes.

OREGON
Beaver State
Harvest Ranking: #42

For more information, contact:
Department of Fish and Wildlife
400 Public Service Bldg.
Salem, OR 97310
(503) 872-5268   www.dfw.state.or.us

HISTORY OF OREGON'S WHITETAIL HARVEST

Year	Firearm	Bow	Total
1992	422	NA	422
1993	594	NA	594
1994	707	NA	707
1995	667	NA	667
1996	893	NA	893
1997	800	NA	800
1998	NA	NA	611
1999	1,011	NA	1,011
2000	1,013	NA	1,013

Editor's Note — *White-tailed deer are rare in Oregon. In fact, the 1992 season was the first time the Oregon Dept. of Wildlife distinguished between mule deer and whitetails in harvest totals. The estimated deer population in the "Oregon Snapshot" on this page includes mostly mule deer and blacktails.*

Oregon Whitetails Are Isolated

Oregon is home to a sizable black-tailed deer population, but some whitetails live in the Umpqua River Basin near Roseburg, on a series of Columbia River islands. Efforts are being made to increase these small herds. Therefore, all of western Oregon is closed to whitetail hunting.

The Idaho whitetail strain is another species found in Oregon. These deer thrive in areas with heavy shrub patches and thick riparian vegetation.

Mule deer are native to eastern Oregon. Explorers in the early 1800s reported a scarcity of big game, but 20 years later gold miners found abundant mule deer herds. This century has seen similar fluctuations. Between 1926 and 1933, Oregon's muley population ranged from 39,000 to 75,000.

OREGON WHITETAIL RECORDS

•**Record harvest:** 1,013 (2000)
•**Record low harvest:** 422 (1992)
•**Bow-hunting record:** Not available
•**Gun-hunting record:** 1,013 (2000)

•**Season to remember:** 1996. Despite having relatively few whitetails, Oregon gun- and bow-hunters kill 893 whitetails.

Oregon Offers Blacktail Hunting Opportunities

Oregon has limited numbers of white-tailed deer, but it does offer some fantastic hunting for black-tailed deer.

Shotgun deer hunting is available by permit only for White Clay Creek, Brandywine Creek, Fort DuPont and Fort Delaware State Parks. Hunters should also check out the Blackbird State Forest, Ennis Tract at Woodland Beach, Cedar Swamp, Ted Harvey-Logan Lane and Buckaloo Tracts and the Assawoman Wildlife Areas. Permits are be issued through a pre-season lottery except at the Assawoman State Wildlife Area, which uses a daily lottery. Elevated stands are provided for each permittee.

Deer hunting is also allowed at Lums Pond State Park by permit only. Applications for the preseason lottery are available in the annual *Hunting Guide* published by the Division of Fish and Wildlife.

Three hunt locations at Assawoman, Ted Harvey and Woodland Beach Wildlife Areas and three locations at Cedar Swamp Wildlife Area are available for nonambulatory handicapped hunters. Deer hunting opportunities without a permit are also available at many other state wildlife areas.

OREGON SNAPSHOT

Deer Population: 647,600, (Includes other species)

Average Harvest: 857, 42nd in U.S.

Harvest Calculation Method: Surveys and camp checks.

Does State Predict Annual Harvest? No

How Close is Annual Prediction? NA

Gun-Hunters: 208,943

Bow-Hunters: 25,829

Muzzleloading Hunters: 3,030

Hunter Education: Required for persons under the age of 18. Bow-hunter education is not required.

Orange Required for Gun-Hunting? No.

PENNSYLVANIA
Keystone State
Harvest Ranking: #3

For more information, contact:

Game Commission
2001 Elmerton Ave.
Harrisburg, PA 17110
(717) 787-4250
www.pgc.state.pa.us

HISTORY OF PENNSYLVANIA'S DEER HARVEST

Year	Firearm	Bow	Total
1949	130,723	0	130,723
1954	40,870	55	40,925
1959	88,845	1,327	90,172
1963	83,028	1,388	84,416
1967	141,164	3,251	144,415

THIRTY-YEAR HISTORY

Year	Firearm	Bow	Total
1970	96,688	2,998	99,686
1971	101,458	2,769	104,227
1972	104,270	2,945	107,215
1973	123,239	3,652	126,891
1974	121,743	3,909	125,652
1975	133,134	5,061	138,195
1976	118,385	3,648	122,033
1977	141,400	4,678	146,078
1978	116,188	5,053	121,241
1979	110,562	4,232	114,794
1980	129,703	5,774	135,477
1981	142,592	5,938	148,530
1982	130,958	7,264	138,222
1983	130,071	6,222	136,293
1984	133,606	6,574	140,180
1985	154,060	7,368	161,428
1986	148,562	8,570	157,132
1987	164,055	8,901	172,956
1988	185,565	9,834	195,399
1989	184,856	10,951	195,807
1990	396,529	19,032	415,561
1991	365,267	22,748	388,015
1992	335,439	25,785	361,224
1993	359,224	49,409	408,557
1994	345,184	49,897	395,081
1995	375,961	54,622	430,583
1996	294,674	56,323	350,997
1997	342,556	54,460	397,016
1998	317,774	59,715	377,489
1999	306,521	72,401	378,992
2000	426,078	78,522	504,600
2001	411,963	74,051	486,014

PENNSYLVANIA DEER RECORDS

•**Record harvest:** 504,600 (2000)
•**Record low harvest:** 40,925 (1954)
•**Bow-hunting record:** 78,522 (2000)
•**Gun-hunting record:** 426,078 (2000)

•**Season to remember:** 1949. Pennsylvania bow-hunters kill no deer. Although bow-hunting's future looked bleak, Keystone State bow-hunters would kill almost 80,000 deer 50 years later.

Pennsylvania Hunters Set Safety Record

In 2000, Keystone State hunters experienced the fewest hunting-related shooting incidents (HRSIs) since 1915, when officials began recording such accidents.

The 2000 hunting season resulted in 69 HRSIs — only three being fatal. With more than 1 million hunters heading afield in Pennsylvania, this equates to 6.72 accidents per 100,000 hunters. The lower rate reflects a continuing downward trend in hunting accidents, which have declined almost 80 percent since Pennsylvania's hunter education program began in 1959.

Researchers Study Buck Dispersal

The Pennsylvania Game Commission and Penn State University recently launched one of the most extensive radio-telemetry studies of male deer dispersal and survival, and the effects of antler restrictions ever attempted. To highlight the significance of this joint research project, representatives of the agency and university today demonstrated one of the dramatic capturing and radio-collaring techniques that will be used as part of this latest joint research project on white-tailed deer.

PENNSYLVANIA SNAPSHOT

Deer Population: 1.5 million, 5th in U.S.

Average Harvest: 428,824, 3rd in U.S.

Harvest Calculation Method: Harvest cards mailed to hunters.

Does State Predict Annual Harvest? Yes

How Close is Annual Prediction? 10%

Gun-Hunters: 1,060,728

Bow-Hunters: 282,700

Muzzleloading Hunters: 136,600

Hunter Education: Required for all first-time hunters. Bow-hunter education is not required.

Orange Required for Gun-Hunting? Yes.

RHODE ISLAND
Ocean State
Harvest Ranking: # 41

For more information, contact:
Department of Environ. Mgmt.
83 Park St.
Providence, RI 02903
(401) 222-6822   www.state.ri.us/dem

HISTORY OF RHODE ISLAND'S DEER HARVEST

Year	Firearm	Bow	Total
1972	93	57	150
1973	46	56	102
1974	62	48	110
1975	57	54	111
1976	61	50	111
1977	95	62	157
1978	91	78	169
1979	103	93	196
1980	145	72	217
1981	155	88	243
1982	112	104	216
1983	123	99	222
1984	139	109	248
1985	144	112	256
1986	299	126	425
1987	252	179	431
1988	323	125	448
1989	466	169	635
1990	701	238	943
1991	857	291	1,148
1992	1,052	417	1,474
1993	945	378	1,323
1994	1,157	252	1,409
1995	1,351	415	1,766
1996	1,689	474	2,163
1997	1,542	243	1,785
1998	1,222	382	1,532
1999	1,661	390	2,043
2000	1,819	488	2,307
2001	1,582	470	2,052

Small State, Big Opportunities

Rhode Island is home to more than 46,000 aces of state management area land. Maps of these areas are available from the Rhode Island Division of Fish and Wildlife.

Deer hunting in the Simmons Mill Pond management area is only allowed during the archery season. Camping is prohibited except in portions of the Arcadia and George Washington management areas.

RHODE ISLAND DEER RECORDS

•**Record harvest:** 2,307 (2000)
•**Record low harvest:** 102 (1973)
•**Bow-hunting record:** 474 (1996)
•**Gun-hunting record:** 1,819 (2000)

•**Season to remember:** 1986. Although the harvest is miniscule when compared to those of other states, Rhode Island's deer hunters kill 425 deer — 40 percent more than the previous year.

Safety is Top Priority for Rhode Island Hunters

In 1956, Rhode Island enacted legislation that mandated first-time hunters receive formal training in safe hunting practices and the handling and use of firearms and archery equipment before receiving a license. Since the program's inception, more than 40,000 individuals have completed the course, resulting in a significant decrease in hunting-related accidents.

Rhode Island's hunter-injury rates have steadily declined through the years as more hunters received the training. The course has evolved over time to include subjects that have become increasingly important, such as landowner relations, hunter ethics and wildlife management.

The Rhode Island Division of Fish & Wildlife, working in conjunction with volunteer instructors and sportsmen's clubs throughout the state, administers the program.

— RHODE ISLAND DIVISION OF FISH & WILDLIFE

RHODE ISLAND SNAPSHOT

Deer Population: 11,000, 34th in U.S.

Average Harvest: 1,966, 41st in U.S.

Harvest Calculation Method: Mandatory registration.

Does State Predict Annual Harvest? No

How Close is Annual Prediction? NA

Gun-Hunters: 5,465

Bow-Hunters: 3,143

Muzzleloading Hunters: 5,754

Hunter Education: Required for first-time hunters. Bow-hunter education is not required.

Orange Required for Gun-Hunting? Yes.

SOUTH CAROLINA
Palmetto State
Harvest Ranking: #10

For more information, contact:

Department of Natural Resources
Box 167
Columbia, SC 29202
(803) 734-3888
http://water.dnr.state.sc.us/

HISTORY OF SOUTH CAROLINA'S DEER HARVEST

Year	Firearm	Bow	Total
1972	NA	NA	18,894
1973	NA	NA	23,703
1974	NA	NA	26,727
1975	NA	NA	29,133
1976	NA	NA	33,749
1977	NA	NA	36,363
1978	NA	NA	39,721
1979	NA	NA	43,569
1980	NA	NA	44,698
1981	NA	NA	56,410
1982	NA	NA	54,321
1983	NA	NA	57,927
1984	NA	NA	60,182
1985	NA	NA	62,699
1986	NA	NA	69,289
1987	NA	NA	86,208
1988	NA	NA	98,182
1989	NA	NA	107,081
1990	NA	NA	125,171
1991	NA	NA	130,848
1992	NA	NA	126,839
1993	NA	NA	142,795
1994	NA	NA	138,964
1995	NA	NA	142,527
1996	NA	NA	155,654
1997	NA	NA	165,000
1998	NA	NA	150,000
1999	284,701	16,299	301,000
2000	278,700	16,000	294,700
2001	289,647	19,181	308,828

South Carolina has Early Season

Deer hunting in South Carolina is characterized by two distinct season frameworks. The Coastal Plain encompasses 28 counties where the deer season begins on Aug. 15, Sept. 1, or Sept. 15, and continues until Jan. 1. In this region, which encompasses about two-thirds of the state, baiting and dog-hunting are legal.

South Carolina's upstate areas have different season dates and hunting laws.

SOUTH CAROLINA DEER RECORDS

•**Record harvest:** 308,828 (2001)
•**Record low harvest:** 18,894 (1972)
•**Bow-hunting record:** 19,181 (2001)
•**Gun-hunting record:** 289,647 (2001)

•**Season to remember:** 1972. Although the 18,894 harvest is miniscule by today's standards, the 1972 season began a series of almost-always increasing deer harvests, which eventually broke the 300,000 mark in 1999.

South Carolina Honors Big Bucks

Since 1974, South Carolina has been recognizing superb bucks through its Antler Records Program. In that time, hunters have entered more than 3,200 bucks onto the prestigious list.

Aside from helping hunters appreciate the state's finest whitetails, the program lets wildlife biologists identify areas that consistently produce quality bucks. With that knowledge, biologists better understand what factors South Carolina whitetails require for optimum growth.

Among other things, the records indicate that low deer densities are crucial for producing large-antlered bucks. For example, although South Carolina had relatively low deer numbers throughout the 1980s, the decade accounts for about 40 percent of records.

To qualify for the South Carolina Antler Records List, a buck must score 125 typical or 145 nontypical after the 60-day drying period. Only about one of every 400 white-tailed bucks harvested in South Carolina qualifies for the records list.

For more information, contact Antler Records, Box 167 Columbia, SC 29202.

SOUTH CAROLINA SNAPSHOT

Deer Population: 1 million, 7th in U.S.

Average Harvest: 243,906, 10th in U.S.

Harvest Calculation Method: Surveys and voluntary registration.

Does State Predict Annual Harvest? Yes

How Close is Annual Prediction? 10%

Gun-Hunters: 175,813

Bow-Hunters: 42,218

Muzzleloading Hunters: 30,704

Hunter Education: Required for all persons born after June 30, 1979. Bow-hunter education is not required.

Orange Required for Gun-Hunting? Yes.

SOUTH DAKOTA
Coyote State
Harvest Ranking: #30

For more information, contact:

Division of Wildlife
Bldg. 445 E. Capital
Pierre, SD 57501
(605) 773-3485
www.state.sd.us/gfp/index.htm

HISTORY OF SOUTH DAKOTA'S DEER HARVEST

Year	Firearm	Bow	Total
1985	43,989	2,738	46,727
1986	40,798	1,953	42,751
1987	32,018	2,456	34,474
1988	33,265	2,327	35,592
1989	42,947	3,081	46,028

TEN-YEAR HISTORY

Year	Firearm	Bow	Total
1990	38,902	2,986	41,888
1991	39,915	2,686	42,601
1992	41,959	2,964	44,923
1993	45,431	2,963	48,394
1994	47,142	2,325	49,467
1995	39,868	2,625	42,493
1996	39,936	3,107	43,043
1997	47,503	2,440	49,943
1998	43,000	2,800	45,800
1999	43,214	2,700	45,914
2000	39,600	2,600	42,200
2001	45,340	3,418	48,758

South Dakota Holds Successful Youth Hunt

South Dakota's 1999 antlerless deer hunt for youths was a big hit — more than 54 percent of participants tagged a deer.

Nearly 2,500 young hunters participated, and they killed 1,339 deer.

The state's most successful hunt occurred in the special buck unit in the West River region. Only 730 tags were issued for the hunt, but 506 hunters killed bucks — a 69 percent success ratio.

Overall, state bow-hunters had a successful season. More than 22 percent of archers harvested a deer in 1999.

SOUTH DAKOTA DEER RECORDS

•**Record harvest:** 49,943 (1997)
•**Record low harvest:** 34,474 (1987)
•**Bow-hunting record:** 3,418 (2001)
•**Gun-hunting record:** 47,503 (1997)

•**Season to remember:** 1996. South Dakota bow-hunters kill 3,107 deer, surpassing the previous record of 3,081, set in 1990.

Hunting in the Black Hills

Although South Dakota isn't usually associated with whitetail hunting, the Black Hills, which reach an elevation of more than 7,000 feet, provide ample opportunities. And unlike much of the surrounding prairie, the Black Hills feature thick stands of aspen, white spruce, bur oak and ponderosa pine, plus rimrock, deep gorges, rolling hills and tall mountains.

South Dakota's Black Hills hunting unit stretches 100 miles from north to south and 40 miles east to west, covering 2.3 million acres — more than 80 percent of which is open to public hunting. Whitetails there make up about 75 percent of the deer herd, with muleys making up only 25 percent.

The area is also ideal for bow-hunters because several roads crisscross the area, making most good hunting spots accessible by pickup truck.

Because of limited harvest quotas, Black Hills deer hunters must apply draw a tag by lottery. Applications become available in early June with and are due in early July. Visit the South Dakota Division of Wildlife Web site for applications.

To obtain a U.S. Forest Service map of the Black Hills, call (605) 673-2251.

SOUTH DAKOTA SNAPSHOT

Deer Population: 153,000, 29th in U.S.

Average Harvest: 46,523, 30th in U.S.

Harvest Calculation Method: Surveys

Does State Predict Annual Harvest? Yes

How Close is Annual Prediction? 10%

Gun-Hunters: 72,600

Bow-Hunters: 11,900

Muzzleloading Hunters: 1,800

Hunter Education: Required for all persons under age 16. Bow-hunter education is required.

Orange Required for Gun-Hunting? Yes.

TENNESSEE
Volunteer State
Harvest Ranking: #18

For more information, contact:
Tennessee Wildlife Resources
Box 407
Nashville, TN 37204
(888) 814-8972
www.state.tn.us/twra

HISTORY OF TENNESSEE WHITETAIL HARVEST

Year	Firearm	Bow	Total
1970	8,258	372	8,630
1971	6,202	365	6,567
1972	7,354	499	7,853
1973	10,937	474	11,411
1974	12,624	685	13,309
1975	13,897	993	14,890
1976	16,374	1,739	18,113
1977	19,527	1,770	21,297
1978	22,819	2,465	25,284
1979	25,970	2,570	28,540
1980	27,196	3,457	30,653
1981	28,885	3,407	32,292
1982	35,726	4,644	40,370
1983	42,528	6,347	48,875
1984	49,493	5,883	55,376
1985	53,118	7,278	60,396
1986	69,044	8,578	77,622
1987	86,777	12,040	98,817
1988	81,469	10,796	92,265
1989	95,475	13,287	108,762
1990	97,172	16,061	113,233
1991	105,832	15,764	121,596
1992	106,168	19,728	125,896
1993	118,946	19,596	138,542
1994	111,598	20,832	132,430
1995	124,179	20,953	145,132
1996	127,129	22,501	149,630
1997	126,233	24,108	150,341
1998	135,261	20,414	155,675
1999	122,497	21,000	143,497
2000	129,580	19,900	149,480
2001	134,765	21,591	156,356

Volunteer State Provides Abundant Public Land

With almost 500,000 acres of public hunting lands, Tennessee is a great place for deer hunters. The state's extensive land holdings have been acquired through a cooperative effort between the Tennessee Wildlife Resources Agency and various landholding organizations, such as Cumberland Forest, Graham, International Paper, Tackett Creek, Westvaco Corporation and Willamette Industries, Inc.

Spread across the state, these lands are as varied as Tennessee. What's more, they are distributed so evenly, most hunters live near at least one. Although some tracts provide better opportunities, most public hunting areas harbor many deer, plus quail, rabbits, squirrels, waterfowl, black bears and wild turkeys.

Because these lands depend on the cooperation of land-owning companies, Tennessee Wildlife Resources encourages hunters to be respectful of the property, the wildlife and other hunters.

If hunters behave irresponsibly, these lands can be closed.

— TENNESSEE WILDLIFE RESOURCES

Tennessee WMAs Offer Fantastic Opportunities

Aside from thousands of acres of public land, Tennessee offers deer hunters 93 refuges and wildlife management areas spread throughout the state. These WMAs are managed by the Tennessee Wildlife Resources Agency and vary in size from 53 to 625,000 acres.

All WMAs are open to public hunting and trapping, although regulations apply.

TENNESSEE DEER RECORDS

•**Record harvest:** 156,356 (2001)
•**Record low harvest:** 6,567 (1971)
•**Bow-hunting record:** 24,108 (1997)
•**Gun-hunting record:** 135,261 (1998)

•**Season to remember:** 1998. Tennessee deer hunters kill a record 155,675 deer — 18 times more than during the 1970 season.

TENNESSEE SNAPSHOT

Deer Population: 990,000 , 8th in U.S.

Average Harvest: 123,050, 18th in U.S.

Harvest Calculation Method: Mandatory registration.

Does State Predict Annual Harvest? No

How Close is Annual Prediction? NA

Gun-Hunters: 209,684

Bow-Hunters: 99,000

Muzzleloading Hunters: 99,000

Hunter Education: Required for persons born after Jan. 1, 1969. Bow-hunter education is not required.

Orange Required for Gun-Hunting? Yes.

TEXAS
Lone Star State

Harvest Ranking: #5

For more information, contact:

Texas Parks & Wildlife
4200 Smith School Road
Austin, TX 78744

(800) 895-4248   www.tpwd.state.tx.us

HISTORY OF TEXAS' ANNUAL WHITETAIL HARVEST

Year	Firearm	Bow	Total
1980	253,993	6,390	260,383
1981	292,525	7,527	300,052
1982	328,678	8,943	337,621
1983	309,409	8,935	318,344
1984	361,811	11,451	373,262
1985	370,732	12,767	383,499
1986	431,002	14,117	445,119
1987	489,368	15,585	504,953
1988	458,576	16,392	474,968
1989	460,896	16,595	477,491
1990	413,910	15,622	429,532
1991	459,083	14,964	474,047
1992	453,361	15,532	468,893
1993	438,934	13,575	452,509
1994	408,780	12,643	421,423
1995	436,975	13,518	450,593
1996	320,819	13,000	333,819
1997	357,832	13,500	371,332
1998	NA	NA	392,573
1999	431,927	6,700	438,627
2000	NA	NA	424,000
2001	NA	NA	NA

Big Bucks Abound in South Texas Brush Country

Texas is comprised of 10 ecological areas: the Edward Plateau, South Texas Plains, Cross Timbers, Gulf Prairies, Marshes, Post Oak Savannah, Blackland Prairies, Rolling Plains, High Plains and Piney Woods.

The South Texas Plains is also known as "Brush Country," and is a level to rolling plain extending south and west from San Antonio to the Gulf of Mexico and the Rio Grande. This area is known for large-antlered bucks.

TEXAS DEER RECORDS

- **Record harvest:** 504,953 (1987)
- **Record low harvest:** 260,383 (1980)
- **Bow-hunting record:** 16,595 (1989)
- **Gun-hunting record:** 489,368 (1987)
- **Season to remember:** 1989. Texas bow-hunters kill a record 16,595 whitetails. In the following years, however, bow harvests steadily declined. In 1999, Texas bow-hunters killed only 6,700 deer.

Texas Urges Hunters to Follow Tagging Procedures

Improper deer tagging is one of the most common game violations in Texas. Although such violations are often innocent mistakes, Texas hunters who tag their deer improperly might receive citations of up to $500.

Texas requires hunters tag deer immediately after the kill. The date and time of kill must be cut from the tag, and the county and location must be written on the back of the tag. Deer must be tagged before being moved or field dressed.

The tag must stay with the carcass and/or the meat. If a hunter removes a buck's head, the tag must remain with the carcass.

Lone Star Bucks Grow Old

Texas' reputation for large-antlered bucks is well deserved. Aside from intensively managed, high-quality habitat, the state's relatively low hunter densities ensure many bucks reach maturity and peak antler growth. For example, the average age of bucks in Webb County, Texas — located along the Mexican border — is 4½. This is vastly different from most of North America, where yearlings make up most of the buck population.

TEXAS SNAPSHOT

Deer Population: 3,543,000, 1st in U.S.

Average Harvest: 392,070, 5th in U.S.

Harvest Calculation Method: Surveys

Does State Predict Annual Harvest? No

How Close is Annual Prediction? NA

Gun-Hunters: 561,415

Bow-Hunters: 38,500

Muzzleloading Hunters: 65,650

Hunter Education: Required for all persons born on or after Sept. 1, 1979. Bow-hunter education is not required.

Orange Required for Gun-Hunting? No.

VERMONT
Green Mountain State
Harvest Ranking: #35

For more information, contact:
Vermont Dept. of Fish and Wildlife
103 S. Main St.
Waterbury, VT 05671
(802) 241-3701   www.anr.state.vt.us

HISTORY OF VERMONT'S WHITETAIL HARVEST

Year	Firearm	Bow	Total
1899	90	NA	90
1909	4,597	NA	4,597
1919	4,092	NA	4,092
1929	1,438	NA	1,438
1939	2,589	NA	2,589
1949	5,983	NA	5,983
1959	11,268	232	11,500
1969	20,753	1,547	22,300

THIRTY-YEAR HISTORY

Year	Firearm	Bow	Total
1970	17,592	1,197	18,789
1971	7,760	604	8,364
1972	8,980	1,073	10,053
1973	8,560	1,040	9,600
1974	11,254	1,580	12,834
1975	9,939	1,606	11,545
1976	10,278	1,200	11,478
1977	10,029	2,094	12,123
1978	7,087	1,688	8,775
1979	14,936	1,587	16,523
1980	24,675	1,257	25,932
1981	19,077	1,169	20,246
1982	9,148	798	9,946
1983	6,092	538	6,630
1984	12,418	630	13,048
1985	13,150	727	13,877
1986	11,943	810	12,753
1987	8,046	958	9,004
1988	6,451	627	7,078
1989	8,030	1,202	9,232
1990	7,930	1,053	8,983
1991	9,993	1,591	11,584
1992	11,215	3,245	14,460
1993	10,043	2,999	13,333
1994	9,177	3,276	12,903
1995	12,769	5,046	18,116
1996	13,632	4,990	18,622
1997	14,836	5,000	19,836
1998	12,000	4,562	16,562
1999	14,487	5,296	19,783
2000	15,975	4,523	20,498
2001	11,340	3,633	14,973

VERMONT DEER RECORDS

•**Record harvest:** 25,932 (1980)
•**Record low harvest:** 90 (1899)
•**Bow-hunting record:** 5,296 (1999)
•**Gun-hunting record:** 24,675 (1980)

•**Season to remember:** 1983. Three years after Vermont hunters killed a record 25,932 whitetails, the overall harvest bottoms out at 6,630 — the lowest since 1949.

Vermont Has A Unique Harvest Structure

In an age when burgeoning deer populations have prompted many state's wildlife managers to issue more antlerless deer tags, Vermont's harvest structure remains remarkably unchanged.

For example, while states with high deer densities like Wisconsin harvest about 60 percent antlerless deer, antlerless deer make up only about 38 percent of Vermont's harvest.

Vermont's harvest is also more traditional in that hunter success rates are much lower than farm-country states with booming deer herds. For example, in 2000, 83 percent of Vermont hunters failed to kill a deer. Fourteen percent killed one deer, and 3 percent killed two deer. Amazingly, no Vermont hunters killed three or more whitetails.

Interestingly, Vermont firearms hunters killed only 50 percent of the total harvest. Twenty-three percent of the remaining 10,249 deer were killed by muzzleloading hunters, 22 percent were killed by bow-hunters and 5 percent were killed in special youth hunts.

— RYAN GILLIGAN

VERMONT SNAPSHOT

Deer Population: 150,000 , 30th in U.S.

Average Harvest: 18,330, 35th in U.S.

Harvest Calculation Method: Mandatory registration.

Does State Predict Annual Harvest? No

How Close is Annual Prediction? NA

Gun-Hunters: 94,908

Bow-Hunters: 40,764

Muzzleloading Hunters: 29,944

Hunter Education: Required for first-time hunters. Bow-hunter education also required.

Orange Required for Gun-Hunting? No.

VIRGINIA
Old Dominion
Harvest Ranking: #13

For more information, contact:
Department of Game & Fisheries
Box 11104
Richmond, VA 23230
(804) 367-1000   www.dgif.state.va.us

HISTORY OF VIRGINIA'S WHITETAIL HARVEST

Year	Firearms	Bow	Total
1935	NA	NA	1,158
1945	NA	NA	4,545
1955	NA	NA	14,227
1965	NA	NA	27,983

THIRTY-YEAR HISTORY

Year	Firearms	Bow	Total
1970	NA	NA	38,138
1971	NA	NA	42,369
1972	NA	NA	48,775
1973	NA	NA	60,789
1974	NA	NA	61,989
1975	NA	NA	63,443
1976	NA	NA	63,671
1977	NA	NA	67,059
1978	NA	NA	72,545
1979	NA	NA	69,940
1980	NA	NA	75,208
1981	NA	NA	78,388
1982	NA	NA	88,540
1983	NA	NA	85,739
1984	NA	NA	84,432
1985	NA	NA	101,425
1986	NA	NA	121,801
1987	NA	NA	119,309
1988	NA	NA	114,562
1989	NA	NA	135,094
1990	NA	NA	160,411
1991	NA	NA	179,344
1992	NA	NA	200,446
1993	185,222	15,900	201,122
1994	190,673	18,700	209,373
1995	202,277	16,199	218,476
1996	193,134	15,974	209,108
1997	182,881	15,074	197,995
1998	164,449	14,578	179,027
1999	173,619	15,370	190,043
2000	168,527	17,210	187,114
2001	196,392	18,191	214,583

Editor's note — *Virginia has one of the most popular "Hunters for the Hungry" programs in the nation. For more information, contact Hunters for the Hungry, Box 304, Dept. DDH, Big Island, VA 24526.*

VIRGINIA DEER RECORDS

•**Record harvest:** 218,476 (1995)
•**Record low harvest:** 1,158 (1935)
•**Bow-hunting record:** 18,700 (1994)
•**Gun-hunting record:** 202,277 (1995)

•**Season to remember:** 2001. Virginia bow- and gun-hunters combine to harvest 214,583 deer — a 14 percent increase from 2000.

Virginia Acquires New WMA

Old Dominion deer hunters have even more prime hunting grounds thanks the the recently acquired Big Survey wildlife management area in Wythe County along Interstate 81. The two-tract, 8,300-acre area includes parts of Sand, Lick, Stuart and Swecker mountains.

The Big Survey WMA is open to hunting without charge. Although hunters must possess appropriate hunting licenses, a National Forest stamp is not required.

The Virginia Department of Game & Fisheries urges hunters using the Big Survey WMA to respect the rights of adjacent prop- erty owners by strictly observing their boundaries.

Disease Periodically Affects Virginia Whitetails

Epizootic Hemorrhagic Disease (EHD) — an often deadly virus — periodically infects Virginia's whitetail herd. EHD, which is spread by no-see-um gnats, causes hemor- rhaging throughout an infected deer's body, often causing the deer to drown in its own blood.

VIRGINIA SNAPSHOT

Deer Population: 950,000, 11th in U.S.
Average Harvest: 193,752, 13th in U.S.
Harvest Calculation Method: Mandatory registration.

Does State Predict Annual Harvest? Yes
How Close is Annual Prediction? 35%

Gun-Hunters: 282,816
Bow-Hunters: 58,513
Muzzleloading Hunters: 103,015

Hunter Education: Required for all persons born after June 30, 1979. Bow- hunter education is not required.
Orange Required for Gun-Hunting? Yes.

WASHINGTON
Evergreen State
Harvest Ranking: #32

For more information, contact:
Department of Fish & Wildlife
600 Capitol Way N.
Olympia, WA 98501
(360) 902-2200   www.wa.gov/wdfw

HISTORY OF WASHINGTON'S ANNUAL DEER HARVEST

Year	Firearms	Bow	Total
1974	49,792	808	50,600
1984	38,416	1,790	40,206

TEN-YEAR HISTORY

Year	Firearms	Bow	Total
1990	41,549	3,606	45,155
1991	52,745	4,367	57,112
1992	50,441	4,856	55,297
1993	31,892	3,789	35,681
1994	42,054	4,948	47,002
1995	34,469	3,296	37,765
1996	35,970	3,472	39,442
1997	29,775	2,366	32,141
1998	27,578	2,675	30,253
1999	32,556	3,204	35,760
2000	37,565	3,411	40,976
2001	NA	NA	NA

Editor's note — Washington is one of several states that has limited numbers of white-tailed deer. The above harvest figures are for all species, including blacktails, whitetails and mule deer.

Washington Harbors Whitetails, Blacktails and Muleys

Mule deer and whitetail populations in southeast Washington are at high levels except for the very southern and mountainous part of the Blue Mountains. In fact, since 1992, whitetail populations have steadily increased in the Spokane area.

In 1991, the state had a record whitetail harvest of about 18,000. Since then, the harvest has leveled off at about 10,000 deer annually. That's an excellent figure considering most deer hunters target blacktails and mule deer.

WASHINGTON DEER RECORDS

•**Record harvest:** 66,000 (1979)
•**Record low harvest:** 30,253 (1998)
•**Bow-hunting record:** 4,948 (1994)
•**Gun-hunting record:** 64,888 (1979)

•**Season to remember:** 1994. Washington bow-hunters kill a record 4,948 deer. Although this number is low compared to other states' archery kills, it's amazing, considering Washington archers killed just 808 deer in 1974.

Washington is Monitoring Herd Closely for CWD

In response to growing threats of chronic wasting disease, the Washington Department of Fish and Wildlife has been sampling deer and elk that died or were killed by hunters after exhibiting symptoms similar to those of CWD, a deadly brain disease found in deer and elk. In 2001, Washington expanded this testing to include checks of some meat processors that handle wild game. In 2002, the WDFW substantially increased CWD testing statewide. To date, no Washington deer or elk have tested positive for CWD.

In the early 1990s, WDFW moved to ban game farming statewide, partly to reduce the risk of transmitting diseases from captive animals to wild herds.

Because the only reliable CWD test requires sampling the brain tissue of dead deer and elk, the WDFW and other state wildlife agencies depend heavily on samples from hunter- and road-killed animals.

CWD-positive animals lose weight, appear lethargic, salivate excessively, drink more water, have droopy ears and isolate themselves from other animals. Afflicted animals invariably die.

Although no Washington deer or elk have been diagnosed with CWD, hunters should wear rubber gloves while field dressing deer and elk and avoiding consuming the animal's brain, eyes, spleen or spinal cord.

— WASHINGTON DEPARTMENT OF FISH & WILDLIFE

WASHINGTON SNAPSHOT

Deer Population: 380,000 (includes other species)
Average Harvest: 35,714, 32nd in U.S.
Gun-Hunters: 129,987
Bow-Hunters: 17,136
Muzzleloading Hunters: 6,804
Hunter Education: Required for all persons born after Jan. 1, 1972. Bow-hunter education is not required.
Orange Required for Gun-Hunting? Yes.

WEST VIRGINIA
Mountain State

Harvest Ranking: #12

For more information, contact:
W. Va. Wildlife Resources
State Capital, Bldg. 3
Charleston, WV 25305

(304) 367-2720   www.wvwildlife.com

HISTORY OF WEST VIRGINIA'S WHITETAIL HARVEST

Year	Firearms	Bow	Total
1939	897	NA	897
1949	6,466	6	6,472
1959	19,588	90	19,678
1969	13,620	470	14,090

THIRTY-YEAR HISTORY

Year	Firearms	Bow	Total
1970	13,399	589	13,988
1971	15,905	714	16,619
1972	20,960	1,443	22,403
1973	24,179	1,684	25,863
1974	27,821	2,119	29,940
1975	32,368	2,968	35,336
1976	38,712	2,323	41,035
1977	37,987	2,531	40,518
1978	40,096	4,350	44,446
1979	49,625	5,461	55,086
1980	47,022	7,144	54,166
1981	65,505	9,003	74,508
1982	74,642	13,454	88,096
1983	78,605	11,235	89,840
1984	94,132	12,578	106,710
1985	71,183	13,416	84,599
1986	101,404	17,207	118,611
1987	109,367	19,742	129,109
1988	112,155	16,537	128,692
1989	129,350	16,217	145,567
1990	148,233	21,715	169,948
1991	149,536	27,448	176,984
1992	177,265	28,659	205,924
1993	142,589	26,425	169,014
1994	120,954	24,448	145,402
1995	173,553	28,072	201,625
1996	157,275	29,637	186,912
1997	200,859	34,446	235,305
1998	165,609	28,430	194,039
1999	197,339	33,942	231,281
2000	162,184	30,752	192,936
2001	182,155	33,622	215,777

WEST VIRGINIA DEER RECORDS

• **Record harvest:** 235,305 (1997)
• **Record low harvest:** 897 (1939)
• **Bow-hunting record:** 34,446 (1997)
• **Gun-hunting record:** 200,859 (1997)

• **Season to remember:** 1984. West Virginia hunters kill 106,710 deer, breaking the 100,000 mark for the first time in state history.

Mountain State Hunters Have Successful Season

In 2001, West Virginia bow- and gun-hunters experienced one of the best deer seasons in history, killing 215,777 deer. The harvest was the third-highest in state history and was 12 percent more than the 2000 harvest. Interestingly, the buck harvest of 99,609 animals was also up 12 percent from 2000 and ranked as the third-highest on record.

With a harvest of 33,622, the 2001 archery harvest was up 9 percent from 2000 and the muzzleloader harvest was up 48 percent.

West Virginians top 10 buck counties were Hampshire, 3,697; Randolph, 3,550; Hardy, 3,355; Greenbrier 3,266; Jackson, 3,206; Preston, 3,106; Ritchie, 3,086; Pendleton, 3,031; Mason, 2,997; and Braxton, 2,816.

The top 10 antlerless counties were Preston, 3,067; Ritchie, 2,772; Jackson, 2,652; Roane, 2,574; Lewis, 2,551; Hampshire, 2,523; Mason, 2,296; Upshur, 2,244; Hardy, 2,220; and Wetzel, 2,178.

— WEST VIRGINIA WILDLIFE RESOURCES

WEST VIRGINIA SNAPSHOT

Deer Population: 890,000, 12th in U.S.

Average Harvest: 213,868, 12th in U.S.

Harvest Calculation Method: Mandatory registration.

Does State Predict Annual Harvest? Yes

How Close is Annual Prediction? 20%

Gun-Hunters: 290,000

Bow-Hunters: 153,793

Muzzleloading Hunters: 74,736

Hunter Education: Required for all persons born after Jan. 1, 1975. Bow-hunter education is not required.

Orange Required for Gun-Hunting? Yes.

WISCONSIN
Badger State
Harvest Ranking: #1

For more information, contact:
Department of Natural Resources
101 S. Webster St.
Madison, WI 53707
(608) 266-2621   http://www.dnr.state.wi.us

HISTORY OF WISCONSIN'S WHITETAIL HARVEST

Year	Firearms	Bow	Total
1897	2,500	--	2,500
1907	4,750	--	4,750
1917	18,000	--	18,000
1928	17,000	--	17,000
1937	14,835	0	14,835
1947	53,520	368	53,888
1957	68,138	1,753	68,138
1967	128,527	7,592	136,119

THIRTY-YEAR HISTORY

Year	Firearms	Bow	Total
1970	72,844	6,520	79,364
1971	70,835	6,522	77,357
1972	74,827	7,087	81,914
1973	82,105	8,456	90,561
1974	100,405	12,514	112,919
1975	117,378	13,588	130,966
1976	122,509	13,636	136,145
1977	131,910	16,790	148,700
1978	150,845	18,113	168,958
1979	125,570	16,018	141,588
1980	139,624	20,954	160,578
1981	166,673	29,083	195,756
1982	182,715	30,850	213,565
1983	197,600	32,876	230,476
1984	255,240	38,891	294,131
1985	274,302	40,744	315,046
1986	259,240	40,490	299,730
1987	250,530	42,651	293,181
1988	263,424	42,393	305,817
1989	310,192	46,394	356,586
1990	350,040	49,291	399,331
1991	352,328	67,005	419,333
1992	288,906	60,479	349,385
1993	217,584	53,008	270,592
1994	307,629	66,254	373,883
1995	397,942	69,158	467,100
1996	388,211	72,313	460,524
1997	292,513	66,792	359,305
1998	332,314	75,301	407,615
1999	402,179	91,937	494,116
2000	528,494	86,899	618,274*
2001	361,264	83,120	446,957*

*Includes tribal harvest

WISCONSIN DEER RECORDS

•**Record harvest:** 618,274 (2000)
•**Record low harvest:** 2,500 (1897)
•**Bow-hunting record:** 91,937 (1999)
•**Gun-hunting record:** 528,494 (2000)

•**Season to remember:** 1999. Wisconsin bow-hunters kill a record 91,937 deer, surpassing the previous year's harvest by 16,636 deer.

CWD Discovered in Wisconsin Whitetails

In February 2002, three Wisconsin bucks killed during the 2001 firearms season tested positive for the fatal brain illness chronic wasting disease.

The discovery marked the first time CWD had been found in a wild deer herd east of the Mississippi. In fact, the area where the bucks were killed — about 20 miles west of Madison, Wis., — is about 900 miles east of where the disease was thought to be isolated, the confluence of northeastern Colorado, western Wyoming, southwestern South Dakota and eastern Nebraska.

Deer, Hunters are Plentiful

Although some hunters yearn for the "old days," most modern deer hunters know those days are here and now.

In 1966, Wisconsin bow and gun-hunters combined to kill 116,048 whitetails. In 2000, they bettered that by a staggering 432 percent.

Wisconsin is also adding hunters. In 2000, 952,948 people hunted whitetails in Wisconsin — a new record. That's 435,723 more hunters than the state had in 1966 — an increase of nearly 84 percent.

WISCONSIN SNAPSHOT

Deer Population: 1.6 million, 3rd in U.S.

Average Harvest: 465,253, 1st in U.S.

Harvest Calculation Method: Mandatory registration.

Does State Predict Annual Harvest? Yes

How Close is Annual Prediction? 5%

Gun-Hunters: 694,712

Bow-Hunters: 258,230

Muzzleloading Hunters: 8,250

Hunter Education: Required for all persons born after Jan. 1, 1973. Bow-hunter education is not required.

Orange Required for Gun-Hunting? Yes.

WYOMING
Equality State
Harvest Rating: Not ranked

For more information, contact:
Wyoming Game and Fish
5400 Bishop Blvd.
Cheyenne, WY 82002
(900) 884-4263   http://gf.state.wy.us/

HISTORY OF WYOMING'S DEER HARVEST

Year	Firearm	Bow	Total
1971	7,806	NA	7,806
1972	4,306	NA	4,306
1973	9,174	NA	9,174
1974	12,832	NA	12,832
1975	14,001	NA	14,001
1976	11,298	NA	11,298
1977	11,049	NA	11,049
1978	7,796	NA	7,796
1979	7,452	NA	7,452
1980	7,014	NA	7,014
1981	7,286	NA	7,286
1982	7,608	NA	7,608
1983	8,498	NA	8,498
1984	9,888	NA	9,888
1985	9,267	NA	9,267
1986	7,983	254	8,237
1987	5,628	192	5,820
1988	7,005	174	7,179
1989	8,903	197	9,100
1990	9,535	147	9,632
1991	10,240	139	10,379
1992	14,533	216	14,749
1993	12,623	1,322	13,945
1994	8,249	228	8,477
1995	6,959	175	7,134
1996	6,857	232	7,089
1997	6,889	200	7,089
1998	6,842	194	7,036
1999	6,883	196	7,079
2000	10,833	290	11,103
2001	9,125	292	9,417

Wyoming Hunters Enjoy High Success Rates

Nonresident deer hunters in Wyoming have a 45.8 percent success rate. Although that's largely because nonresident hunters rely heavily on guides and outfitters, it's also testament to Wyoming's often-underestimated hunting opportunities.

WYOMING DEER RECORDS

•**Record harvest:** 14,749 (1992)
•**Record low harvest:** 4,306 (1972)
•**Bow-hunting record:** 1,322 (1993)
•**Gun-hunting record:** 14,533 (1992)

•**Season to remember:** 1993. Wyoming bow-hunters shatter the standing archery harvest, killing 1,322 deer. Since that year, Wyoming's highest archery occurred in 2000, when bow-hunters killed 290 deer — only 22 percent of the 1993 harvest.

'Walk-In' Areas Offer Ample Hunting Opportunities

Like most Western states, Wyoming offers hunters extensive public lands. However, aside from these state and federal lands, Wyoming also offers "walk-in areas," tracts of private lands on which the state's Game and Fish Commission has leased public hunting rights. In exchange for the use of their land, participating landowners receives a monetary reward in proportion to the number of acres enrolled in the program.

As the name states, public access on most walk-in areas is restricted to foot traffic, although several large walk-in areas allow horseback access. Hunters need not seek permission from the landowner to hunt walk-in areas. In fact, for landowner convenience, the Wyoming Game and Fish Commission encourages hunters to walk right in. All walk-in areas will have signs posted to mark their boundaries.

The Walk-in Area program is a result of a concerted effort on the part of the Game and Fish Commission to enhance hunting opportunities in Wyoming. To ensure the success of this program in providing public hunting opportunities, cooperation from sportsmen using Walk-in Areas is greatly appreciated
— WYOMING GAME AND FISH

WYOMING SNAPSHOT

Deer Population: 65,000 (includes other species)

Average Harvest: 8,345, (not ranked)

Harvest Calculation Method: Surveys

Does State Predict Annual Harvest? Yes

How Close is Annual Prediction? 10%

Gun-Hunters: 53,940

Bow-Hunters: 6,790

Muzzleloading Hunters: 7,700

Hunter Education: Required for all persons born after Jan. 1, 1966. Bow-hunter education is not required.

Orange Required for Gun-Hunting? Yes.

FOR SERIOUS HUNTERS, deer hunting is a year-round pursuit — not a seasonal distraction. Studying deer and deer hunting year-round provides unparalleled satisfaction and knowledge.

7

Whitetail Facts

Make Deer Hunting
a Year-Round Pursuit

Mention deer hunting, and most hunters imagine fallen leaves, clashing antlers and saplings rubbed ragged by rut-crazed bucks. They remember the Indian Summer afternoons of early archery season and cold, snowy mornings of gun-hunting.

And for good reason.

After all, few things top the feeling of donning a blaze orange parka, thumbing shells into a rifle magazine and tip-toeing through the predawn darkness toward your stand. And nothing beats the heart-thumping adrenaline rush that comes when a buck appears out of nowhere and steps into your shooting lane.

Unfortunately, because of seasonal limitations, many hunters experience such stimuli only a few days each year. For casual hunters, this might be OK, but as most serious whitetail enthusiasts know, pulling a trigger or releasing an arrow is only part of a year-round pursuit. For such hunters, there is no off-season — there are just the pre-season and post-season, times reserved for scouting, practice-shooting and expanding one's knowledge of whitetail habits.

If you love aspects of deer and deer hunting like fine-tuning equipment, butchering your own venison and hashing over deer behavior theories to learn what makes whitetails tick, you'll love to sink your teeth in the following pages.

Can the Internet help you find more deer? Find out on Page 206.

How does your hunting area measure up when compared to other counties across the country? The Quality Deer Management Association has the answer. Just turn to Page 186.

Aside from a sunrise/sunset chart, weight-estimation tips, deer biology insights and information about the moon's influence on deer activity, you'll also find a unique blood-trailing log on Pages 192 to 196. Filling out these pages after you shoot a deer might help you recover more whitetails. Plus, it will provide vital insight on how shot angles and other factors affect blood trails and recovery percentages.

Standard Time Differences Across North America

City, State	Time
Akron, Ohio	12:00 p.m.
Albuquerque, N.M.	10:00 a.m.
Atlanta, Ga.	12:00 p.m.
Austin, Texas	11:00 a.m.
Bismarck, N.D.	11:00 a.m.
Boise, Idaho	10:00 a.m.
Buffalo, N.Y.	12:00 p.m.
Butte, Mont.	10:00 a.m.
Charleston, S.C.	12:00 p.m.
Chattanooga, Tenn.	12:00 p.m.
Cheyenne, Wy.	10:00 a.m.
Chicago, Ill.	11:00 a.m.
Colorado Springs, Colo.	10:00 a.m.
Dallas, Texas	11:00 a.m.
Detroit, Mich.	12:00 p.m.
Duluth, Minn.	11:00 a.m.
Erie, Pa.	12:00 p.m.
Evansville, Ind.	11:00 a.m.
Fort Wayne, Ind.*	12:00 p.m.
Frankfort, Ky.	12:00 p.m.
Halifax, Nova Scotia	1:00 p.m.
Hartford, Conn.	12:00 p.m.
Jacksonville, Fla.	12:00 p.m.
Juneau, Alaska	8:00 a.m.
Kansas City, Mo.	11:00 a.m.
Lincoln, Neb.	11:00 a.m.
Little Rock, Ark.	11:00 a.m.
Los Angeles, Calif.	9:00 a.m.
Milwaukee, Wis.	11:00 a.m.
Mobile, Ala.	11:00 a.m.
Montreal, Quebec	12:00 p.m.
New Orleans, La.	11:00 a.m.
Norfolk, Va.	12:00 p.m.
Oklahoma City, Okla.	11:00 a.m.
Phoenix, Ariz.	10:00 a.m.
Pierre, S.D.	11:00 a.m.
Portland, Me.	12:00 p.m.
Portland, Ore.	9:00 a.m.
Reno, Nev.*	9:00 a.m.
St. John's, Newfoundland	1:30 p.m.
Salt Lake City, Utah	10:00 a.m.
Santa Fe, N.M.	10:00 a.m.
Savannah, Ga.	12:00 p.m.
Seattle, Wash.	9:00 a.m.
Sioux Falls, S.D.	11:00 a.m.
Toledo, Ohio	12:00 p.m.
Toronto, Ontario	12:00 p.m.

Sunrise and Sunset Times

Calculated for Milwaukee, Wis. (Central Time)
Corrected for Daylight Saving Time

Month	2002		2003	
October	Sunrise	Sunset	Sunrise	Sunset
01	6:49 a.m.	6:33 p.m.	6:49 a.m.	6:34 p.m.
02	6:50 a.m.	6:31 p.m.	6:50 a.m.	6:32 p.m.
03	6:51 a.m.	6:30 p.m.	6:51 a.m.	6:30 p.m.
04	6:52 a.m.	6:28 p.m.	6:52 a.m.	6:28 p.m.
05	6:54 a.m.	6:26 p.m.	6:53 a.m.	6:27 p.m.
06	6:55 a.m.	6:24 p.m.	6:54 a.m.	6:25 p.m.
07	6:56 a.m.	6:23 p.m.	6:56 a.m.	6:23 p.m.
08	6:57 a.m.	6:21 p.m.	6:57 a.m.	6:21 p.m.
09	6:58 a.m.	6:29 p.m.	6:58 a.m.	6:20 p.m.
10	6:59 a.m.	6:18 p.m.	6:59 a.m.	6:18 p.m.
11	7:01 a.m.	6:16 p.m.	7:00 a.m.	6:16 p.m.
12	7:02 a.m.	6:14 p.m.	7:01 a.m.	6:15 p.m.
13	7:03 a.m.	6:12 p.m.	7:03 a.m.	6:13 p.m.
14	7:04 a.m.	6:11 p.m.	7:04 a.m.	6:11 p.m.
15	7:05 a.m.	6:09 p.m.	7:05 a.m.	6:10 p.m.
16	7:06 a.m.	6:08 p.m.	7:06 a.m.	6:08 p.m.
17	7:08 a.m.	6:06 p.m.	7:07 a.m.	6:06 p.m.
18	7:09 a.m.	6:04 p.m.	7:09 a.m.	6:05 p.m.
19	7:10 a.m.	6:03 p.m.	7:10 a.m.	6:03 p.m.
20	7:11 a.m.	6:01 p.m.	7:11 a.m.	6:02 p.m.
21	7:13 a.m.	6:00 p.m.	7:12 a.m.	6:00 p.m.
22	7:14 a.m.	5:58 p.m.	7:13 a.m.	5:58 p.m.
23	7:15 a.m.	5:57 p.m.	7:15 a.m.	5:57 p.m.
24	7:16 a.m.	5:55 p.m.	7:16 a.m.	5:55 p.m.
25	7:18 a.m.	5:54 p.m.	7:17 a.m.	5:54 p.m.
26	7:19 a.m.	5:52 p.m.	7:18 a.m.	5:53 p.m.
27	7:20 a.m.	5:51 p.m.	6:20 a.m.	4:51 p.m.
28*	6:21 a.m.	4:49 p.m.	6:21 a.m.	4:40 p.m.
29	6:23 a.m.	4:48 p.m.	6:22 a.m.	4:48 p.m.
30	6:24 a.m.	4:47 p.m.	6:23 a.m.	4:47 p.m.
31	6:25 a.m.	4:45 p.m.	6:25 a.m.	4:46 p.m.
Nov.	Sunrise	Sunset	Sunrise	Sunset
01	6:26 a.m.	4:44 p.m.	6:26 a.m.	4:44 p.m.
02	6:28 a.m.	4:43 p.m.	6:27 a.m.	4:43 p.m.
03	6:29 a.m.	4:41 p.m.	6:29 a.m.	4:42 p.m.
04	6:30 a.m.	4:40 p.m.	6:30 a.m.	4:40 p.m.
05	6:31 a.m.	4:39 p.m.	6:31 a.m.	4:39 p.m.
06	6:33 a.m.	4:38 p.m.	6:32 a.m.	4:38 p.m.
07	6:34 a.m.	4:36 p.m.	6:34 a.m.	4:37 p.m.
08	6:35 a.m.	4:35 p.m.	6:35 a.m.	4:36 p.m.
09	6:37 a.m.	4:34 p.m.	6:36 a.m.	4:34 p.m.
10	6:38 a.m.	4:33 p.m.	6:38 a.m.	4:33 p.m.
11	6:39 a.m.	4:32 p.m.	6:39 a.m.	4:32 p.m.
12	6:40 a.m.	4:31 p.m.	6:40 a.m.	4:31 p.m.
13	6:42 a.m.	4:30 p.m.	6:41 a.m.	4:30 p.m.
14	6:43 a.m.	4:29 p.m.	6:43 a.m.	4:29 p.m.
15	6:44 a.m.	4:28 p.m.	6:44 a.m.	4:28 p.m.
16	6:46 a.m.	4:27 p.m.	6:45 a.m.	4:27 p.m.
17	6:47 a.m.	4:26 p.m.	6:46 a.m.	4:27 p.m.
18	6:48 a.m.	4:26 p.m.	6:48 a.m.	4:26 p.m.
19	6:49 a.m.	4:25 p.m.	6:49 a.m.	4:25 p.m.
20	6:51 a.m.	4:24 p.m.	6:50 a.m.	4:24 p.m.
21	6:52 a.m.	4:23 p.m.	6:51 a.m.	4:23 p.m.
22	6:53 a.m.	4:23 p.m.	6:53 a.m.	4:23 p.m.
23	6:54 a.m.	4:22 p.m.	6:54 a.m.	4:22 p.m.
24	6:55 a.m.	4:21 p.m.	6:55 a.m.	4:21 p.m.
25	6:57 a.m.	4:21 p.m.	6:56 a.m.	4:21 p.m.
26	6:58 a.m.	4:20 p.m.	6:57 a.m.	4:20 p.m.
27	6:59 a.m.	4:20 p.m.	6:59 a.m.	4:20 p.m.
28	7:00 a.m.	4:19 p.m.	7:00 a.m.	4:19 p.m.
29	7:01 a.m.	4:19 p.m.	7:01 a.m.	4:19 p.m.
30	7:02 a.m.	4:18 p.m.	7:02 a.m.	4:19 p.m.

*Denotes end of Daylight Saving Time.
Source: United States Naval Observatory

How Does the 'Rutting Moon' Affect Deer Behavior?

Throughout much of the whitetail's range, the rut usually peaks in late October or early November.

Charles J. Alsheimer, Northern field editor for *Deer & Deer Hunting*, and Vermont wildlife biologist Wayne Laroche believe it's possible to accurately predict the peak times for deer activity. The following chart, provided by Alsheimer, lists the "rutting moon" dates for the next several years. Use this guide to help plan future rut-time hunts.

Peak deer activity usually starts about a week after the rutting moon.

Alsheimer's lunar insights are included annually in *Deer & Deer Hunting's Whitetail Calendar*. Here's a sample of the responses the *D&DH* editors have received concerning Alsheimer's lunar predictions:

YEAR.....	RUTTING MOON
2002	OCT. 20
2003	NOV. 8
2004	OCT. 28
2005	OCT. 17
2006	NOV. 5

➤ After reading Charles Alsheimer's article "2001 Rut Forecast: Another Barnburner?" in the October 2001 issue, I had to respond. Come on, guys! The moon has no more bearing on the rut than does the sun! Temperature, dwindling daylight, weather patterns, and changing food supplies play the greatest role in the rut's timing.

In his article, Alshiemer noted that 1999 was a poor year for rutting behavior. He also noted that year's extreme temperature difference from previous years. What did the moon have to do with it? Nothing.

He also stated that his 2000 studies indicate deer activity was good Nov. 9 to 24. That sounds like the local meteorologist saying the temperature for tomorrow will be between 50 and 80 degrees! His findings are too vague to support the theory that the moon affects the rut. Regardless of moon phase, most hunters will observe more rubbing and scraping activity starting the week of Oct. 12 to 15. Chasing usually increases the last week of October.

Incidentally, such findings are even less accurate in states like Pennsylvania, where an out-of-balance herd structure makes the rut last longer than normal. There, hunters often find fresh rubs and scrapes long after Jan. 1. Does the moon have anything to do with it? You decide.

Todd Harman
East Berlin, Pa.

➤ I have found that the rutting moon plays a major role in triggering the rut. In Fall 2001, Alsheimer's rutting moon prediction was perfectly timed to the rut's chase phase. My hunting partners' experiences and my trail-timer data confirm this.

There has been too much evidence about how deer movement is affected by the moon recorded and observed to prove against it.

Ryan Pelowski
Trempealeau, Wis.

Editor's note: *For Alsheimer's most recent predictions, see the October 2002 issue of* Deer & Deer Hunting.

Deer Hunting Guide to Full-Moon Dates* in 2003

Month	Date	Day
January	18	Saturday
February	16	Sunday
August	12	Tuesday
September	10	Wednesday
October	10	Friday
November	9	Sunday
December	8	Monday

*Based on Central Standard Time

Plan Your Hunts by the 'Rutting Moon'

In most areas, the rut usually peaks in late October or early November.

Many deer biologists and hunting experts believe it's possible to accurately predict the peak times for deer activity during the rut. Three in-depth research articles on this topic were published in the August, September and October 1997 issues of *Deer & Deer Hunting*. These articles revealed a new theory on the moon's influence on deer activity.

The dates on this page are nearest to the full-moon phases for the rutting months. This guide will help you plan this year's hunts, enabling you to be in the woods when deer are most active.

For an in-depth look at how the moon influences deer behavior, check out Charles Alsheimer's book, *Whitetails by the Moon*.

To order, call (888) 457-2873, or visit our Web site: www.deeranddeerhunting.com.

Use the Internet to Locate Big Bucks

Although there's no substitute for in-the-field scouting when patterning deer, you might glean some of the most useful information about whitetails on your property from your home computer.

One of the latest and most valuable resources for deer hunters is Microsoft TerraServer, a Web site that provides U.S. Geological Survey aerial photos and topographic maps of most of the United States.

After logging onto the site (http://terraserver.homeadvisor.msn.com/default.asp), find your hunting area by entering the state and nearest town, or by inputting global positioning system coordinates. The site will then display an aerial photo for the area. TerraServer lets you zoom in or out, toggle between a topographic map or an aerial photograph, and adjust the image location to include your hunting area.

By showing roads, clear-cuts and transition zones between thick and sparse vegetation, aerial photos help reveal funnels, bedding areas, travel corridors and other vital hunting areas you might miss while viewing the property from ground level.

In addition, if you use these aerial photographs in conjunction with a county plat book, which shows property lines and landowner names, you might find a new place to hunt.

— RYAN GILLIGAN

ALMANAC INSIGHTS

➤ **NORTH AMERICA'S** whitetail population dropped from an estimated 20 million in 1690 to 390,000 in 1890. By the turn of the century, the population had rebounded to bout 500,000. The herd increased because, in the late 1890s, conservationists realized the whitetail's plight, and as a result, many states enacted hunting laws. Another boost to whitetail herds was the passage of the Lacey Act of 1900, which prohibited interstate trafficking of wild game — essentially ending market hunting.
— *Deer Hunters' Almanac*

➤ **FROM 1715 TO 1735**, South Carolina exported 75,000 deer hides a year. In neighboring Georgia, 100 tons of whitetail hides were exported to Europe between 1755 and 1773. And, by the end of that century, Quebec was exporting more than 100,000 deer hides a year to European markets.
— *Deer Hunters' Almanac*

➤ **HUNTING MORTALITY** of whitetailed does is the most important factor determining whether a deer population increases, decreases or remains stable. One buck can mate with many does, so bucks can remain at much lower numbers than does without affecting reproductive rates. This can be shown by simulating a deer population under various buck-and-doe-harvest rates. Harvests of 10 percent and 40 percent of the antlered deer from a herd has little effect on the overall population growth. Similar harvests of does, however, affect population growth.

If hunting mortality is eliminated, and all other mortality and reproductive factors remain the same, a deer population increases rapidly, nearly quadrupling in size in just 10 years. Growth at this rate, however, could not continue indefinitely. As the deer population increases, it eventually reaches and exceeds the land's carrying capacity — the number of animals a habitat can support on a sustained basis.
— *Missouri Dept. of Conservation*

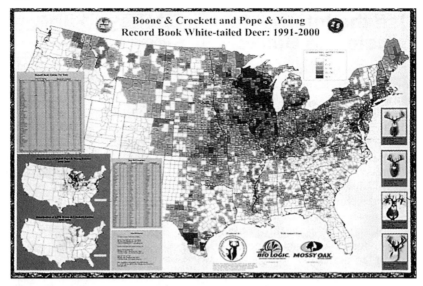

Boone & Crockett and Pope & Young Record Book White-tailed Deer: 1991-2000

Quality Deer Management Association Offers Map of Record-Class Whitetail Kill Densities

Have you ever wondered which areas produce the most Boone and Crockett and Pope and Young bucks? Well, today, answering that question is easier than ever, thanks to detailed maps recently compiled by the Quality Deer Management Association.

The maps, created by QDMA intern Joel Helmer, reflect how many record-class bucks each county in the Unites States produced from 1991 to 2000. To illustrate concentrations of record-class buck kills during the 10-year period, each county is color-coded in shades of red, with the darkest shade indicating the most big-buck kills.

The map reveals some fascinating aspects of how geography, climate and soil conditions affect deer size. For example, some of the highest concentrations of record-class bucks have been killed along the Ohio and Upper Mississippi rivers, where mineral-rich soils encourage antler growth.

The map also illustrates the fantastic hunting and big-buck potential of states like Wisconsin and Illinois, where almost every county produces high numbers of B&C and P&Y bucks.

In addition, the map lists the top 50 counties for record-class buck kills, and shows how many P&Y and B&C bucks each of those counties produced from 1991 to 2000.

To obtain a copy of the poster, contact the QDMA at Box 227, Watkinsville, GA 30677.

Successful Blood Tracking Begins at the Shot

It's bound to happen. Despite your shooting proficiency, you will eventually shoot a deer in a less-than-ideal spot, resulting in a difficult tracking job. Recovering a poorly hit deer is an exercise in patience and attention to detail, and it begins when you shoot.

As you pull the trigger or release your arrow, watch the deer's reaction and make mental notes of landmarks it passes as it leaves the area. Although this sounds simple, the excitement of the moment and the erratic path of a rapidly fleeing deer require that you pay especially close attention.

The next — and often most difficult — element of tracking is simply giving the wounded deer sufficient time to lay down and expire. Unless it is extremely hot or heavy precipitation is washing away the blood trail, wait at least an hour before tracking a poorly hit deer. If you hit the deer in the paunch, wait at least three hours before trailing. By waiting, you have nothing to lose and everything to gain.

Carry that patience with you when you begin tracking. Move slowly and keep your eyes and ears open for movement or sound that might give away a wounded deer's presence.

Mark the blood trail clearly with flagging tape or toilet paper, and if the blood trail dries up, use the trail you've marked to get an impression of the deer's route.

Finally, if your efforts don't pay off quickly, don't give up. Any deer you shoot deserves your best effort.

— RYAN GILLIGAN

Maintain Shaving-Sharp Hunting Knives

A good knife is an invaluable deer hunting tool. Whether used for skinning, field dressing, cutting shooting lanes or performing deer-camp tasks, a knife's sharpness is critical to its performance.

With the array of easy-to-use sharpening products on the market, keeping a shaving-sharp edge is easy. Just follow these simple steps:

➤ Begin by cleaning the blade. Obviously, your sharpening stone will not grind the blade evenly if dried tallow or other materials are coating the knife.

➤ Use the lightest-grit stone possible for the job. In other words, if a blade is extremely dull or damaged, begin sharpening it with a coarse stone. When the blade is almost sharp, switch to a fine stone.

If the knife needs only a minor touch-up, use a fine stone throughout the process. Using a coarser stone than necessary removes too much metal, shortening blade life.

➤ Grind the blade against the sharpening stone the same direction on each pass. Use moderate pressure and match each stroke's angle to the knife's existing edge — changing the angle will dull the blade.

➤ As you reach the desired edge, use increasingly less pressure on each stroke until the blade is razor-sharp.

Finally, remove any burr edge created while grinding by running the blade against a leather strop, such as an old belt.

— RYAN GILLIGAN

Use Browse to Pattern Elusive Whitetails

Whether you hunt in big woods or farm country, deer in your area likely obtain some of their nutrition from woody browse. However, from a deer's perspective, browse species are not created equal.

Taste and nutritional value make some browse species more desirable than others. Deer will feed on the best browse available and ignore other species until preferred sources are exhausted. Therefore, it's important to identify the browse sources in your hunting area and tailor your hunting strategies to take advantage of them as the season progresses and food sources change. Use the following information on Northern browse species to guide you to more whitetails this fall.

Optimum browse: Northern white cedar, red maple, Eastern hemlock, American mountain ash and alternate-leaf dogwood.

Second-level browse: Eastern white pine, yellow birch, mountain maple, jack pine and serviceberry.

Last-resort browse: Aspen, Northern red oak, beaked hazel, paper birth, balsam fir, red pine, speckled alder, black spruce, white spruce and tamarack.

Of course, finding preferred browse species doesn't guarantee deer sightings. However, by locating stands of preferred browse and pinpointing deer activity within those areas using tracks, trails, droppings and/or rubs and scrapes, you'll increase your odds of ambushing deer.

Field-Dressed Deer Weights Are Deceptive

Although we'd all like to mentally add a few pounds to our deer when estimating their field-dressed weights, it's important to realize that deer often look deceptively heavy. As a result, hunters often have unrealistic expectations of how much venison they should receive from their butcher.

Many aspects combine to determine venison yields. Although a neck-shot mature buck can yield a big amount of steaks, chops, hamburger and stew meat, the amount of meat seems minuscule when compared to the meat yield of domestic animals.

A recent survey of meat processors revealed insights into meat yields. Among other things, the processors agreed deer hunters often have false expectations of how much venison they'll get from their deer.

"A customer wanted to watch his first deer get processed," said one meat cutter. "We started by weighing his field-dressed doe. It was 95 pounds. We processed his order, freezer-wrapped the cuts — basic chops, steaks, roast with bone attached and hamburger — and weighed all of the meat. We came up with 45 pounds. The customer was amazed at how much waste was in the hide, bones, head and hoofs."

— Dan Schmidt

Too Much Fiber Isn't Healthy For Whitetails

Researchers P. Brian Gray and Frederick A. Servello at the University of Maine in Ornono note that Northern Forest whitetails generally cannot meet their daily energy requirements in winter when eating only woody browse. Why? One vital reason is that deer struggle to digest a woody diet, so fiber from the woody browse takes up a lot of space in a whitetail's digestive system. As a result, deer cannot pack in enough high-energy food to meet their needs.

This is especially obvious in fawns. However, relatively small amounts of high-quality leaf litter during winter might be enough to adequately supplement a fawn's woody-browse diet.

Girth Charts Are Inaccurate

For decades, some hunters have relied on chest-girth charts to estimate live weights of deer. Unfortunately, such charts are often inaccurate because — among other things — they don't account for fluctuations in the body sizes of bucks before and after the rut. Most biologists put no stock in weight estimates based on chest-girth measurements.

Hunters can obtain a more accurate estimate of their deer's live weight by multiplying its field-dressed weight by 1.28. For example, a yearling buck with a field-dressed weight of 125 pounds will have an estimated live weight of 160 pounds. Remember, this is just an estimate — many variables can skew the actual live-weight figure.

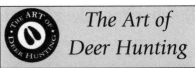

The Art of Deer Hunting

BY TOM CARPENTER

The Secret of Deer Hunting Success

Here is one final insight into being a successful deer hunter. It has nothing to do with the best rifle, the fastest bow, the highest stand, a pack-full of calls and rattling antlers and other gear, a high-cost hunting lease, the fastest ATV in the woods or any other technology.

None of those modern advantages makes a real difference if you start comparing yourself and your hunting to other hunters. There will always be people with more inches of antler on their buck. There will always be people with more venison in their freezer.

Find your own satisfaction. Don't turn the hunt into a competition with other hunters, or with the almighty tape measure. If you do, there will always be someone else to be jealous of, and something else to attain.

If you're going to compete, do it with the whitetail. Hunt him fair and square, on his (and her) terms. Measure success on your standards — how well you hunted and how happy you are with what you brought home, whether it wore big antlers, small antlers or no antlers at all.

And if all you bring home are memories of hours in the glory of autumn's woods then, well, you have a trophy worth keeping!

Butcher Your Own Deer for Safe, Tasty Venison

For great-tasting venison, allow your deer to hang at least 24 hours. Professional butchers agree that butchering and freezing a deer in less time usually results in "gamey" venison because all of the natural body heat was not allowed to escape the carcass.

It is not necessary to "age" venison, and, in fact, proper aging can only occur under tightly regulated conditions. Do not attempt to age a deer unless you have access to a walk-in cooler.

When processing your deer, be sure to double-wrap meat and label it with the date. Two layers of wrapping paper provide better insulation and keep the meat from getting freezer burn.

Give yourself plenty of time to process a deer. Carefully remove sinew and fat from the meat before wrapping it. Fat begins to break down once meat is frozen, and it can taint the meat. It's also wise to bone as much meat as possible. Bones not only take up space in your freezer, they too can cause an off-flavor in meat if left in the freezer too long.

Processing tasks become much easier, even fun, with quality knives. However, the best knife is useless if you don't also invest in a sharpening steel or set of stones.

Other useful items include a tape dispenser, waxed-paper dispenser, hog hooks, gambrel bar, small ax, plastic meat lug, apron with pockets and numerous pairs of disposable rubber gloves.

If your budget allows it, invest in a quality stainless-steel table. Butcher shops use these tables because they offer years of service and they're easy to clean. However, a homemade cutting table will work in a pinch, and save you time and sore back muscles. Make your table out of wood, and construct it at a height that allows you to perform tasks without straining your back.

It's crucial to keep all utensils and work areas clean to prevent contamination. Knives should be frequently washed with hot, soapy water. Work areas can be kept bacteria-free by

---

Meat-Processing Tips

The well-prepared home butcher keeps a variety of quality knives in his processing tool box:

✓ Fillet knife
✓ Boning knife
✓ Butcher knife
✓ Meat cleaver
✓ Skinning/caping knives
✓ Meat saw (hand or electric)

When processing your deer, be sure to double-wrap meat and label it with the date. Two layers of wrapping paper provide better insulation and keep the meat from getting freezer burn.

---

wiping them down with a water-bleach solution and drying them before beginning another task.

Another tip: Buy knives made specifically for butchering, and use them only for processing deer. Nothing makes a butchering job easier than a set of well-honed knives.

After skinning your deer, use a slightly moistened towel to remove hair from the carcass. It's much easier to remove hair at this point than wait until the carcass has been quartered. It's also wise to use a fillet knife to skin away as much fat and sinew from the hind quarters and backstraps before they are removed from the carcass.

Although the backstraps and hind quarters contain the most desirable cuts, a whitetail carcass provides equally valuable venison in the neck, ribs and front legs/shoulders. Spend the time to bone out each section. These often-overlooked scraps make great additions to stew, chili, burger and sausage. Most butcher shops will gladly make sausage for a reasonable charge if you supply them with clean, boned venison.

— Daniel E. Schmidt

Deer Harvest Records

Year _____ Name of Camp _____

Month & Day	Time of Day	Hunter Name	Buck (points)	Doe	Dressed Weight	Bow or Gun	Shot Distance	Tracking Distance

Blood-Trailing Log

Hunter: _____

Location: _____

Deer/Age: _____ Shot Distance: _____

Bow/Gun: _____ Broadhead/Bullet: _____

Pass-Through?_____ Time Allowed: _____

Trail Distance: _____ Recovery? _____

Indicate Shot Placement:

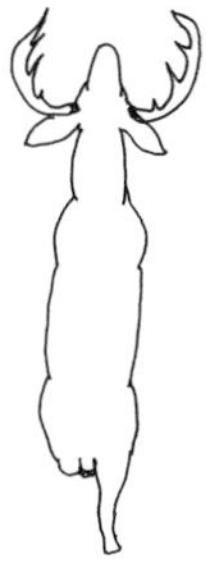

Trail details:

_____

_____

_____

_____

_____

_____

_____

_____

_____

_____

__ One Lung   __ Both Lungs
__ Liver   __ Heart
__ Paunch   __ Ham
__ Shoulder Blade

_____

_____

_____

_____

_____

_____

_____

_____

_____

_____

_____

_____

Blood-Trailing Log

Hunter: _____

Location: _____

Deer/Age: _____ Shot Distance: _____

Bow/Gun: _____ Broadhead/Bullet: _____

Pass-Through?_____ Time Allowed: _____

Trail Distance: _____ Recovery? _____

Indicate Shot Placement:

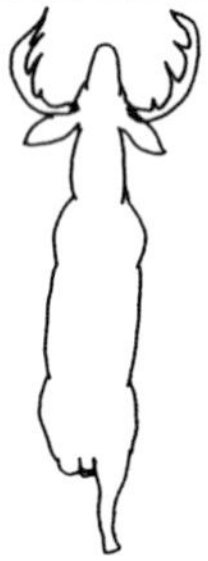

Trail details:

_____

_____

_____

_____

_____

_____

_____

_____

__ One Lung   __ Both Lungs
__ Liver   __ Heart
__ Paunch   __ Ham
__ Shoulder Blade

_____

_____

_____

_____

_____

_____

_____

_____

_____

_____

_____

Blood-Trailing Log

Hunter: _____

Location: _____

Deer/Age: _____   Shot Distance: _____

Bow/Gun: _____   Broadhead/Bullet: _____

Pass-Through? _____   Time Allowed: _____

Trail Distance: _____   Recovery? _____

Trail details:

Indicate Shot Placement:

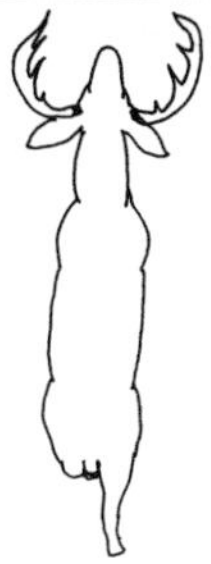

_____ One Lung   _____ Both Lungs
_____ Liver   _____ Heart
_____ Paunch   _____ Ham
_____ Shoulder Blade

_____

_____

_____

_____

_____

_____

_____

_____

_____

_____

_____

_____

_____

_____

_____

_____

_____

_____

_____

_____

_____

Blood-Trailing Log

Hunter: _____

Location: _____

Deer/Age: _____ Shot Distance: _____

Bow/Gun: _____ Broadhead/Bullet: _____

Pass-Through? _____ Time Allowed: _____

Trail Distance: _____ Recovery? _____

Indicate Shot Placement:

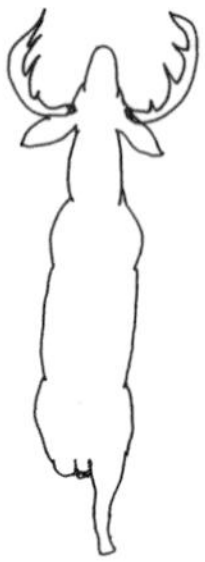

Trail details:

_____

_____

_____

_____

_____

_____

_____

_____

__ One Lung   __ Both Lungs
__ Liver   __ Heart
__ Paunch   __ Ham
__ Shoulder Blade

_____

_____

_____

_____

_____

_____

_____

_____

_____

UNLIKE HUNTING'S FOREFATHERS, today's hunters often have expendable income and leisure time, letting many hunters travel out of state or even out of the country for a chance at bucks like this Illinois 9-pointer.

8

Deer Hunting References

The Age of the Traveling Deer Hunter

Y ou don't have to be a veteran hunter to realize how much hunting has changed. Since the mid-20th century, North America's deer population has more than doubled, the compound bow has introduced generations to bow-hunting, and harvest strategies like quality deer management have turned hunters into amateur wildlife biologists. What's more, between the time most of our parents were born and today, hunting has transformed from an activity rural folks used to put food on the table to a high-dollar recreational activity. As a result, many of today's hunters have pursued whitetails outside of their home state — and maybe in Canada or Mexico. Furthermore, threats from urban sprawl, habitat loss, declining hunter numbers and animal-rights activists have forced hunters to become more political. As a result, millions of hunters have joined conservation and hunter-advocacy groups.

If you're such a hunter, this chapter will suit you well. It begins with a comprehensive guide to planning Canadian hunting trips, and answers questions regarding guides, weather, license fees, hunting regulations and how you should transport your once-in-a-lifetime buck home.

Traveling deer hunters will also want to check out the travel tips on Page 204. The article provides updated airline rules regarding traveling with firearms and ammunition, some of which have changed after the terrorist attacks of Sept. 11, 2001. Following the article's recommendations will ensure that your out-of-state hunts won't be put on hold because of a mix-up at the airport terminal.

Have you every wanted to view your favorite manufacturer's most up-to-date products but lacked a current catalog? If so, check out the extensive list of Web pages for the hunting industry's leading companies on Page 206. The sites provided will keep you on the cutting edge of hunting technology.

Finally, every political-minded hunter will want to refer to the list of hunting-organization contact information on Page 207.

Things You Should Know Before Booking a Deer Hunting Trip to Canada

It's no secret that Canada offers some of the best deer hunting in North America. From British Columbia to Quebec, hunters not only find huge whitetails, they hunt pristine wilderness areas with little or no competition from other hunters.

What's more, most Canadian deer hunts are relatively inexpensive, considering many outfitters offer fantastic accommodations and top-notch guide services. However, it's unwise to book any hunt without doing a lot of homework. Although most outfitters offer hunting packages, many details are left to the hunter.

The following items are just a few you should investigate before booking a Canadian hunt. For more information, contact the bureaus and information centers listed within this article.

Tax-Refund Policy

Before writing a check for what seems like an affordable hunt package, double-check to see what taxes you still owe. In many cases, package hunts are quoted on price, but they do not include the applicable federal and provincial taxes.

Nonresidents are eligible for a reimbursement of 50 percent of the taxes paid on a package. An outfitter who sells a package directly to non-residents can request this reimbursement on their behalf and deduct it from the price of the package.

For more information, contact your outfitter or call Revenue Canada at (613) 991-3346.

Canada's Updated Gun Law

Canada requires visitors to register their firearms. This law took effect Jan. 1, 2001. The registration form can be completed in about 10 minutes. However, because it is a declaration, visitors should not sign the form until they are before a customs officer. A fee of $37 ($50 Canadian) per gun is required.

Trip Cancellation

Whether you are dealing with an outfitter or an intermediary, inquire about cancellation policies. These conditions should appear in the agency's guidelines or the outfitter's brochure.

Responsibilities of Agencies and Outfitters

Canadian hunting agencies serve as intermediaries between travellers and travel service organizations. Because they do not exercise any control over suppliers, agencies cannot be held responsible if the suppliers fail to provide services.

Neither intermediaries nor outfitters can be held responsible for any damage, loss, delay, illness, injury or inconvenience arising from:

✓errors, negligence or omissions on the part of other suppliers, such as carriers, hotels, etc.

✓strikes, mechanical failures, a quarantine or other restrictive government action, meteorological conditions or other factors beyond human control such as forest fires.

✓failure on the part of the customer to carry necessary travel documents.

✓any airport delays on the customer's day of departure, for whatever reason.

✓material damage, loss of property or theft.

✓illness, injury and/or death.

Insurance

Most agencies offer trip cancellation, medical and baggage insurance. For information on such policies, contact the fishing and hunting agency of your choice.

Terms of Payment

If the trip has not been completely paid for before your departure and you do not intend to settle the bill with cash, you should verify whether the outfitter accepts personal checks, traveler's checks and/or credit cards.

Baggage

Before departure, check if the airline has weight limits and baggage allowances. Most airlines tightly monitor baggage regulations.

Climatic Conditions

While every effort is made to

CANADA OFFERS some of the best whitetail hunting on the planet. However, your dream hunt could become a nightmare if you don't make the proper preparations before your trip.

comply with published timetables, irregularities in flight operations can occur in some regions, due to poor weather. Such conditions can also affect the schedule of activities at an outfitter's camp. There is no refund for adjustments to activities resulting from such irregularities.

Permits and Quotas

Hunters must purchase provincial hunting licenses, generally available at sporting goods stores in most cities and towns, and from many outfitters.

Nonresidents are not obliged to produce a hunter's safety certificate to purchase a hunting license.

Deer Hunting

Nonresidents are limited to purchasing particular hunting licenses and frequenting specific hunting zones

Where to Write

Alberta
Department of Forestry,
Lands and Wildlife
Main Floor North Tower
Petroleum Plaza
9045 108th St.
Edmonton, Alberta CAN T5K 2G6

British Columbia
Ministry of Environment,
Fish and Wildlife
780 Blanchard St.
Victoria, British Columbia
CAN V8V 1X5

Manitoba
Dept. of Natural Resources
Wildlife Branch
200 Saulteaux Crescent
Winnipeg, Manitoba,CAN
R3J 3W3

New Brunswick
Bureau of Natural Resources
Fish and Wildlife Branch
Box 6000
Fredricton, N.B. CAN E3B4X5

Newfoundland
Dept. of Culture, Wildlife Division
Box 8750
St. Johns, N.F. CAN A1C 5 7

Nova Scotia
Dept. of Lands and Forests
136 Exhibition St.
Kentville, N.S. CAN B4N 4E5

Ontario
Ministry of Natural Resources
Room 1-73, MacDonald Block
900 Bay St.
Toronto, Ontario CAN M7A 2C3

Quebec
Dept. of Recreation, Hunting
Box 2200, 150 E. St. Cyrille
Quebec City, Quebec, CAN G1R 4Y1

Saskatchewan
Parks and Renewable Resources
3211 Albert St.
Regina, Saskatchewan
CAN S4S 5W6

or areas, according to the species hunted.

Nonresidents pursuing whitetails can hunt in all zones where hunting is allowed. However, nonresidents cannot participate in computer drawings to obtain a hunting license for antlerless deer during gun season.

Deer Registration
When returning to the United States from Canada, U.S. hunters must register their kill when going through the U.S. Customs.

Transporting Game
All successful deer hunters must immediately detach the appropriate transportation tag from his or her license and affix it to the deer. The tag must remain affixed throughout the registration process and until the animal has been dressed and stored.

Safety Regulations
All hunters must wear at least 400 square inches of blaze-orange material — covering their back, shoulders and chest — while gun-hunting for deer. The clothing must be visible from all angles at all times.

In addition, a life jacket must be provided for each person using any kind of boat. All boats must be equipped with a bailer, a sound-signaling device and a pair of oars.

Money
It's wise to change your currency into Canadian dollars before leaving the United States. Traveler's checks and major credit cards are accepted in most establishments, but it's advisable to check with your outfitter in advance.
— Daniel E. Schmidt

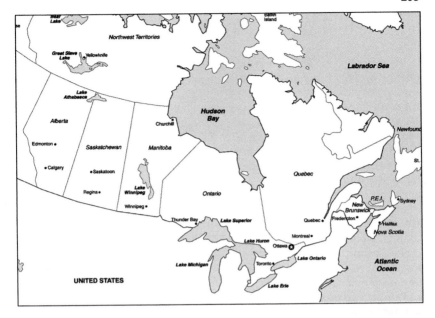

Miscellaneous Tips and Notes

✓When deer hunting in Manitoba, nonresidents must be accompanied by a licensed Manitoba guide. No more than three hunters can use the services of the same guide at the same time. In addition, nonresident deer hunters must book their hunts through a registered lodge or outfitter.

✓Planning a hunt in Saskatchewan? Topographic maps and aerial photographs can be purchased for all areas of the province from Saskatchewan Environment and Resource Management district offices (except the Regina office). Hunters can also order maps from: Sask Geomatics, 2151 Scarth St., Regina, SK, CANADA S4P 3V7, or call (306) 787-2799.

✓For current weather conditions and extended forecasts in any province, visit Canada's most popular weather Web site: www.weatheroffice.com.

✓Alberta whitetail hunters enjoy tremendous success. Nearly 80,000 hunters pursue whitetails in the province each year, and they harvest about 32,000 deer, a success rate of 40 percent.

Nonresident Fees for Deer Hunting

Province	License*
British Columbia	$75
Alberta	$183
Saskatchewan	$280
Manitoba	$185
Ontario	$123
Quebec	$260

*Nonresident fees as of February 2001. Other fees might apply. For example, Ontario charges a $30 export fee for taking deer out of the province, while Alberta requires hunters to purchase a Wildlife Identification Number for $8. If you plan to hunt deer in Canada, contact the respective province's department of wildlife for complete cost information. Contact information is on Page 195.

Traveling With Heightened Airport Security

The Sept. 11, 2001, terrorist attacks probably affected air travel forever, especially for those traveling with firearms and ammunition. If you're planning an out-of-state hunt and are depending on air travel to get you to your big-buck destination, follow these precautions to ensure your trip goes smoothly.

First, when traveling with a firearm, declare the weapon immediately when you check in at the ticket counter. Also, store the firearm in a locked, airline-approved gun case.

Whenever possible, purchase ammunition when you reach your destination instead of buying it at home and bringing it with you on the plane. However, when flying to remote areas, this might be impossible. In such instances, pack ammunition separately from your firearm in the manufacturer's original package, or locked in a fiber, wood or metal box.

Also, call your airline for specific information on its current policies regarding transporting guns and ammunition. These regulations often change without notice.

When you declare your firearm at the check-in counter, you must show the gun is unloaded and sign a "Firearms Unloaded" declaration.

Keep entry permits in your possession for the country or countries of destination or transit.

Ammunition Restrictions

The amount of ammunition you can check varies by airline. For example, Delta permits passengers to check 11 pounds of ammunition — 10 pounds on its SkyWest flights.

Ammunition weighing more than 11 pounds or containing incendiary projectiles is prohibited.

If necessary, you may purchase a hard-sided, 12-by-52-by-$4^{7}/_{8}$-inch gun case with suitcase-type locks for $75 plus tax at most Delta ticket counters.

Airlines generally permit passengers to check one item of shooting equipment as part of their free checked-baggage allowance. One item of shooting equipment is defined as one or a combination of the following:

One firearms case containing:

✓ two or fewer firearms — rifles, pistols or shotguns. Cases containing more than two firearms will be assessed an excess baggage charge.

✓ one shooting mat
✓ one small pistol tool kit
✓ noise suppressors
✓ pistol telescopes

Finally, remember that each airline might have different firearms restrictions and regulations change, especially in the wake of terrorist activity. Therefore, always call ahead or check your airline's Web site for its latest regulations before packing for your hunting trip.

— NATIONAL WILD TURKEY FEDERATION

ALMANAC INSIGHTS

➤ **CAUTION IS VITAL FOR** preventing hunting accidents like those that occurred last fall in Wisconsin. Despite the large number of hunter education graduates, fatalities remain constant.

In west-central Wisconsin, a hunter faces 15 years in prison and a $10,000 fine, stemming from charges of second-degree reckless homicide. The hunter shot a woman in the head while she was walking her dogs, during the 2001 muzzleloading season.

During Wisconsin's firearm season, a young hunter was shot by his companion while they hunted from the same blind. As the victim lifted his head after shooting at a deer, his partner took a consecutive shot, hitting the victim at point-blank range. It is believed the shooter could not see the victim in his riflescope due to the close range.

➤ **THE FIRST AMENDMENT** and hunting aren't normally a hot issue. However, in as tensions between animal-rights activists and hunters escalated in the 1980s, the U.S. Sportsman's Alliance began drafting hunter-harassment laws and has introduced legislation in each state since.

A woman from Missouri, the first in her state to be convicted of hunter harassment, was charged with a class A misdemeanor for repeatedly driving past a wooded area, blasting her radio, and continuously honking her car horn near a hunter's tree stand. The woman was fined $50 and must pay $53.50 in court costs.

In Connecticut, four anti-hunting activists arrested for hunter harassment in 1995, appealed to the state Supreme Court claiming the statute impeded their first and 14- amendment rights.

The court ruled the activists' speech was restricted, "only to the degree necessary to prevent interference in taking game," and decided the statute did not hinder any constitutional rights because state parks and other public hunting grounds were not intended for public forums, such as protests or debates.

Web Site Addresses for Hunting Gear

Clothing

10X Products	www.10xwear.com
Gore-Tex	www.gore-tex.com
Mossy Oak	www.mossyoak.com
Realtree	www.realtreeoutdoors.com

Calls

Knight & Hale	www.knight-hale.com
Primos	www.primos.com
Woods Wise	www.woodswise.com

Bows

Darton	www.Dartonarchery.com
Browning	www.browning.com
BowTech	www.bowtecharchery.com
Golden Eagle	www.beargoldeneagle.com
Fred Bear	www.beararch.com
High Country	www.highcountryarchery.com
Hoyt USA	www.HOYTUSA.com
Barnett	www.barnettcrossbows.com
Mathews	www.mathewsinc.com
McPherson	www.mcphersonarchery.com
Parker	www.parkerbows.com
PSE	www.pse-archery.com/ddh

Broadheads

Ballistic Archery	www.steelforce.com
Barrie Archery	www.RockeyMtBroadheads.com
Innerloc	www.Innerloc.com
Muzzy Products	www.BadToTheBone.com
New Archery Products	www.newarchery.com
Satellite	www.gearchery.com

Guns and Ammo

Barnes Bullets	www.barnesbullets.com
Federal Cartridge	wwww.federalcartridge.com
Marlin	www.marlinfirearms.com
Hornady	www.hornady.com
Modern Muzzleloading	www.knightrifles.com
Nosler Bullets	www.nosler.com
Remington	www.remington.com
Savage	www.savagearms.com
Thompson/Center	www.tcarms.com
Weatherby	www.weatherby.com
Winchester	www.winchester.com

Tree Stands and Accessories

Aerospace America	www.aerospaceamerica.com
Bear River	www.up-north.com/bearriver
Ameristep	www.ameristep.com
API	www.apioutdoors.com
Ol'Man Treestands	www.ol-man.com
Blackwater Creek	www.blackwatercreek.com
Summit	www.summitstands.com
Warren & Sweat	www.warrenandsweat.com

*This is only a partial listing of the Web sites featured on the Deer & Deer Hunting links page. For more listings, visit **www.deeranddeerhunting.com**

National Hunting Organizations

**American Shooting Sports
Council**
101 D. Street SE
Washington, DC 20003
(202) 544-1610
(202) 543-5865 fax

**Archery Manufacturers
Organization** (AMO)
304 Brown St. E, Box 258
Comfrey, MN 56019
(866) 266-2776
(507) 877-2149 fax

Archery Hall of Fame
1555 S. 150 West
Angola, IN 46703

**Archery Range
and Retailers Organization**
156 N. Main St., Suite D
Oregon, WI 53575
(800) 234-7499

Archery Shooters Association
Box 399
Kennesaw, GA 30144
(770) 795-0232

**Becoming
an Outdoors-Woman**
UW-Stevens Point
College of Natural Resources
Stevens Point, WI 54481-3897
(715) 228-2070

Boone & Crockett Club
The Old Milwaukee Depot
250 Station Drive
Missoula, MT 59801
(406) 542-1888

**Christian Bowhunters
of America**
3460 W. 13th St.
Cadillac, MI 49601
(616) 775-7744

**Christian Deer Hunters
Association**
Box 432
Silver Lake, MN 55381
(320) 327-2266

**Congressional
Sportsman's Foundation**
303 Pennsylvania Ave. SE
Washington, DC 20003
(202) 543-6850

Ducks Unlimited
1 Waterfowl Way
Memphis, TN 38120
(901) 758-3718

Hunter Education Association
Box 490
Wellington, CO 80549
(970) 568-7954
(970) 568-7955 fax

**International Association
of Fish & Wildlife Agencies**
Hall of the States
444 N. Capitol St. NW, Suite 544
Washington, DC 20001
(202) 624-7890

**International Bowhunters
Organization**
3409 E. Liberty, Box 398
Vermilion, OH 44089
(216) 967-2137

**International Sportsmen's
Expositions**
Box 2569
Vancouver, WA 98668-2569
(800) 545-6100
(360) 693-3352 fax

**Izaak Walton League of
America**
707 Conservation Lane
Gaithersburg, MD 20878-2983
(301) 548-0150
(301) 548-0146 fax

**National Association
of Sporting Goods
Wholesalers**
400 E. Randolph St., Suite 700
Chicago, IL 60601
(312) 565-0233
(312) 565-2654 fax

**National Bowhunter
Education Foundation**
101½ North Front St.
Townsend, MT 59644
(406) 266-3237

**National Crossbow Hunters
Organization**
Box 506, Verona, OH 45378
(937) 884-5017

**National Field Archery
Association**
31407 Outer I-10
Redlands, CA 92373
(909) 794-2133
(909) 794-8512 fax

**National Muzzleloading
Rifle Association**
Box 67, Friendship, IN 47021
(812) 667-5131
(812) 667-5137 fax

National Rifle Association
11250 Waples Mill Road
Fairfax, VA 22030-7400
(703) 267-1000

**National Shooting Sports
Foundation**
Flintlock Ridge Office Center
11 Mile Hill Road
Newton, CT 06470-2359
(203) 426-1320

Natl. Wild Turkey Federation
770 Augusta Road, Box 530
Edgefield, SC 29824-0530
(803) 637-3106
(803) 637-0034 fax

**Outdoor Writers
Association of America**
27 Fort Missoula Road, Suite 1
Missoula, MT 59804
(406) 728-7445

**Physically Challenged
Bowhunters of America**
Box 57, Gorham, KS 67640
(785) 637-5421

Pope & Young Club
15 E. 2nd St., Box 548
Chatfield, MN 55923
(507) 867-4144

**Quality Deer Management
Association**
Box 227
Watkinsville, GA 30677
(800) 209-3337

Safari Club International
4800 W. Gates Pass Road
Tucson, AZ 85745
(520) 620-1220

U.S. Fish & Wildlife Service
1849 C St. NW
Washington, DC 20240
(202) 208-4131

Wildlife Legislative Fund
801 Kingsmill Parkway
Columbus, OH 43229-1137
(614) 888-4868

Wildlife Management Institute
1101 14th St. NW, Suite 801
Washington, DC 20005
(202) 371-1808

**Women's Shooting Sports
Foundation**
4620 Edison Ave., Suite C
Colorado Springs, CO 80915
(719) 638-1299

Catch More Fur and Get a
<u>FREE GIFT</u> While Doing It!

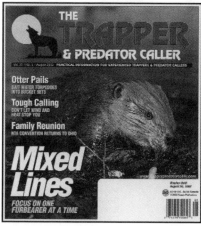

Ten times a year you'll get expert opinion on sets, baits and lures, trapline strategies, predator calling, ambush techniques, fur market reports, nuisance control, chances to enter incredible contests, and sweepstakes!

Plus, if you subscribe right now, you'll set the 2003 Trapper Yearbook absolutely FREE! This attractive full-color book is loaded with stunning photos, super-secrets of old-time trappers, fur handling improvements and a whole lot more! It's information you won't find anywhere else!

Only $16.95
for 10 issues plus a
FREE 2003 Trapper
Yearbook!

Order Now!

76 pages of all-new & exciting trapping stories!
Innovative techniques, fur handling tips &
loaded with photos!
Yours **FREE** with paid subscription.

Credit card customers call toll-free

800-258-0929 offer ABA942

write for non-U.S. rates to:
Krause Publications, 700 E. State St., Iola, WI 54990-0001
Or visit us online at www.trapperpredatorcaller.com